CV 01.23.2024 1223

"Elegantly and thoughtfully, Stanley takes us behind the mask of Starchild, his KISS persona, and shares intimately his own insecurities about his physical appearance and his emotional life."
—*Publishers Weekly*

"Most people will probably not associate sensitivity with the flamboyant heavy-metal rock band KISS, and yet in his memoir, front man, rhythm guitarist, and cofounder Paul Stanley succeeds in making a connection with the reader, KISS fan or not."
—*Booklist*

"For years the members hid their true identities behind cartoon personas and hard rock anthems that were powerful and exciting, but did little to reveal the men behind the music . . . After years of carefully maintaining his Starchild superhero identity, Stanley lets down his guard and unleashes a torrent of pent-up feelings that erupt and flow over 400 pages like molten lava."
—*Guitar World*

Face the Music

Face the Music

A LIFE EXPOSED

Paul Stanley

HarperOne
An Imprint of HarperCollins*Publishers*

HarperOne

FACE THE MUSIC. Copyright © 2014 by Paul Stanley. All rights reserved. Printed in the United States of America. No part of this book may be used or reproduced in any manner whatsoever without written permission except in the case of brief quotations embodied in critical articles and reviews. For information, address HarperCollins Publishers, 195 Broadway, New York, NY 10007.

HarperCollins books may be purchased for educational, business, or sales promotional use. For information, please e-mail the Special Markets Department at SPsales@harpercollins.com.

HarperCollins website: http://www.harpercollins.com

FIRST HARPERCOLLINS PAPERBACK EDITION PUBLISHED IN 2016

ISBN 978–0–06–211405–1

24 25 26 27 28 LBC 11 10 9 8 7

To my family

Contents

Prologue   1

Part I: No place for hiding, baby, no place to run   11

Part II: Out on the street for a living   75

Part III: I've been up and down, I've been all around   185

Part IV: Under the gun   285

Part V: The highway to heartache   353

Part VI: Forever   417

About the Author   457

About the Collaborator   459

Acknowledgments   461

Prologue

Adelaide, Australia, March 3, 2013

I sit down and look in the mirror, staring for a moment into the eyes peering out at me. The mirror is surrounded by high-watt theater-style bulbs, and on the table in front of the brightly lit mirror is a small black makeup case. We hit the stage in about three hours, which means it's time for the ritual that has defined my professional life for forty years.

First, I wipe my face with an astringent, to close the pores. Then I grab a container of "clown white," a thick, cream-based makeup. I dip my fingers into the tub of white goo and start applying it all over my face, leaving some space open around my right eye, where the rough outline of the star will be.

There was a time when this makeup was a mask—hiding the face of a kid whose life up to then had been lonely and miserable. I was born with no right ear—I'm deaf on that side, too—and the most searing early memories I have are of other kids calling me "Stanley the one-eared monster." It was often kids I didn't even know. But they knew me: the kid with a stump for an ear. When I was out among people I felt naked. I was painfully aware of being constantly scrutinized. And when I came home, my family was too dysfunctional to provide any kind of support.

Once the white is on, I take the pointed end of a beautician's comb, one with a metal point, and sketch the outline of the star, freehand, around my right eye. It leaves a line through the white makeup. Then with a Q-tip I clean up the inside of the star. I also clean up the shape of my lips.

The character taking shape on my face originally came about as a defense mechanism to cover up who I really was. For many years when I first put this makeup on, I had a sense of another person coming out. The insecure, incomplete kid with all the doubts and all the internal conflicts suddenly got painted away, and that other guy came out, the guy I had created to show everybody that they should have been nicer to me, that they should have been my friend, that I was someone special. I created a guy who *would* get the girl. People I'd known earlier in life were astonished by my success with KISS. And I understand why. They never knew what was going on inside me. They never knew why I was the way I was, what my aspirations were. They never knew any of that. To them I was just a fuck-up or a freak. Or a monster.

Next, I get up and go into another room—there's usually a bathroom adjoining the dressing rooms. I hold my breath and powder my entire face with white powder. This fixes the white to my face and allows me to sweat through it during the show. At this point I can touch the white and it doesn't come off on my finger. I learned this part of the process by trial and error—early on I would be blinded by the makeup running into my eyes.

As a young kid I used to dream that when I got older, I would become a masked crime-fighter. I wanted to be the Lone Ranger. I wanted to be Zorro. I wanted to be the guy up on a hill on a horse, with a mask on—that vision I saw in movies and on television.

This lonely kid wanted to do that, and this lonely kid ended up doing that. I made my own reality. The character I created—the Starchild—would go up on stage and be *that guy*, the superhero, as opposed to the person I really was.

I reveled in being *that guy*.

But sooner or later, I had to go back down the stairs. I had to come off stage. When you come down those steps you are confronted with the totality of your life. For many years, all I could think when I left the stage was, *Now what?* Back then, home was a sort of purgatory. During the short periods when KISS was not on the road I would sit on the sofa in my New York City apartment and think, *Nobody would believe that I'm home and have no fucking place to go.* The band was my life-support system, but it was also a way to stave off establishing the types of relationships that constitute a real life. At home, all I felt was a hunger: an important need wasn't being addressed, wasn't being filled by anything else. In one sense, I was always on my own—remote and inaccessible; but in another sense, I couldn't stand to be on my own.

With time, the line between the character and the man blurred. I began to take part of that guy offstage with me. Girls wanted that guy. People just assumed I *was* that guy. Still, I knew I really wasn't that guy. I could suspend reality onstage, but I couldn't sustain it; getting through a whole day as the Starchild was difficult. Because I didn't believe it. I knew the truth. I knew who I really was.

I was also very defensive. When people around me poked fun at each other, I could dish it out but I couldn't take it. I knew it must be much nicer to be able to laugh at yourself, to laugh about your own quirks and shortcomings, but I still couldn't get myself to that place. I couldn't let go—it was an instinctive reaction to having been constantly scrutinized and ridiculed as a child. I was still too insecure, too self-conscious. Though I didn't fully understand it myself (and nobody around me did either, since I never revealed anything about my ear), I was still fueled by the bitterness of my past. I imbued my jokes with undertones of maliciousness at other people's expense.

Hit me once and I'll hit you twice.

It's easy to live your life with your hand closed. But you get nothing with a fist that you can't get in multitudes with your hand open. Unfortunately, that message was lost on me for a long, long time. And throughout that time, I felt a sense of struggle within, a sense of dissatisfaction, inadequacy, and profound loneliness.

After the white makeup is fixed with powder, I go back into the dressing room, sit down at the mirror again, and brush away any powder inside the shape of the star around my eye. Next, I trace the outline of the star with a black eyebrow pencil. Then I take black grease paint, which is a little waxier than the clown white, and use a brush to paint in the star. I go into the other room again and fix the black makeup with talcum-based baby powder, which is less opaque than the white theatrical powder on the rest of my face. I return to the dressing room and line my left eye and eyebrow with black waterproof eyeliner. As it dries, I look in the mirror.

In earlier periods of my life, I didn't necessarily like the person I saw when I looked in the mirror. But I was trying—trying to become the person I wanted to be as opposed to remaining complacent. The problem was, no matter what I tried, nothing seemed to get me where I wanted to go. As KISS endured its ups and downs, I realized at various turns that many of the assumptions I held about what would satisfy me—or perhaps just make me comfortable with myself—had been wrong. I thought the fix was being famous. I thought the fix was being rich. I thought the fix was being desirable. By 1976, with the success of the *KISS Alive!* album, we became famous. But I found that rubbing my fame in people's faces didn't make me feel any better. By the end of the 1970s, we had made millions of dollars. But I found that the money—and the clothes, and the cars, and the collectible guitars I bought with it—didn't make me happy either. And as far as being desirable, from the moment of the release of our first album, sex was available any time and all the time. But I found I could be with somebody and still feel alone. I once heard someone say that you're never more alone than when you're sleeping with the wrong person. That's true. And while there are worse ways to suffer than bedding *Penthouse* Pets and *Playboy* Playmates, the happiness of those experiences proved transient. Exhilarating, yes, but momentary. I learned that none of it—while enjoyable—could take the place of whatever I felt was missing inside of me.

When KISS eventually took off the makeup in 1983, I occupied the Starchild character even more—or rather, the character occupied me. My own face became the face of the Starchild. I had banished to some extent the shy, defensive, unpopular kid inside, but I hadn't replaced or rebuilt him. I was something of a shell, an empty vessel. I was still searching for the person I might become, and the Starchild—now without the visible star—remained very much the mask I wore to interact with the world. But I still found—or at least, I *believed*—that keeping people at arm's length was easier than dealing with them in a more personal and intimate way. After all, in order to be comfortable with other people, you have to be comfortable with yourself. And I still wasn't. As a result, my life wasn't adding up correctly. Where was the family? Where were the friends? Where was the place to call home?

There was simply no getting away from the fundamental truth that I still wasn't comfortable in my own skin. When you can't get away from the truth, you either numb yourself or fix yourself. It's that simple. And it's in my makeup—no pun intended—to fix myself, not numb myself. Even at the most painful moments of my life—when my band seemed to be falling apart, when people around me fell by the wayside because of drugs, when I lay crumpled on the floor in despair after I got divorced from my first wife—a sense of self-preservation and an urge to improve myself always overrode any other impulses.

For some people, a near-death experience causes the epiphany that changes the course of their life. In fact, if you page through a stack of rock and roll memoirs, you might think every musician is required to have a close call with the beyond that becomes the definitive milestone in his or her life.

But I never tried to kill myself. And I never did much in the way of drinking or drugs, so I can't say I ever woke up in a hospital after being resuscitated, forced to take stock of my life. Still, I have had a few brushes with death. And in those moments the gravity of the situation certainly triggered soul-searching. But to tell you the truth, none of those near-death experiences had as powerful an effect on me as something that might not seem so rock and roll. Instead of coming when I had a gun in my mouth or a defibrillator on my chest, my epiphany came to me on the set of a Broadway musical.

In 1999 I landed the lead role in the Toronto production of Andrew Lloyd Webber's *Phantom of the Opera*. The title character is a music composer who wears a mask to hide a horrible facial disfigurement. And there I was—the kid born without an ear, Stanley the monster, who had spent his life playing music with his face obscured by makeup—playing that character. One scene in particular touched a psychological nerve in me. In his cape and mask, the Phantom has a dangerous but elegant appeal. Just before he steals away his love interest, Christine, and takes her to his lair, he leans in close to her and she pulls off his mask, revealing his horrid face. Something about his being unmasked and her touching him in that moment of intimacy struck a deep chord inside me.

One day during my run as the Phantom, I received a letter addressed to me at the theater. It was from a woman who had recently seen the production. "You seemed to identify with the character in a way I haven't seen in other actors," the woman wrote. She went on to say that she worked for an organization called About-Face, which was devoted to helping children with facial differences. "Would you possibly have any interest in getting involved?" she asked.

Wow. How did she pick up on that?

I had never spoken about my ear. As soon as I'd been able to grow my hair long, as a teenager, I'd simply hidden my ear and never addressed my deafness. It was something I kept private, secret. It was too personal and too painful. But I decided to call the woman. I wasn't sure what to expect. I wasn't sure what to say. But I opened up to her, and it felt good. Soon I started working with her organization, talking with children and their parents about my birth defect and my own experiences, sharing in their experiences. The effect it had on me was amazing.

I felt freed by talking about something that had always been so private and personal and painful. The truth had set me free—the truth and *The Phantom of the Opera*. Somehow, putting on the Phantom's mask had allowed me to uncover myself. In 2000, I became a spokesman for AboutFace. I found that helping others helped me heal myself. It created a calm in my life that I had never known before. I had been looking for external factors to pull me out of the abyss when all along the problem was inside me.

You can't hold someone else's hand when your own hand is balled in a fist.
You can't find beauty around you when you don't find it inside.
You can't appreciate others when you are immersed in your own misery.

I realized it wasn't people who *showed* their emotions who were weak, but the ones who *hid* their emotions who were weak. I needed to redefine what it meant to be strong. Being a "real man" meant being strong, yes: strong enough to cry, strong enough to be kind and compassionate, strong enough to put others first, strong enough to be afraid and still find your way, strong enough to forgive, and strong enough to ask for forgiveness.

The more I came to terms with myself, the more I was able to give to others. And the more I gave of myself to others, the more I found I had to give.

Not long after this transformation, I met Erin Sutton, a smart, confident, practicing attorney. From the very start, we were totally open and honest with each other; there was zero drama. She was understanding, nurturing, stimulating, and above all, consistent and self-assured. I'd never met anyone like her. We didn't rush into a relationship, but after a few years we both realized we couldn't imagine not being together. "I never hoped for a relationship like this," I told her, "because I didn't know something like this even existed."

This is the life I was searching for.
This is the payoff.
This is what it feels like to be . . . whole.

It was a quest, an unending push for what I thought I should have—not only materially, but in terms of who I should be—that enabled me to reach that point. It was a quest that began with the aim of becoming a rock star, but that ended with something else entirely.

And that's really what this book is about. It's also why I want my four kids to read this book someday, despite the fact that the path I took was long and arduous and meandered through some pretty wild places and times. I want them to understand what my life was like, warts and all. I want them to understand that it really is up to each one of us, that anyone can make a wonderful life for himself or herself. It may not be easy. It may take longer than you think. But it is possible. For anyone.

I collect my thoughts and look into the mirror again. There, staring back at me, is the familiar white face and black star. All that's left to do is empty a bottle or two of hairspray into my hair and vault it up to the ceiling. And put on the red lipstick, of course. These days, it's hard to stop smiling when I wear this face. I find myself beaming from ear to ear, content to celebrate together with the Starchild, who has now become a dear old friend rather than an alter ego to cower behind.

Outside, forty-five thousand people wait. I picture taking the stage. *You wanted the best, you got the best, the hottest band in the world* . . . I count in "Detroit Rock City" and off we go—me, Gene Simmons, and Tommy Thayer, descending onto the stage from a pod suspended forty feet above as the huge black curtain drops and Eric Singer beats the drums below us. Fireworks! Flames! The initial gasp of the crowd hits you like a physical force. *Kaboom!* It's the greatest rush imaginable. When I get out there on stage, I love to look out and see people jumping, screaming, dancing, kissing, celebrating, all in a state of ecstasy. I bask in it. It's like a tribal gathering. KISS has become a tradition, a ritual passed down from generation to generation. It's an amazing gift to be able to communicate with people on that level and have so many of them out there, all of them, all of us, together, decades after we started. The smile will not leave my face through the entire set.

Best of all, that smile will remain on my face as I walk off the stage to return to the totality of my life.

There are people who don't want to go home—who *never* want to go home. And once upon a time, I didn't, either. But these days, I love going home. Because somewhere along this long road, I finally figured out how to create a home, a real home, the kind of home where your heart is.

Part I

No place for hiding, baby,
no place to run

I.

Home is an interesting concept. For most people it is a place of refuge. My first home was anything but. I was born Stanley Bert Eisen on January 20, 1952. The New York apartment my parents took me home to was on West 211th Street and Broadway, at the very northern tip of Manhattan. I was born with an ear deformity called *microtia*, in which the outer ear cartilage fails to form properly and, to varying degrees of severity, leaves you with just a crumpled mass of cartilage. I had nothing more than a stump on the right side of my head. And my ear canal was also closed, so I was deaf. That left me unable to tell the direction of sound, and more importantly, made it incredibly difficult for me to understand people when there was any kind of background noise or conversation. These problems would lead me to instinctively avoid social situations.

My earliest memory is being in our darkened living room, with the shades drawn—as if to keep the conversation a secret between only my mother, my father, and myself. "If anyone ever asks you

*In the beginning . . .
there was a Starchild.*

*My sister, Dad, and me, at Inwood
Hill Park near our apartment,
Uptown Manhattan, 1952.*

With Mom and Dad in Lake Mohegan, New York.

what happened to your ear," my parents told me, "just tell them you were born that way."

If we ignore it, my parents seemed to intimate, *it doesn't exist.* That philosophy would rule our house and my life for much of my childhood. I got simple answers for complex situations. And despite the fact that my parents wanted to ignore it, nobody else did.

Children seemed to detach the person from the deformity—I became an object instead of a little kid. But children weren't the only ones staring at me. Adults did, too, and that was even worse. One day in a market on 207th Street, just down the road from our place, I realized one of the adults in line was staring at me like I was a thing instead of a person. *Oh, God, please stop,* I thought. When somebody stares at you, it's not limited to you and that person. Treatment like that draws attention. And becoming the center of attention was horrific. I found the scrutiny and relentless attention even more excruciating than being taunted.

Needless to say, I didn't have a lot of friends.

On my first day of kindergarten, I wanted my mother to leave as soon as she got me to the door of the class. She was proud. But I didn't want her to leave for the reason she thought. It wasn't because I was independent and sure of myself. I just didn't want her to see me being stared at. I didn't want her to see me treated differently. I was in new surroundings with new kids, and I didn't want to go through that in front of her. The fact that she was proud of me told me that she didn't understand anything about me—my fears went over her head.

One day I came home crying. "Somebody spat in my face," I wept. I had come home looking for support and protection from my mom. I assumed she would ask who had done it and then go out and find the kid's parents and tell them such behavior was unacceptable. But instead she said, "Don't come crying to me, Stanley. Fight your own battles."

Fight my own battles? I'm five!

I don't want to hurt anybody. I just want people to leave me alone.

But I went back out, and about an hour later I found the kid who had spit on me. I punched him in the eye. But he barely seemed to remember the incident and couldn't figure out what the big deal was.

One thing was clear after that: home was not a place where I could find help. Whether I was beaten up or taunted or anything else, I had to handle it on my own.

Top row, third from left: *doing my baseball player pose in first grade. P.S. 98, 1958.*

We lived practically next door to PS 98, my public elementary school. The school complex had three different yards, each separated from the others by chain-link fences. There was a kid whose name I didn't know, but who knew mine, who shouted at me from behind the fences between the yards. Whenever he spotted me someplace where I couldn't get at him, he'd shout: "Stanley the one-eared monster! Stanley the one-eared monster!"

I had no idea how this kid knew me, and all I could think was, *Why are you doing this? You're hurting me.*

You're really hurting me.

He was a normal, nondescript kid about my age, with brown hair, small enough that I thought I could beat him up if I ever caught him. But he was always out of reach, always on the other side of a fence or on the other side of the yard and able to run away into one of the nearby apartment complexes before I could get to him.

If only I could catch this kid.

And then one day, I finally did. I heard him shout, "Stanley the one-eared monster," and as always, the first thing I did was cringe. I heard the voice in my head pleading: *Stop doing that! Other people can hear you! Other people are looking at me now!*

And as always, there was no place to go to escape the stares.

But this time I managed to run him down and grab him. He was suddenly terrified. "Don't hit me!" he cried, looking like a frightened rabbit.

"Stop doing that!" I said, grasping him. "Stop doing that to me!"

I didn't hit him. Suddenly, facing him like that, I didn't want to. I hoped not hitting him would be enough to put me in his good graces. So I let him go. He couldn't have been thirty yards away before he turned back and yelled, "Stanley the one-eared monster!"

Why?

Why are you doing this to me?

Why?

Although unable to articulate it, I felt incredibly vulnerable and naked, unable to protect myself from the stares, taunts, and scrutiny that seemed everywhere. So I developed an explosive temper as a little boy.

Rather than recognize my temper as a sign that I needed help and support and guidance, my parents dealt with it by threatening me. "If you don't get that under control," they said in a darkly menacing tone, "we're going to take you to a psychiatrist." Now, I had no idea what a psychiatrist was, but it sounded ominous. It sounded like a diabolical form of punishment: I pictured going into a hospital room and having somebody torture me.

Not that I felt safe at home, anyway. My parents frequently went out at night and left me and my sister, Julia, who was only two years older than I was, home alone. "Don't open the door for anybody," was all they'd say, leaving a six-year-old and an eight-year-old all on their own. We were so scared we slept with knives and hammers under our pillows. We would wake up early the next day to sneak the weapons back to where they belonged so our parents wouldn't yell at us.

I shared the one small bedroom of our apartment with Julia; my parents slept on a pullout sofa in the living room. Julia started to have mental problems at a very early age. My mother said she'd always been "different," even as a baby. She was wild and prone to violence. My sister scared me. And as my own problems intensified, I spent a good deal of time worrying I might end up *like her*.

My parents may not have been very supportive of me, but then again they were not very supportive of each other, either. My mom, Eva, was domineering, and my dad, William, resented it. My mom portrayed herself as strong and my dad as meek. She considered herself the smart one. In actuality my dad was very bright and well-read. He had graduated from high school at age sixteen. Had circumstances been different, he would have gone to college. But his family insisted he start working to help pay the bills, and he did. By the time I came along, my dad worked nine-to-five as an office furniture salesman. Taken out of necessity, the job was one that with time he came to accept, but never to embrace.

My mother was a stay-at-home mom when I was little, but she had previously worked as a nurse and as a teacher's aide at a school for children with special needs. Eventually she started back to work at a redemption center where people went to collect merchandise after filling books of stamps accumulated through various customer loyalty programs offered by supermarkets in the 1950s.

My mother's family had fled from Berlin to Amsterdam with the rise of the Nazis. They'd left everything behind, and my mom's mother had divorced, which was rare at the time. After my grandmother had remarried, they'd moved to New York. Members of my mother's family were condescending toward other people, and they weren't beyond ridiculing me about my hair and clothes. I slowly came to realize there was no foundation for the arrogance and sense of self-righteousness shared by my mother's side of the family. They weren't successful, they were just dismissive. If you didn't agree with my mother, you frequently heard a derisive "Oh, please," delivered with a contempt that made it clear your opinion carried no merit at all.

My dad's parents were from Poland, and he was the youngest of four children. My dad told me his oldest brother, Jack, was a bookie and an alcoholic; his other brother, Joe, suffered from uncontrollable manic mood swings that crippled him throughout his life; and my father's sister, Monica, apparently surrendered to pressure from their mother not to leave the nest, and never married. Even as a child I couldn't help but see that expectation as manipulative and selfish on my grandmother's part. My dad spoke of a very difficult and unhappy childhood; he despised his father, who died before I was born.

My parents were not happy people. I don't know what the basis for their marriage was beyond what later became known as codependency. They didn't provide anything positive for each other. There was no warmth or affection in the house. Fridays were often the worst day of the week. My dad would be agitated, and the outcome was inevitable: my parents would get into a fight, and then my dad wouldn't talk to my mom for the entire weekend. It's childish to act like that for an hour. It's insane to see your own parents acting like that for days on end.

In addition to whatever issues they had between themselves, my parents were also consumed with my sister, who got into a lot of trouble and eventually spent many years in and out of mental institutions. Since I was always viewed as the good kid, I got progressively less attention at home. In my case, being the good kid didn't mean I was praised; it meant I was ignored. As a result, I pretty much had free license to do anything. I did not find this a very secure feeling. Security comes from having boundaries and limitations, and without any, I felt lost and unprotected, exposed and vulnerable. I didn't want or relish the freedom. In fact, it was almost the opposite: I was nearly paralyzed by fear because nobody was there to tell me I was safe.

I was alone a lot. I approached every day with a sense of foreboding, as I faced the unknown without any safety net. Every new day was uncertain, every new day was unprotected, every new day meant dealing with a world I wasn't equipped to deal with and trying to decipher the unspoken messages at home.

I found refuge in music.

Music was one of the few great gifts my parents gave me, and I will be forever grateful to them for it. They may have left me feeling completely adrift, but they unknowingly provided me a lifeline. I'll never forget hearing Beethoven's Piano Concerto no. 5 in E-flat major—the *Emperor Concerto*—for the first time. I was five, and I was completely blown away.

My parents made culture and the arts seem a natural part of life. Their appreciation of classical music was palpable. They had a big wooden Harman Kardon radio-phonograph console and listened to Sibelius and Schumann and Mozart. But it was Beethoven that left me dumbfounded.

On the weekends I listened to *Live from the Met* on WQXR with my mom, a tradition I continued even as I got older. Once I started listening to the radio, I also discovered rock and roll. Whether it was Eddie Cochran, Little Richard, or Dion & the Belmonts, it was pure magic—they sang about a glorified life of teenagers that I quickly came to dream of. All that singing about an idyllic concept of youth touched me emotionally. It filled me with the wonder of being a teen and transported me to a wonderful place, a place where life's angst concerned relationships and *love*. Man, what perfect lives these young people lived!

One afternoon I went for a walk with my grandmother. We crossed the 207th Street bridge into the Bronx, heading toward Fordham Road. On the far side of the bridge was a record shop. We went inside and my grandmother let me pick out my first-ever record: a 78 RPM shellac single of "All I Have to Do Is Dream," by the Everly Brothers.

When I want you to hold me tight . . .

If only.

While most of the other kids in the neighborhood were out playing cowboys and Indians, I sat indoors and listened obsessively to things like "A Teenager in Love" and "Why Do Fools Fall in Love." For a time, a lot of standards were also turned into doo-wop tunes, and I used to get irritated with my mom when she sang the original versions around the house. "That's not how it goes, Mom. It goes like this . . ." Then I would sing, say, the "dip da dip dip dip" part from the Marcels' version of the 1930s classic "Blue Moon." Sometimes she was dismissive about the modern stuff, but for the most part she just seemed to find it funny.

And then I *saw* some of the singers and bands I liked.

The famous rock and roll DJ Alan Freed started appearing on TV around the same time as the national debut of Dick Clark's *American Bandstand*. The wildness and danger of somebody like

Jerry Lee Lewis wasn't lost on me as he kicked his piano stool away and flung his hair around. What *was* lost on me was the sexuality of the music—not surprisingly, given what I saw at home. The romantic fantasy I envisioned was clean and sterile, and even as I got older, that's how I continued to view life. It would be many, many years before I realized what a song like the Shirelles' "Will You Still Love Me Tomorrow" was really about.

Still, there was no argument these people were cool. They were cool because they were singing. They were cool because people were watching them and screaming for them. In that audience these musicians had everything I craved as a young kid. *Adulation. Wow!*

A few Jewish immigrant families, like ours, lived in the part of upper Manhattan where I lived, but it was predominantly Irish. Our next-door neighbors were two lovely old Catholic sisters, Mary and Helen Hunt, who had never married. They became something like aunts or grandmothers to me. As my compulsion to perform like my new heroes increased, I frequently went over to their apartment and sang and danced for them. As soon as I could master *any* song, I knocked on their door and sang it for them while doing a little choreographed two-step, hopping from one foot to the other.

When I sang, it momentarily tempered some of my doubt and pain.

Everything just felt right.

2.

When I was eight, just before I started third grade, my family moved from upper Manhattan to a working-class Jewish neighborhood in a distant section of Queens. I had never seen anything like it—trees lined the block, coming right up out of the pavement, and across the street from us was a plant nursery that took up an entire block. I kept looking for forest rangers. Or Lassie.

Most of the adults in the area went into Manhattan for work, but the neighborhood functioned like a small town in the middle of nowhere. Within a few tree-lined blocks were a library, a post office, a butcher, a baker, a shoe store, an A&P grocery, a toy store, a hardware store, a pizza parlor, and an ice cream shop. I noticed one thing missing, though: a record shop.

Most of the buildings were two-story houses. Some were divided in half to form adjoining row houses; others, like ours, were divided into four apartments, two upstairs and two downstairs, with a yard in the front. I still shared a bedroom with my sister, Julia, but my parents had a room of their own now. There were lots of kids in the area.

My new school was PS 164. Instead of individual chairs and desks, the classrooms had two-person desks. I prayed the teachers would put me on the right-hand side so the kid I shared a desk with would see my left ear—the good one. I didn't want anyone looking at what I considered my bad side. Not to mention that I couldn't hear people if they were speaking into my deaf side all the time.

At some point on the first day, a teacher named Mrs. Sondike called me up to her desk. I walked to the front of the class. She was looking at my ear.

Oh, God, please don't do this.

"Let me look at your ear," she said.

No, no, no!

She started examining me like a scientific specimen. This was my worst nightmare. I was petrified. I was shattered.

What should I do?

I desperately wanted to open my mouth and say, "Don't do that." But I remained silent. I took a deep breath and waited for it to be over.

If I ignore it, it doesn't exist.

Don't show your pain!

Not long after that incident, I was taking a walk with my father. "Dad, am I good looking?" He seemed taken aback. He stopped in his tracks and looked down at the ground. "Well," he said, "you're not bad looking."

Thanks.

Ten points for my dad. It was just the perfect sort of encouragement that an isolated, hopelessly self-conscious young boy needed. Unfortunately, it would become a familiar pattern with my parents.

I started to build a wall around myself. My way of dealing with other kids became to preemptively push them away. I started to act like a smart-ass or a clown, putting myself in a position where nobody wanted to be around me. I wished I weren't alone all the time, but at the same time, I did things to keep people away from me. The conflict inside could be excruciating. I was helpless.

A lot of the other kids in the neighborhood went to Hebrew school together, which reinforced their friendships from PS 164 and created others beyond school. My family lit candles and observed Jewish holidays in some vague ways, but we weren't very observant. I was never bar mitzvahed. But the reason I didn't go to Hebrew school had nothing to do with any of that. I simply told my parents I didn't want to go. What I didn't say was *why:* sure, I felt Jewish, but I didn't want to subject myself to being around any more people. Life was bleak enough without putting myself into even more situations where I would be paralyzed by the fear of humiliation.

OK, school lets out at three o'clock? Hey, how about more of the same at three-thirty from a different batch of kids? Great.

PS 164 did have a glee club that interested me. A chance to sing! Every year they put on a musical, and they auditioned anyone who wanted to try out for a part. The first year, I decided to audition. When it was my turn, I stood up on the stage in front of other people, opened my mouth, and expected to sing. But all that came out was a little squeak. I ended up in the chorus, an able seaman in *HMS Pinafore* or whatever. Every year after that—fourth, fifth, and sixth grades—I wanted a role in one of those productions. But every year I choked at the audition—that same tiny voice was all that came out. I ended up in the chorus every time, despite the fact that when I sat through the auditions, I knew I could out-sing many of the students who managed to land the leads.

PS 164 was also the home to a scout troop. After I saw a few schoolmates in their blue uniforms, I thought about joining. When a new friend of mine, Harold Schiff, showed up in his uniform, I took him up on an offer to go with him to a meeting. Harold ran with the mainstream kids but had also befriended a few loners, like me. He was tight with some other guys in the troop, like Eric London, who played in the school orchestra with Harold, and Jay Singer, who played piano. I had run across Eric and Jay in glee club, but their friendship with Harold was based more on attending Hebrew school together. I stuck to myself for the most part. Even

when I joined something, I operated at the periphery.

Everybody in the scouts was trying to get merit badges—for tying knots or helping old ladies cross the street—but I didn't give a crap about that stuff. The only thing that appealed to me was going camping. And sure enough, we took some weekend camping trips. But I had a problem when I lost sight of the other people when we were out hiking. That was really the first time I realized that being deaf on one side meant I had no sense

I realized that I was better suited to own a team than to play on one.

of direction. I remember standing in a clearing listening to someone yell, "We're over here!" I had no idea where the voice was coming from. Without the ability to triangulate the sound, it was impossible. I felt vulnerable because I didn't know where I was—yet another way I couldn't place myself.

My instinct was still to cling to my parents. But whenever I got home from a situation like that looking for a sense of security, they let me down. "Ignore it and it will go away" remained the household mantra. Same old story. I would have loved more assurance and less hitting, but it just wasn't going to happen. My parents steadfastly refused to acknowledge the trouble I was having despite the fact that it was so obvious. I sleepwalked at home. Sometimes at night I would sort of come to and realize I was in the living room. Sometimes I was aware of my parents turning me around and directing me back to my bed. They knew; they just never acknowledged it or tried to figure out what was wrong.

I also had two recurring nightmares. In one, it was pitch black and I was on a floating dock in a huge body of water, far from any shore. I was stranded and alone. I started yelling for help.

Night after night.

I'm alone on a floating dock, far from shore, surrounded by darkness . . .

I would wake up screaming in my bed.

In the other nightmare I was sitting in the driver's seat of a car barreling down a dark, empty highway. The car had no steering wheel. I had to try to maneuver it by leaning from side to side, but there was no way to control it.

Night after night these nightmares left me suddenly awake, screaming, confused, deathly afraid.

Things with my sister were going south, too. By the time I was in junior high, Julia was getting more and more self-destructive. My parents started periodically committing her to state mental facilities. After she bounced in and out of state facilities, my parents spent what for them was a fortune on an expensive private psychiatric hospital. When she was at home, she ran away a lot, and my parents could spend days looking for her. Sometimes I woke up in the morning to see that my parents had gone yet another night without sleep and I wondered: *Will all of this kill them?*

Julia would hang out in the East Village and crash at people's apartments and take drugs. Once when she was home, she stole a drawer of silver dollars my mother had been collecting and sold

I'm twelve years old and my sister fourteen years old in front of our apartment on 75th Road in Queens . . . dressed to star on The Sopranos.

them to buy drugs. I know now that what she was doing would be called self-medicating, but back then I didn't analyze it much. When she was gone, she was gone. And when she was there, I was scared.

One afternoon after my parents brought Julia home from an institution where she had received electroshock therapy, they left us home alone. They just dropped her off and left me with a violent nutcase only a few hours removed from a mental hospital—who just happened to be my sister. While they were out, Julia got angry at something and started chasing me around with a hammer. I was terrified. I ran into a bedroom and locked the door. I sat there listening at the door, swallowing hard, praying my parents would come home.

Oh, God, please come home.

Then I heard a crashing sound as Julia started swinging the hammer wildly at the door. She kept at it.

Bang! Bang! Bang!

The wood cracked and splintered, and the hammer began to wedge its way through the door as she continued to flail at it with all her strength.

Then suddenly she stopped. The hammer was lodged in the wood and everything went quiet. I curled up and counted the minutes and then the hours.

Will they come home before she starts up again?

They did.

"What happened here?" they asked.

I told them that Julia had come after me with the hammer. But then they lashed out at *me*, as if it was *my* fault. They yelled at me. Then they hit me. I had been so scared, and now my head reeled in confusion.

You left me with her! That was your choice, not mine!

She tried to KILL me!

School continued to be a challenge, too. When I was in grade school I had tested my way into the "gifted and talented" track. At the start of junior high I was once again placed with the gifted children. I wouldn't have made it on the basis of my grades—I was never a good student. But entrance to the gifted track was gauged purely on some sort of intelligence test. While my IQ apparently qualified me, I remained at the bottom of the class. I was the one they scratched their heads about—I guess they thought I didn't want to learn. What they failed to realize was that my ear put me at a terrible disadvantage. I simply couldn't hear a lot of what was said in class. And if I missed a sentence, I was lost. Once I got lost, I surrendered. I gave up because I'd lost the thread.

At parent-teacher conferences the teachers always told my parents the same things: "He's bright but he doesn't apply himself," or,

"He's bright but he doesn't work to his potential." No teacher ever told them, "He's bright but he can't understand what I'm saying." Back then, kids didn't benefit from the recognition of learning disabilities.

But my parents *knew* I was deaf in one ear. And yet, after every parent-teacher conference, they came home and admonished me: "God gave you this wonderful brain and you're not using it."

I cried. I felt guilty. "Tomorrow I'll turn over a new leaf," I vowed.

Which was all well and good—until I went back to school the next day and still couldn't hear. At which point I couldn't follow what the teacher was saying. And there I was, feeling like a quitter all over again.

I knew that if I didn't do something, things were going to end badly. Did that mean failure? Did that mean taking my own life? I wasn't sure. To live in misery, to live a lie, to take it out on other people—I knew this was all bad. And I knew it was untenable. I didn't know where it would end, but I knew it would end badly.

It was a horrible situation, and I stewed over it at night. In addition to the nightmares and sleepwalking, I became a hypochondriac—in the extreme: I believed I was dying. I would lie awake at night, afraid to fall asleep lest I never wake up. Eventually I would doze off, unable to keep my eyes open any longer. It was the same every night.

You're dying. You're in trouble.

Then, lo and behold, I got my first transistor radio. It opened an entirely different world, a separate place where I could go whenever I put the single earpiece in my functioning left ear. Music once again became my sanctuary, giving me at least a fleeting sense of safety and solitude.

And in February 1964, a few weeks after my twelfth birthday, I saw the Beatles on *The Ed Sullivan Show*. As I watched them singing, it hit me: *This is my ticket out.* Here was the vehicle I could use to rise out of misery, to become famous, to be looked up to, to be liked, to be admired, to be envied.

And with no rational basis, I convinced myself: *I can do that. I can touch that nerve.* I had never played a guitar in my life, and I certainly had never written a song. And yet . . . this was my ticket out.

I just knew it.

Immediately I started to grow my hair out, aspiring to a Beatles mop-top. Partly I did it for style, but it was obvious why the style appealed to me: I could cover the stump I had instead of a right ear. Somehow, this was lost on my parents. They badgered me as my hair grew out and threatened to cut it.

One afternoon, not long after I saw the Beatles on *Ed Sullivan,* I bumped into a kid from my neighborhood named Matt Rael. He told me he had an electric guitar and played music. He was a grade behind me in school, but I was very impressed. All I needed now was an electric guitar and I, too, could start playing music. And I thought I knew how to get one. For the next eleven months—as the British Invasion quickly brought not only the Beatles, but the Dave Clark Five, the Kinks, the Rolling Stones, the Searchers, Manfred Mann, Gerry and the Pacemakers, the Animals, the list was endless—I pestered my parents for an electric guitar for my thirteenth birthday.

"It means the world to me," I told them.

3.

On the morning of January 20, 1965, I woke up excited. My birthday had finally arrived. Finally, an electric guitar! "Look under your bed," my mom told me. I leaned over excitedly and peered under the bed. I saw a big alligator-print cardboard case—it looked like an *acoustic* guitar.

My heart sank.

I pulled it out from under the bed and opened the case. Sure enough, it was a used Japanese acoustic guitar with nylon strings. The top had been cracked and shoddily repaired. I was crushed. I closed the case and pushed it back under the bed. I didn't want to play it.

My parents came from families that emphasized the need to keep kids down rather than lift them up. That was how they thought kids should be raised. They had made a point of not giving me something I wanted before—despite the fact that it would have been just as easy for them to do. They didn't want me to get a big head, I guess.

Once I had rejected the guitar, they made me feel guilty about it—never acknowledging their role in this enormous disappointment.

My friend from scouts, Harold Schiff, did get an electric guitar for his birthday a few weeks later—a powder blue Fender Mustang with a mother-of-pearl pick guard. He immediately started a band. And he asked me to be the singer!

Harold's friends Eric London and Jay Singer, whom I knew casually from glee club and scouts, soon joined. Eric played bass in the school orchestra and just plucked the same instrument as a stand-up bass. Jay, who already knew how to play piano, had recently gotten an electric keyboard—a Farfisa organ. Harold got another kid he'd gone to Hebrew school with named Arvin Mirow to be the drummer. It turned out that I recognized him from glee club, too. Then I suggested we talk to Matt Rael, who lived next door to Eric. So Matt joined as the lead guitar player. Matt and I were the only ones in the group whose parents weren't doctors of one kind or another.

Harold and Matt lived in houses as opposed to apartments—their places had basements. Matt's older brother Jon already had a band, too, and his parents were pretty tolerant about noise. Harold's mom didn't mind the noise, either, and we'd have the Schiff's basement to ourselves, so that was where we set up first. Harold's basement was finished—the walls were lined with knotty pine wood paneling, there was a linoleum floor, and even a window. There was a door to the backyard, too, which was below street level.

Harold and Matt would plug both of their guitars into one amp, and my vocals went through the amp used by Jay Singer's keyboard. I often banged a tambourine as I sang—that was something you saw singers on TV do a lot. Eric just had to pluck the bass as loud as he could. We ran through "Satisfaction," by the Stones, and other songs by British Invasion bands like the Kinks and the Yardbirds. And to take advantage of Jay's Farfisa sound we learned "Liar, Liar," by the Castaways.

I loved it from the start. And even though all the kids had vague dreams of being rock musicians at that time—given the frenzy over the Beatles and the Stones—their parents had their lives planned out for them. These kids were going to become dentists and optometrists like their parents, and for them the band was a lark.

But I kept telling them, "I *am* going to be a rock star."

Matt Rael and I started hanging out a lot at his house. In addition to practicing together, sometimes we got to sit around during rehearsals of his brother Jon's band. Matt and I played music so much at his house that his mother eventually proposed a deal: if we refinished an old bookshelf she had bought upstate, we could officially call the basement our practice space. So we stripped the white paint off that old bookshelf and kept playing.

Matt's parents were sort of proto-hippies. His mom had actually sung on the first Weavers recordings and was friends with Pete Seeger. She had babysat for Woody Guthrie's children. By the time I got to know his parents, his mom was still booking prominent folk and blues musicians for hootenannies in Manhattan—people like Sonny Terry, Brownie McGhee, and Lead Belly, as well as Seeger.

I listened obsessively to the radio and knew the pop hits of the day, but at Matt's place I was exposed to his parents' amazing collection of folk music. They had tons of country blues and old-time music and lots of contemporary folk by the likes of Bob Dylan, Eric Andersen, Tom Rush, Phil Ochs, Buffy St. Marie, and Judy Collins. Eventually I pulled my acoustic guitar out from under the bed, and Matt showed me some chords. Then I took a couple lessons from a woman who had placed an ad in the local paper. The first song I learned to play was "Down in the Valley." Soon I had a harmonica around my neck and was trying to mimic the folk music I now knew from Matt's house.

The band continued to practice, too, and that summer of 1965 we got our first gig. There was a mayoral election that year, and John Lindsay's campaign had a local office in our neighborhood. It was housed in a storefront—just an open room with bright lights. Harold was volunteering for the campaign, distributing pamphlets—I think he thought it was something mature and cool to do. And one day the guy in charge of the office was talking about some kind of party or rally, and mentioned they needed entertainment. Even though he hadn't been talking to Harold, Harold piped up: "Um, I have a band."

They invited us to play at the event. I guess it looked good for the Democratic Party to have neighborhood kids playing. We didn't get paid, and not many people were there, but still, it was a gig. My first gig!

Sometimes when the band practiced, I got Harold to show me barre chords on his Fender Mustang. The basics came pretty easily, but if I had realized then how long it would take me to become a somewhat proficient guitar player, I probably would have given up on the spot. At the time, though, it just drove me on; messing around in the basement was fine, but I wanted to get an electric guitar of my own and get serious. I started taking the subway into Manhattan whenever I could to scour the music stores on 48th Street for affordable guitars.

Those trips into town became pilgrimages for me. Between Sixth and Seventh Avenues, independent music stores lined both sides of 48th Street. And a block up, on 49th Street and Seventh Avenue, was a sandwich shop called Blimpie's. I'd get a sub sandwich there, or a Texas chili dog—covered in gooey yellow cheese and chili and onions—at Orange Julius, and then I'd wander the music stores. Back then you weren't allowed to touch anything. If you wanted to play an instrument, they asked, "Are you buying today?" And if someone didn't look the part, like me, they'd say,

"Let me see that you really have the money on you."

So those trips to 48th Street were not about playing but about soaking in the trappings of rock and roll: drum kits, guitars, basses. And once in a while I spotted a musician I recognized from TV or from the music magazines I was starting to collect. I was in heaven.

As junior high progressed, I started skipping school more and more to hop the bus to the subway and head for 48th Street. I would arrive early in the morning, before the shops were open—so this Jewish kid would go sit in a pew in St. Patrick's Cathedral, on 49th Street and Fifth Avenue, and wait. I also found a record store a block from the cathedral, called the Record Hunter, where they let you listen to records. They had banks of turntables with headphones, and you could have them open anything up and play it. That became my idea of a perfect day—waiting in the cathedral for the record store to open, listening to music, having a chili dog, and looking at guitars.

Exploring closer to home, I found that if I took the southbound Q44 bus from my apartment to the last stop in Jamaica, Queens, there was a huge, two-story record store called Triboro Records. They had thousands of albums. And since it was a predominantly black neighborhood, I was able to pick up things I had not been exposed to before: James Brown, Joe Tex, and Otis Redding, as well as black comedians like Redd Foxx, Pigmeat Markham, and Moms Mabley. I didn't always have money to buy something, but just being able to hold the records and look at the covers was enough to make it worthwhile.

After I saved money for a year, and added the money I got for my fourteenth birthday, I went to 48th Street one day and walked into a music store called Manny's. Eying a guitar, I said, "Can I see that one, please?"

"You buying today?" came the response.

"Yes."

"Show me the money."

I plunked down all the money I had. And the man behind the counter handed me the guitar I was going to buy: a three-quarter-size, two pick-up Stratocaster knock-off built by Vox. It wasn't much of a guitar, but it was the one I could afford—it was cheaper than anything else because it wasn't full-size. And besides, I knew nothing about guitars and could barely play.

But now I *really* had my ticket out.

4.

I began to try to write songs as soon as I had the electric guitar. Somehow it just seemed like the natural thing to do—playing the instrument and writing songs went hand in hand. Whenever I heard songs I liked, I tried to emulate them. One of my first attempts was an homage to the Who's "The Kids Are Alright."

I also studied the song structures of Brill Building writers like Barry Mann and Cynthia Weil, Gerry Goffin and Carole King, Jeff Barry and Ellie Greenwich. Songs with a verse, chorus, and bridge, with great hooks; songs so catchy you knew them already by the time the second chorus arrived. They were about melodies and telling a story.

Harold Schiff's basement band had stalled, but Matt Rael and I jammed together constantly once I got my guitar. Sometimes a kid named Neal Teeman would join us on drums. We called ourselves Uncle Joe and continued to add songs to our repertoire. Matt was having problems of his own, however, and at some point his parents enrolled him in a private school in Manhattan.

My hair was really long now, but it was very curly. At the time, I hated the curls because the style was straight hair. So I'd buy a relaxer cream called Perma-Strate—it was available in nearby black neighborhoods. Perma-Strate smelled like ammonia and heavy chemicals, and it burned your scalp like nobody's business. You had to apply it to your hair, comb it back, let it sit, and then comb it forward. On occasions when I left it in too long, my scalp would bleed. Sometimes I'd iron my hair, too. Anything to straighten it out. The mother of another kid I became friends with, David Un, called me "Prince Valiant" because of the look. My dad, meanwhile, had taken to calling me "Stanley Fat Ass."

I'd met David Un at Parsons junior high, and his family, like Matt's, were nurturing and artistic. His dad was a painter, his mom a teacher. Like me, David had really long hair. Sometimes when I skipped school to go into Manhattan and haunt 48th Street, he went with me. He was big into music, too. David and I also started mixing as best we could with the budding counterculture.

One day, walking down Main Street in my neighborhood, I noticed a new shop called Middle Earth. It was a head shop, selling water pipes and glass bongs and all sorts of drug paraphernalia. The people behind the counter inside had long hair, too.

Maybe I would fit in here?

I didn't fit in with normal people, that was sure, but here, right in my own neighborhood, was an alternative. I started to hang out there and talk with the owners as well as a few of the customers who came and went. It wasn't about the drugs—though I did start to smoke pot once in a while—it was about seeking acceptance. To an outcast, or someone in a sort of self-imposed exile, Middle Earth felt comfortable. Eventually I started taking my acoustic guitar to the shop and playing it while hanging out.

One girl in my school, Ellen Mentin, treated me with an extraordinary amount of patience and understanding. I trusted her enough

"Be-in" at age fifteen in Central Park . . . blissed out with a little help.

to try to explain some of my inner demons, but hinting at my problems didn't reduce my anxiety. Ellen wanted us to become a normal
junior high couple—go to the movies together or whatever—but I
was incapable of doing things with her in public. It felt too risky,
too suffocating, too claustrophobic.

What if someone started making fun of me while we were together?

I also couldn't understand why she wanted to be with someone
like me—with or without the long hair, I was a freak after all. I
even asked her, "Why do you like me? Why do you want to be
around me?" It made no sense to me at all.

Ellen and I stayed friends, but being with someone who was
steadfastly caring was all but unbearable. Even riding the bus together
to go see a movie involved risks I couldn't get myself to take.

My dad decided to give me his version of the birds and the bees
around that time. Out of the blue, on one of our walks, he said, "If
you get someone pregnant, you're on your own."

Did that mean I'd be out on the street at age fourteen?

Great.

I barely knew how to get someone pregnant, but now I knew it was a one-way ticket to getting thrown out.

As if I'm not already on my own.

I spent the bulk of my time *on my own*, at home, in my room, shutting everything out and immersing myself in music—listening to my transistor radio, playing guitar, reading music magazines. My mom, feeling guilty about the way my sister's plight was consuming all her time, also bought me a stereo.

I became an avid follower of Scott Muni's radio program, *The English Power Hour,* one of the early FM radio shows to highlight the latest sounds from the UK. In the spring of 1967, Jimi Hendrix, who had moved to the UK, was dominating the English scene and charts, and his music started to filter back to the States on shows like Muni's. When his first album finally arrived, it hit me like an atom bomb.

I loved to put the *Jimi Hendrix Experience* album on my new stereo and lie down and press the big speakers against both sides of my head. Even though I was deaf on the right side, when I pressed the speaker against my head, I could hear through bone conduction. I also painted my room purple and strung a set of flashing Christmas lights along the ceiling. I played my guitar and looked at myself in the mirror, lights flashing, and tried to perfect jumps and windmills like Pete Townsend of the Who.

But perhaps the greatest effect Hendrix had was on hair styles. His hair was teased up in a huge puff, and soon Eric Clapton and Jimmy Page had done the same to their hair. Suddenly that became the look. I remember the first day I blew out my hair. No more Perma-Strate for me. As I emerged from my room and got ready to leave the house with my hair now exploding around my head like my heroes' hair, my mom said, "You're not going out like *that,* are you?"

"Yep, see you later."

It was time to let my freak flag fly.

As junior high neared the end, I auditioned for the High School of Music & Art, a public alternative school on West 135th Street and Convent Avenue in Manhattan. I had been one of the best visual artists in my junior high—drawing was my thing. But equally important, I hoped this specialized school would be a more comfortable environment than the meat grinders I had attended up to that point. I had gone from being stared at for something beyond my control—my ear—to being stared at for something of my own making—my outlandish hair and clothes. Most schools still had dress codes in those days, but the philosophy at Music & Art was that it didn't matter what you came to school wearing as long as you came to school.

As I saw it, instead of being the freak in school, I'd go to a school of freaks.

5

Even though drawing was my ticket into Music & Art, I wasn't thinking very seriously about trying to make a career of art. Which turned out to be a good thing, because it was sobering to show up at school in the fall of 1967 and see not only so many people who were as good as I was, but also plenty who were clearly better.

I had pursued art primarily because there was no school for aspiring rock stars—art was a backup plan. No longer. I knew now it was music or bust. Even so, when I headed off to school each day, my musical aspirations stayed behind, carefully stashed in my purple bedroom. Though I never told fellow students at school about my aspirations or tried to switch to the music curriculum, I was aware that Music & Art students had an impressive track record of making a musical impact—and not just on Broadway and in orchestras. A band called the Left Banke, who had a big hit with "Walk Away Renee," were recent grads. As was the brilliant singer-songwriter Laura Nyro. Janis Ian, who had just had a hit with "Society's Child," was still enrolled when I arrived.

One day Matt Rael's older brother, Jon, came around to see me. He'd already had several bands and we all looked up to him. His first band was influenced by the Ventures—surf music—but these days he was leading one called the Post War Baby Boom that sounded like some of the stuff coming out of San Francisco—a hippie take on folk, blues, and jug band sounds. They had a girl singer who took leads on some songs—that stuff was a bit like Grace Slick's first band, the Great Society. And the Post War Baby Boom actually played gigs.

Out of nowhere, Jon asked me to join the band. They needed a rhythm guitar player. My mind raced: why hadn't they asked Matt, who at that point was a better guitar player than I was? Maybe because I'm in high school and Matt has another year of junior high? Is Matt going to be pissed?

Holy shit, a real band! This is huge!

I didn't hesitate for another second. I said yes. Next thing I knew we were rehearsing in the same basement where Matt and I had pre-

Playing Tompkins Square Park in the East Village with "The Baby Boom."
I'm on the left, at age fifteen, Jon Rael on the right.

viously practiced. We worked on an up-tempo cover of Gershwin's "Summertime." I also worked out a version of "Born in Chicago" by the Paul Butterfield Blues Band, and even sang lead vocals.

Everybody else in the band was at least two years older than me, which, at that age, seemed like a lot. What didn't occur to me at the time was that they would graduate high school at the end of that school year. But in the short term, I was all in. We had a few gigs in "our" new lineup, and then I suggested we try to get a recording contract. I said we should have some pictures taken—and I knew just who to call. That summer of 1967 I'd spent two ill-fated weeks at a summer camp near the Catskills Mountains. Or at least, it was supposed to be a summer camp. It turned out to be a scam—some guy got a bunch of parents to *pay* him to have their kids come up to his farm, camp out, and, it turned out, help him tear down an old barn. He called it a work camp, implying that his program represented a chance for city kids to work on the land. In the end, though, it had been kind of fun, and I had become friends with one of the counselors, who were as duped as the campers. His name was Maury Englander, and he was now working for a famous photographer in Manhattan.

Maury had access to the photographer's studio whenever it wasn't being used—that was one of the perks of the job, since Maury was in the process of becoming a photographer himself and in fact would be working for magazines like *Newsweek* less than a year later. So I called him, and we arranged to go into the studio one weekend and have Maury take some promo shots. Maury was pretty wired-in politically as well, and we parlayed the photo session into a few gigs playing parties for various antiwar organizations in early 1968, as protests against the Vietnam War were picking up steam.

Club gigs were tough to come by, because they still wanted Top 40 cover bands for the most part. We played a lot of our own songs, and the covers we did were not the sorts of songs at the top of the charts. I arranged an audition for us at a place called the Night Owl; I had read that the Lovin' Spoonful had played there, and the Spoonful's jug band roots and good-time sound weren't so far off from what the Post War Baby Boom was trying to do. But at the audition, the guy who was making the decision walked out while we were still playing. We didn't get that gig.

Despite the slow-going, I wanted to succeed and worked at it ceaselessly. Eventually I managed to pass some materials to somebody with an in at CBS Records, and an exec from the label called me. "If you guys can play as good as you look, you'll be great," he said. He was referring to one of the studio shots Maury Englander had taken of the band.

Before the guy ever saw us in person or heard us, he arranged for us to record a demo at CBS. I wrote a song for us to record called "Never Loving, Never Living," but I was too shy to play it for the band until the day before we were supposed to cut it. And then our female vocalist decided to go for a swim in the fountain in Washington Square Park in Greenwich Village the night before, and she caught a cold and lost her voice. When we showed up in the studio the next day, my first time ever in a real recording studio, she couldn't sing.

To top it all off, the CBS exec told us he wanted to rename the band the Living Abortions. The demo never got finished.

Meanwhile, at Music & Art, despite keeping to myself, the chance to see girls in T-shirts and no bras—another advantage of the lack of a dress code—was more than enough to get me to school every day. But I soon found I was at odds with myself and everybody else. I looked hipper than I really was because of my hair and clothes. But my hair was blown out in part for one very specific reason, and I felt intimidated by the kids I thought were genuinely hip. As I slowly learned, covering my ear didn't change anything. Like everything else in life, ultimately it wasn't about what other people saw, it was about what I knew and what I felt.

One day at school, one of the cool girls called out to me. Victoria was curvy and blond, with disarming blue eyes. It was well known that she had the coolest friends, in and out of school. I was wearing a leather jacket with fringe, which was a hip look at the time, and a look not many people were rocking yet, even at Music & Art. "Hey, fringe!" she said.

I went over to talk to her and somehow mustered the courage to ask her out. It was like an out-of-body experience—somebody was talking, and it was me, but I felt totally disconnected because it was such a leap into uncharted territory. She said yes, and I walked away in a state of exhilaration and terror.

We went to a concert at the Fillmore East. But when we got there, she knew tons of other people in the audience. We wound up sitting with her friends. I was immediately intimidated because they were hip, and I was an uptight kid from Queens. They started passing a joint. I took a hit each time it was passed to me, and I got pretty high. Soon I was talking nonstop, until Victoria said, "What the hell are you talking about?"

That shut me up for the rest of the show.

After the concert we went back to her parents' apartment. I was still really stoned and also paranoid because Victoria had seen a chink in my armor and questioned my coolness. I ended up talking to her dad—and continuing to talk to him long after she had slipped off to her room and gone to bed. I eventually slithered out of the apartment feeling like a complete jerk.

From then on in school she snickered whenever we ran into each other. I don't think she meant to be mean, but she wasn't laughing *with* me.

Another girl I saw briefly lived in Staten Island. She was half Italian and half Norwegian and lived in an Italian neighborhood.

She was hooked on speed—between me being a bit stocky and her having no appetite, I often got to eat her lunch, which her mom lovingly prepared, not knowing who would actually end up savoring it. The first time I met her mom, she seemed to like me; the next time I went over to her house to pick her up, I wasn't allowed into the house.

"I can't go inside?" I said to the girl.

"No, my mom thought you were Italian, but she found out you're a Jew."

That was my introduction to the wonderful world of anti-Semitism.

After a while, the double-whammy of my insecurity and my inability to hear what was going on in class had me falling into the same old pattern in school of getting lost, getting frustrated, isolating myself, and eventually cutting school as often as I could get away with it. I knew how many days I could be absent, how many classes I could miss, how many times I could be late—and I used them all to their fullest. Those were the school statistics that mattered most to me.

I became a ghost—hardly ever in school, and when I was there, nearly invisible. I sat in the back of my classes and barely spoke to

My rank: 552 out of 587 students. If you can't graduate at the top of your class, distinguish yourself by graduating at the bottom. It's a miracle they let me graduate at all.

anybody. Once again, I was living in self-imposed exile as a result of my defensiveness and social anxiety. Once again, I was beginning to shut down. Life was poisonous and desolate. My sleeping problems returned. Once again, I would wake up screaming from the familiar nightmares, sure that I was dying.

I'm alone on a floating dock, far from shore, surrounded by darkness . . .

6.

One night while my mom was on her first trip back to Germany, my dad came home late, smelling of booze. He started talking to me. "We all sometimes do things we shouldn't do," he said.

Oh, God.

"But that's okay, right?"

I'm your kid. Are you looking for absolution from me? Me? You want me to rid you of guilt for something you just did?

I knew by this stage that I couldn't turn to my parents for help or support or approval. But I didn't expect them to dump their own problems on me.

Suddenly I remembered an incident that had happened a few years before. My dad had answered the phone one evening and was clearly disturbed by what he heard. He spoke quietly to my mom, and then they called the police. When the cops arrived, they asked my dad to recount what he had heard on the phone, and he told them that the man on the other end of the line had told him if my

Me at sixteen with my mom and dad in our apartment on 75th Road.

dad didn't stop seeing some woman he would hurt my dad. "He said he'd cut his balls off," piped my mother. We all just treated it as a case of mistaken identity, but now I wondered.

Home felt like an even more dangerous place after that. It would be decades before I finally found out what was going on, but I knew right there and then that our house had become a potentially deadly whirlpool.

I'm drowning.

It was bad enough picturing myself barreling down the road in a car with no steering wheel, or alone on a floating dock, far from shore, surrounded by darkness. Now it felt as if the floating dock was sinking.

Whatever was going on with my sister was being exacerbated

by my parents; whatever was going on with me was being exacerbated by my parents. My home felt as fraught with danger as school and other social situations. I could not escape a pervasive sense of fear. I was only fifteen years old and I was losing it. And I had nobody to talk to.

Nobody. Totally alone. Petrified.

What should I do?

I could sense that it was going to end very badly if things went on like this.

Am I going to take my own life? Am I going to go nuts like my sister?

Julia had reacted to her profound issues by choosing a path that led to self-destruction and numbing herself. Obviously, that was a road to ruin. How I dealt with things was up to me. Sure, I was on my own, but I had choices. If I did nothing, that, too, was a choice—and I knew the consequences would be dire.

I refuse to be a victim.

I wanted to fix myself. I wanted to roll up my sleeves and get my shit together. I wanted to make things work, to transform my world into one I liked.

But how?

I was riding my bike when it hit me. As I turned the corner near our house, a thought hit me like a sledgehammer.

I need to get help.

Otherwise, I suddenly realized, I wasn't going to make it. Otherwise, I was going to make bad choices. Or no choice. I would just keep spiraling downward.

Do something.

Then one night I overheard a friend of my sister's talking about an outpatient psychiatric clinic at Mount Sinai Hospital in Manhattan. Here was something concrete. A place you could go. It had a name and an address. I looked the hospital up in the phone book. I waited until nobody was home one day and called the psychiatric clinic. I made an appointment.

On the day of the appointment, I took two subways and a bus to get there. I walked in, alone, and said, "I need help." They had me sign in. Fortunately, I didn't need parental authorization. And it cost only three dollars.

Someone took me back to meet a doctor wearing a white lab coat over his clothes. I didn't know anything about therapy. I just hoped someone would tell me how to live. I was surprised when all I got during our first conversation was questions, not answers. Everything was turned around. I wanted the doctor to tell me what to do, and instead he basically turned my questions back on me. It would be quite a while before I realized this was the basis of therapy—it wasn't about someone leading you through life by the hand.

This doctor, a complete stranger, kind of furrowed his brow and looked away when I talked.

Is he looking at me like I'm crazy?

After that first session, I wasn't sure what to make of it. Still, I decided to try it again. Whatever it took.

Roll up your sleeves.

The next time I went, though, I asked to see a different doctor. Thankfully, they obliged. The second doctor was named Jesse Hilsen. I didn't feel self-conscious around Dr. Hilsen. He didn't look at me like I was nuts. He quickly made me realize that even though I thought the rest of the world was "normal" and that I was the outlier, that wasn't true. Plenty of other people had issues that plagued them, too. I wasn't alone. I wasn't the one person in a million who felt his world caving in, felt himself imploding. Thank God. This was progress.

I was still yearning for some support and reassurance at home, and I told my dad that I had started seeing a psychiatrist. He was dismissive. "You just want to be different," he scowled.

Then he got angry. "You think you're the only one with problems?" he shouted.

No, I knew I wasn't. My sister had problems. And I suspected my dad did, too—though who knew what he was talking about that night when he wanted my forgiveness. But I wasn't going to succumb to my problems or surrender in the face of them. I was going to try to tackle them. I was going to fight.

I started meeting with Dr. Hilsen every Wednesday after school. I would stop at a deli near the hospital, buy a turkey sandwich with Russian dressing, sit on a bench in Central Park, and eat it—and then go see Dr. Hilsen. Each afternoon when I left, I was already looking forward to the next week. Talking with Dr. Hilsen represented a rope I could hold on to.

Finally, I was doing something—taking charge of my destiny and improving myself. I was rising to the challenge.

7.

In early 1968, not long after I turned sixteen, Scott Muni's *English Power Hour* broadcast a new hit on the British charts called "Fire Brigade," by the Move. It was about a girl who was so hot that you need to call 9-1-1—run and get the fire brigade.

Now, I was a dyed-in-the-wool Anglophile, and the Move was one of my favorite groups. And what I was doing at that point in terms of song writing was taking inspiration from songs I remembered from the radio. When I heard "Fire Brigade," I loved the concept. So I sat down and began to hash out a song of my own using the same idea. I hadn't heard the song enough to actually copy it musically, but I had grasped something that I really liked, and my chorus went like this:

Get the firehouse
'cause she sets my soul afire

I called the song "Firehouse." This was real progress. With every new song I wrote, my sense of purpose grew stronger. I may not have had a social life, but I had music and a dream.

So many people are miserable. They need someone to entertain them. Why can't it be me?

One day at high school a teacher pulled me aside. "Why aren't you showing up for class? Why aren't you applying yourself?" he asked me.

"Because I'm going to be a rock star," I said.

As the guy looked at me, his face betrayed his thoughts: *You poor fool.* Then he forced a half-smile and said, "A lot of people want to be rock stars."

"Yeah," I told him, "but I *will* be one."

Outside of my band, the Post War Baby Boom, I didn't have anything else in my life—just my guitar, my stereo, and, more and more often, concerts. I envied the kids who had social circles and weekend get-togethers, but I didn't have any of that. I had not figured out how to be part of things. So I often went to shows by myself. It was something fulfilling.

In 1968 I saw Jimi Hendrix live in a small auditorium at Hunter College on the Upper East Side of Manhattan. I saw the Who, the Yardbirds, and Traffic. I saw Otis Redding and Solomon Burke. I saw Hendrix a second time. Virtually every weekend there were multiband bills at the Fillmore East or Village Theater where I could see three bands for three or four dollars. I found myself bathing in music every weekend.

There was a debauched kind of elegance to the British bands: they had great haircuts, they wore velvets and satins, and they were cohesive not only in their musical style, but in their attire and personas. They had individual identities but also a band identity—band members were stylish in a way that complemented one another. They also had a sexuality that American bands of the time didn't have.

I saw a lot of those American bands, too, like Jefferson Airplane, the Grateful Dead, Moby Grape, and Quicksilver Messenger Service. Most of those groups looked like bums who had just rolled out of bed, alone. Seeing some fat guy with pigtails didn't appeal to me. When I saw a band with a bearded guy in it, I thought, *What's Sigmund Freud doing in a rock band?* I think the initial reason for the lightshows they used onstage was to focus attention on the pulsating oils and colors on the screen instead of on a bunch of slobs who looked like they had just finished panhandling. Most American bands looked like a commune gathering. It just didn't work for me. Combine the look with the way they sounded, and it's no wonder people took acid at their shows.

I knew, however, acid was not for me. I saw a few people freak out on it at concerts, and I saw a kid from my neighborhood committed after he took it. I figured I was a prime candidate for a one-way ticket to the insane asylum. Better to stay in control. I had too many issues eating at me—too much turmoil—and I'd seen what drugs had done to my sister. I had a steadfast belief that losing control like that would lead me down a bad, bad path.

The British bands became part of the template for what I wanted to do moving forward. And that template became more and more complete in the coming year or so as I saw Humble Pie, Slade, and Grand Funk Railroad, who all created a churchlike atmosphere, a religious connection to their audience. A frontman like Humble Pie's Steve Marriott was leading a congregation, evangelizing for rock and roll.

I believe!

Of course, while I felt the music in my blood, I needed money to buy concert tickets and guitar strings and imported English music magazines, like *Melody Maker, New Music Express,* and *Sounds,* which I bought at specialized newsstands after taking the bus and subway to Greenwich Village. But jobs were hard to find. So when my mother's cousin, who owned a Sinclair gas station off the Palisades Parkway, offered me a job at his station, I took it. The first thing I did was buy a rickety old Rambler from him so I could drive to the job after school. I had to go from Harlem, where Music & Art was, across the George Washington Bridge and up to Orangeburg, New York, where the gas station was, work a shift, and then drive all the way home to Queens, several times a week.

It was hard work, partly because of the distance, but also partly because I knew absolutely nothing about cars. I was the most unmechanical, un-handy person. On one of my first days at work, a car pulled up and the driver said, "Check the oil." So I opened up the hood and pulled out the dipstick—I knew how to do that. And I knew how to read it. "You're down a quart," I said.

"Okay," he said, "go ahead and put in a quart."

"Sure," I said, and I got to work.

After a few minutes the driver asked, "Hey kid, what's taking so long?" Well, I had a funnel poised above the dipstick hole and was trying to drip the oil in there. I didn't know there was another place for adding oil. Despite my initial difficulties, this arrangement worked fine for a while—there was even an attractive female attendant whose regulation jumpsuit unzipped as quickly as mine.

Then one weekend, one of the local newspapers—which cost five cents a copy—ran a Sinclair ad with a one-dollar voucher toward gas. Readers could present the voucher for a buck of gas, then the gas station owners would send in the vouchers to get the dollar back from Sinclair. My mom's cousin had me buy as many copies of the paper as I could, transport them to his station in a borrowed station wagon, and cut out the vouchers. He planned to claim the dollar from Sinclair's corporate office without ever pumping the dollar's worth of gas. In exchange, he said he would reimburse me for all the five-cent newspapers I bought and pay me a cut of the money he got from the gas company when he redeemed all the vouchers. I brought in many carloads of papers, and he made thousands of dollars, but he never paid me back for the papers, much less a cut of the money he made. Swindled by my own relative. So I quit.

After that, I got a job at an upscale deli called Charles and Company. It specialized in gourmet cold cuts, cheeses, and canned goods and had locations all around New York. I had to wear a wig to hide my hair. It was tight and gave me a headache, but I worked behind the counter, preparing sandwiches and putting salads and spreads in containers, so it was necessary.

A district manager of the chain came in one day, and after he had conducted his business, he came over to me and said, "You know, you could wind up a manager of one of these stores one day." I think this was his idea of a motivational speech, but it had the opposite effect on me. I knew this wasn't where I belonged. God, no. Anything but that.

In the fall of 1968, at the start of my junior year of high school, I learned that the Post War Baby Boom wasn't where I belonged, either. At least they didn't think so. Jon Rael and the other members had gone off to college, most of them to Bard and SUNY New Paltz—upstate but not at the ends of the earth. I had figured we might keep playing during their breaks and that maybe I would go up on weekends and play with them. They had other plans. They didn't tell me I was out of the band; I figured it out when they came home one weekend with another guy—who was a guitar player.

They were still playing together up at college, and this new guy hanging around was part of it now. That hurt, especially because they didn't tell me. I took stock of the situation and thought about what to do.

I'm going to become a better guitar player.

But just as important: *I'm going to keep writing songs.*

No, there was something more to it than that: *Make the most of what you have. There's no reason to wait for a band.*

So what if I didn't have a band? I had songs, and I was writing more of them. By this point I had a reel-to-reel tape recorder I used to make recordings of my songs. With me, the music and melody had always come first, and I filled in the dots—including the lyrics—from there.

Maybe I can get other people to record my songs?

Some of the magazines I bought, like *Hit Parader* and *Song Hits*, printed song lyrics. And at the bottom of the pages where the lyrics were printed was always information on the publishing company and the songwriter.

Well, if I'm a songwriter and need to find an outlet for my songs—and don't have a band—I guess I need a publishing deal.

I was such a loner that making a career in music on my own somehow made perfect sense. So I spent a good deal of my junior year calling around to publishing companies and talking my way into auditions to showcase material. The one I remember best was at the Brill Building, because the place was already legendary to me. I went in with my guitar, sat in an office opposite someone who had agreed to meet me, and played songs to this stranger.

The funny thing was that while I had always been extremely wary about opening myself up by bringing songs to the band, I found it easy to play them for people I didn't know. But even though some of the people were very nice and encouraging, nobody signed me.

I still had a lot to learn about my craft.

8.

I found myself hanging around Middle Earth, the head shop, and often I visited the couple who owned the place at home in their nearby apartment. We would shoot the shit and hang out, and I'd play my acoustic guitar. They had a friend in the same building who also played guitar, and some days I'd go to his place and jam. I never called first—I just showed up at their places.

I smoked pot sometimes, and it was kind of fun sitting on the floor thinking of ridiculous things, suddenly becoming a genius and philosophizing about life on other planets or about the bark on trees. It wasn't very productive, and I realized that if I wanted to write songs, I couldn't spend time smoking pot and eating sandwiches. I still had a goal.

Socializing with older people, though, became an outlet for me. It kept at bay some of my neurosis about socializing with kids my own age. And it could be on my own terms—it wasn't like I had to see these adults at school every day. Around the same time I became friends with a woman down the block named Sandy. She was married to a guy named Steven, had three kids, and was in her mid-twenties. I started hanging out with her and her husband—like the couple at Middle Earth. I spent a lot of time with them. It was great not to have to be at home all the time.

One day when I was hanging out with Sandy, she said, "I have something to tell you."

Okay . . .

"Steven left me."

"That's terrible!" I said, and gave her a big hug. We wound up holding each other on the sofa. And then . . . she led me into the bedroom.

Whoa, what's happening here?

This is awesome!

My sexual technique was nonexistent, but I'm sure Sandy appreciated my enthusiasm: I was a human jackhammer. Or a love gun. At that age, just taking my pants off got me excited. Having someone else there was a bonus.

Up until that moment when I slept with Sandy, sex had seemed like something that would be impossible to find. This changed everything. Luckily for me, Steven didn't have a change of heart about leaving her, so I started to drop by Sandy's house more and more. Her door was only a few steps from my own, and now it was the entrance to a sexual fun park, with a thrill ride like nothing I'd ever experienced.

These rendezvous could be pretty late because we waited for her kids to go to sleep. One night I called my house from Sandy's and told my mom, "I'm going to be late." Again.

"Honestly, Stan, what's going on?" she asked.

"Mom, she has a lot of problems." My mom knew that the couple had split up and seemed suspicious of our connection, but she didn't really want to know the truth.

Once I understood that I had some sort of appeal as a young man to older women, my situation changed dramatically. The only thing my dad had ever said to me about sex was that I'd be on my own if I ever got someone pregnant. Sex, I was taught, was deviant and unclean. But, man, did I want it. And once I got it, man, did I like it. And now, getting it this way, I didn't have to deal with any intimacy issues I would have to work through to persuade a girl my own age to have sex. I couldn't handle that. No way. I still saw intimacy as invasive—I didn't want anyone inside the psychological fortress I had built around myself. I did not want to be close to anyone. But now, I realized, with older women, I could enjoy the act and then immediately hit the road.

Do it and get out.

And that suited them just as well as it did me. The floodgates were open.

Soon enough, another woman from the neighborhood saw me with my guitar and asked me whether I knew somebody who could give her son guitar lessons. She was a divorcee.

"Well, gee, I can give him lessons," I said.

I spent her thirty-ninth birthday in bed with her. I was seventeen.

My instincts and hormones drove me into more and more situations like that. It was like a drug. And what a great drug. I now had access to something magical, without having to let down my guard and deal with a meaningful relationship or any kind of real intimacy. I never had to worry about anyone wanting more from me emotionally.

I didn't see any rules; I never considered the ethics of what I was doing. If somebody's wife wanted to sleep with me, hey, that's fine because she wants to do it. The fact that someone else was often involved meant nothing to me. That was *their* issue, or would be. If a woman made herself available, that was good enough for me.

The husband of the couple who owned Middle Earth seemed captivated by a girl who came in to the store a lot. Then one night, at a party at the couple's apartment, he started hitting on that girl. I think the couple was moving in the direction of an open relationship anyway, but that night the wife seemed upset about her husband going off with another person. So I wound up in another bedroom with the wife and a German shepherd that seemed as interested in me as she was.

Hey, these people are all adults.

I didn't want a girlfriend. I didn't want a relationship. That was scary. But I could still get what I craved in a completely unattached, unemotional way. And situations that might have seemed intimidating to others—there was, after all, a chance that somebody's husband might want to cut off my balls, as my dad had been threatened, or even kill me—seemed ideal to me.

I didn't confide in anyone. I continued to exist in my own little world. But sex was now one of the forces that drove me. It didn't matter where or with whom. I remember inviting myself to a party at a neighbor's house one night. I just walked in. They were using one of the bedrooms as the coatroom—throwing all the guests' coats on the bed. And I ended up taking a woman into that room and screwing on top of all the coats. A few people came looking for their coats as we were going at it, and they were absolutely aghast. But I didn't care. Boundaries as far as what was appropriate simply did not exist to me. Where I had been alone with my music not long before, now I had sex. *Sex!* The beast had awakened in me.

Another time a girlfriend of my sister's slept over at our house, and I tried to crawl into bed with her. She pushed me out of the bed. The next day my sister told my mom. I thought it was hilarious. In fact, it was a bonus to me that my parents were put off by my behavior. That just made it all the more appealing.

I saw music differently now, too. When I saw Led Zeppelin in

Corona Park, in Queens in August 1969, in front of fewer than two thousand people, the sexuality of what they were doing was palpable. The show was in the New York State Pavilion from the 1964 World's Fair, a strange semi-open-air facility with a mosaic tile map of the state on the floor, a multicolored Plexiglas roof above, and flying saucer–shaped forms perched on columns nearby. Jimmy Page's sound hit me with the same impact that Beethoven had when I was a little kid. He wasn't just a great guitar player, he was a visionary who composed and pieced together sonics to perfection. Led Zeppelin took a music form that was by then familiar—blues-based rock—and made it into something new, and something all their own.

Robert Plant sang like a banshee—I didn't know anyone could sing like that. I'd seen Terry Reid and Steve Marriott, who had sort of laid the groundwork for what Plant was doing, but Plant was better, more commanding, more magnetic, more consummate. He created a style that didn't exist before. And for all his qualities as a singer, he was more than just a singer. Robert Plant was the physical embodiment of a rock god. Nobody *looked* like that. He was an archetype in the making. I remember the next time I saw the Who, Roger Daltrey had grown out his bouffant hairdo into long curls— *aha, he wants to look like Plant*, I thought. Everybody wanted to look like Plant and sound like Plant.

Everything on that summer stage was stunning. It was the closest thing I've ever had to a religious experience.

I had gone to the show with David Un, whom I still saw sometimes, and afterwards I said to him, "Let's not even talk about that. Let's not talk about the show because anything we say will cheapen it."

I'll never, ever, see something this perfect again.

Music, I knew, still represented my salvation and the ultimate solution to my deep-seated insecurities. I wanted the validation I had felt playing in front of crowds. While the Post War Baby Boom hadn't made a penny, we had played some gigs at places like the Beehive; I also liked playing the showcases at publishing companies. So I started playing with Matt Rael again, the little brother of Jon from the Post War Baby Boom. I had played with Matt a lot a few years before, and now we both cranked up our Fender blackface amps and started experimenting, sometimes joined on drums by Neal Teeman. Often, we turned all the tone and volume controls on the two amps all the way up and created a trebly wall of noise.

We managed to score a few gigs at a hippie venue called the Bank, in Brooklyn. The building was the headquarters and home of some sort of commune, spread over several floors of an abandoned bank building. One of the floors was covered in hay, and kids could get donkey rides there. We played on another floor, creating a loud wall of noise, our guitars screaming nastily. Matt didn't even face the audience for most of the performances.

It was fun to be playing again, but clearly this wasn't the group I was going to bet my future on. Thoughts of the future began to eat at me as the end of high school loomed. I was coasting through senior year and had to think about my next steps. The pressure I began to feel wasn't about money per se. What bothered me was that other people were laying the groundwork for their future security. They were making plans to go to college and learn trades. I wasn't.

Much as I believed in myself, there were no guarantees about making a career in music. Kids in my neighborhood were following their parents into medicine or law. Meanwhile, my hair was below my shoulders and I was an aspiring rock god. The percentages, I knew, were not in my favor. I spent countless scary nights sitting up thinking, *What the hell am I doing?* No matter how sure you are of yourself, you're going to have some dark moments of doubt. Your self-belief gets questioned, even if it doesn't disappear.

I lay in bed, thinking. I had a plan. Sort of. It was more of a goal than a plan, really. I had something I knew I was working toward, and something I was gambling on. But there were no milestones along the way to check off—it wasn't like working toward becoming an optometrist.

What if? What if I don't make it?

The fears came at night.

Eventually I plotted out a scenario of last resort. I would work for the phone company. That was a well-paid union job with good benefits. And if I could get a job as a phone installer—and they were advertising for them at the time—I would be able to work on my own, away from people, away from any bosses. I could do that. I would drive around in a van and install phones. On my own.

9.

Matt and I began to argue at rehearsals. I thought that we were just messing around more than creating something or moving forward. I also felt that he should face the audience instead of his amp when we played gigs. Things came to a head one day when Neal and I asked him to turn down his amp while we were practicing.

"Turn down!" we shouted.

"No!" Matt shouted back and kept playing, as loud as he could.

So Neal and I called it quits. We walked out, and the group was done. Matt and I remained friends—even started working together as taxi drivers—but I think it was a relief for him in some ways not to be playing with us anymore.

Of course, I wanted to keep playing, and since I'd been turned down when I went solo to the publishing companies, I felt a band was the right way to go again. Neal, who was working part-time at a recording studio by now, heard from a friend of his about a guy named Steve Coronel who played lead guitar. So we called Steve and got together, worked out a few covers, played a few of my originals, and started booking gigs.

The band with Matt had never had a bass player, but Steve wanted to bring one in. "I know this other guy," Steve said.

The guy's name was Gene Klein, and he and Steve had played together as teens in a band called the Long Island Sounds. Gene was living somewhere out of town now, Steve said. He was apparently a few years older than I was and had already graduated from college. I didn't care whether he lived in Sullivan County or Staten Island; if there was a possibility that we'd be moving toward creating a real band, I was all for it.

One night I went over to Steve's Manhattan apartment in Washington Heights, not far from where I had lived as a little kid. Steve's room was painted black. And in the room was a big, burly guy.

"Stan," said Steve, "this is Gene Klein."

Gene had long hair and a beard under his double chin. He was very overweight. I was pretty stocky back then, but this guy was huge. He was wearing overalls and sandals and looked liked something from the then-new country music TV show *Hee Haw*.

Gene made it clear right away that he didn't see us as his musical equals. He played some songs for us that I thought were sort of goofy. Then he challenged me to play one of my songs, so I played something called "Sunday Driver," which I later retitled "Let Me Know." He seemed completely thrown that someone besides John Lennon, Paul McCartney, and Gene Klein could write a song. It was a moment of realization for him—here was another guy who wasn't famous who could actually write a song. He was visibly taken aback. He mumbled, "Hmmmm."

I was annoyed that he saw himself as operating at a level that qualified him to pass judgment on me—as though all that mattered was his approval. Particularly because I hadn't thought much of his songs, the idea that he was judging me seemed arrogant, condescending, and ludicrous. He made it clear that he felt himself to be judging from a higher plane, and I didn't like that at all. Gene, of course, had no clue about my ear, which was covered up by my hair, but I was preprogrammed to dislike being scrutinized and judged. It wasn't a nice thing to do as far as I was concerned, and I wasn't eager to work with the guy.

Another night, Steve, a bass player named Marty Cohen, and I played a free gig at a coffee shop on Broadway and 111th Street called Forlini's Third Phase. The place was lined with Styrofoam, and we played with a bunch of amplified gear. We played some originals and some covers, including Mountain's "Mississippi Queen," and the crowd got into it. Gene came to that gig, too, because Steve had borrowed some of his gear, and he was clearly impressed.

At some point after that, I answered an ad in the alternative weekly the *Village Voice* for a guitar player. When I rang the number, I found out the guy who had placed the ad, Brooke Ostrander, was the keyboard player in a band looking for a lead guitarist, not a rhythm guy like me. That was the end of that.

But not long afterward, Gene called me and asked whether I would come over to New Jersey and work on a demo tape his group was trying to finish. He wanted me to come for a day or two. I agreed. Strangely, it turned out the group was working at the home of their keyboard player, Brooke Ostrander, and this was the same band Brooke had placed the ad about. Brooke was already a school music teacher. Gene, too, bragged about some white-collar job he had that paid five dollars an hour—a fortune at the time. They had a home tape recording machine as opposed to something fancier that might be used in a studio, but we worked all day. Toward the end of the night, Brooke and I smoked some weed using a big fish-shaped bong. I was absolutely out of my head, and with the workday done, we listened to Pink Floyd and Jethro Tull until it occurred to me that I didn't know where I was sleeping that night.

"Come on into the bedroom," Brooke said to me.

Uh-oh.

That was one of the longest walks I'd ever taken. I wasn't sure what to do. But when he opened the door, I saw two beds in the room. *Phew! Thank you, Lord.*

Working with Gene like that, I could see that we had some things in common. His family were Holocaust survivors. He was smart and serious. Even though he and Brooke were working in New Jersey, Gene turned out to live only about fifteen minutes away from me in Queens. It also turned out that he'd had a band upstate during college, and they had played live quite a lot. He had a lot to offer. He could sing well and play bass well. He could write songs. Perhaps most importantly, Gene was focused.

One thing I had figured out by then was that talent, like everything else, was just a starting point. What counted was what you did with it. I knew I wasn't the most talented guitar player or the best singer or the best writer, but I could do all of those things, and I had a complete *vision* of what it was going to take to succeed—a vision that included working, working, working.

Gene wrote a lot of very odd songs. Maybe it was because he was originally from another country? I wasn't sure. He had one called "Stanley the Parrot" and another called "My Uncle Is a Raft." He even had one called "My Mother is the Most Beautiful Woman in the World."

Um, okay, that's a bit weird.

Still, the more we played together, the better it got. Gene and I liked the same kind of music, and we could sing harmonies well together. I decided I wanted to work with him. I could see a bigger picture now, and despite his idiosyncrasies—as an only child, teamwork was not Gene's strong suit—we both were intelligent enough to know how to harness ambition. And after all, it would be a lot easier to slay the dragon with a second person to help.

As we continued to rehearse together, Steve Coronel ended up joining us, too, and we slowly started to become something more and more like an actual band.

10

In June 1970 I graduated from the High School of
Music & Art, finishing just a few dozen people from
the bottom of a very sizable class. I was, in fact, amazed that I had
graduated at all, given how little I showed up to class.

Graduating was a mixed blessing. I was glad to have school
behind me, but I was scared shitless about being drafted. The Vietnam War was in full swing, and the last thing I wanted was to be
drafted. I didn't need to go to Vietnam any more than I needed to
take acid.

During years of building fear, I had managed to accumulate
some medical documentation of various problems—like back pain
and other things I'd seen a doctor about. One day I went down to
Whitehall Street in lower Manhattan with my draft card for induc-
tion. They reviewed my records and quickly dismissed me. All my
fears, the years I spent anguishing over being sent to Vietnam, had
been for nothing. I told my parents the great news, how I had taken
all my medical records to prove I wasn't fit for service. They looked

at each other quizzically and said, "Didn't you know you can't be drafted?"

"Why?" I asked.

"You're deaf in one ear."

Aha.

Shocked, I thought of all the times I had brought up the subject of the draft during high school. Every male approaching draft age was concerned with what was to come. I had made my fears clear to my parents on many occasions. That was one fear they could have laid to rest for me if they had ever told me I was ineligible for the draft.

"Why didn't you ever tell me?" I asked.

They turned to each other, looked back at me, and shrugged their shoulders. Ten more points for my parents.

It was true that I couldn't tell the direction of sound, but I had never put two and two together. And nobody else had ever put two and two together for me.

At that time, New York state had decided to make college available to any resident, and I thought that despite my bravado about making a career in music, I had better apply to the city college system. I had already stacked the deck so much against myself—maybe this new opportunity could be the safety net I might still need.

Since I hadn't taken any of the preliminary tests and I had terrible grades, I was admitted to Bronx Community College. I got a student loan and promptly used it to buy a second-hand blue Plymouth Fury to replace my broken-down Rambler.

When I showed up for the first week of classes, I didn't think many of the people looked like what I considered "college material." They probably thought the same about me.

Despite the change of scenery, college quickly proved to be a continuation of everything I had hated about school. I still had the same basic problem: I couldn't hear well enough to follow what was going on. And it wasn't as if classes took up an hour a day; I was supposed to be there nearly all day. And then there were assignments on top of that. When I thought about the time I would have to devote to college, I began to see it as an obstruction. I was willing to put that much time—and more—into reaching my goal, but this wasn't helping me do that. In fact, it was detracting mightily from it. It made it impossible. And for what? I was never going to succeed in the classroom. It was just a waste of time, and time, I reasoned, was the most precious thing I had.

This is just more of the same. I don't belong here.

This is not for me.

I thought about the new band, the fact that I was no longer going it on my own. I thought about the ideas I had discussed with Gene—about getting a full-time rehearsal space. Sure, Gene had grown up an only child, his mother telling him he was God's gift to the world, and Gene believing it. Sure, he had his quirks. But then again, we had real chemistry, and the two of us together were much stronger than either of us on his own. We had a battle plan.

This is not for me.

To leave yourself no Plan B is a dangerous thing to do. But going to college was taking away from my focus. For a band, focus was success. I needed to live it twenty-four hours a day, not just nights and weekends. Wasting time at Bronx Community College was sabotaging what I was trying to accomplish. I had my Plymouth now, which meant I had transportation to get to and from rehearsals at all hours.

This is not for me.

After the first week of classes, I never went back.

Part II

Out on the street for a living

II.

Gene Klein lived with his mother and her husband in Bayside, Queens. She called me "the bum." The three of them lived in a three-story house: a tenant lived on the ground floor, and Gene and his family lived upstairs. One day I was standing in the front yard talking to Gene, who was hanging out the window. His mother leaned out and, in her thick Hungarian accent, said, "Stan, please, this is a quiet neighborhood."

In other words, I was from the wrong side of the tracks and didn't understand that things were different here in this nice area of town.

In his mother's eyes, Gene could do no wrong. If I happened to call when he was in the bathroom, she would say, "the king is on the throne." Even when he was on the toilet, she believed he created masterpieces. I, on the other hand, couldn't get a compliment out of my parents if my life depended on it. They went out of their way *not* to compliment me—I think they thought they were toughening me up that way. Gene could do no wrong; I could do no right.

Of course, when you considered the particulars of my situation, it wasn't so surprising that Gene's mom thought I was a bum.

My sister and her boyfriend drove around in a van apparently selling drugs and also dropped acid daily, sniffed glue, and did whatever else they did. Ultimately she got pregnant, but by the time she gave birth, she had separated from the guy. I was at the hospital with my parents when my niece, Ericka, was born.

My sister was in no shape to raise a child. She was still struggling with mental illness and still heavily self-medicating. One weekend my father and I rented a van, drove to Boston—where she lived in some sort of commune—loaded all the baby things into it, and carted it all back to my parents' apartment. The baby was already living with my parents anyway.

From that point on, interaction with Julia almost completely stopped. There was still fear and uncertainty about whether she would try to take Ericka back or start a custody battle with my parents. Once, Julia came to the house to visit and was clearly not well. She was holding Ericka, and suddenly I heard the front door bang open and saw Julia running down the street with the baby. We had to run after her and grab Ericka back. It was terrifying.

As part of my parents' philosophy of not acknowledging problems, my niece grew up calling my mom—her grandmother— "Mom." And because my dad wasn't comfortable choosing what to be called, he became by default "Honey," which was what my mom called him.

Whereas Gene was a college grad earning good money as an assistant teacher or a clerk—he held several jobs during the first few years I knew him—I had bounced from gas station to deli and dropped out of college. Now I was getting ready to take the exam to become a part-time New York City taxi driver. While other kids in our neighborhoods were studying to get credentials for long-term careers, I had left myself no alternative but to succeed in music. I had no choice but to spend twenty-four hours, seven days a week, plotting how I was going to accomplish that. For me, it was all about work. You can gauge how important something is to you by how hard you are willing to work to get it.

Fortunately for me, despite his mother's opinion of me, Gene seemed to agree that he and I were better together than on our own. I think our partnership meant more to me at the time, though. With a modicum of approval and somebody to hang out with, I eventually stopped going uptown to see my psychiatrist, Dr. Hilsen. Gene, on the other hand, seemed to have more going on in his life than I did, whether it was girlfriends or jobs or whatever. On the surface, he also seemed more content than I was, more happy-go-lucky. From my perspective, I saw Gene as important to the plan—and the plan was all I had in my life. I had realized after being rejected by publishing companies that I needed a band as a vehicle to get my material out there. On my own, I was at least three people short of the team I needed. In Gene, I felt I had found another key member of the team.

By that stage I had met or seen a lot of people who wanted to be musicians and said they were going to be stars, but most of them didn't have the discipline and weren't willing to commit to doing the work. Talent was all well and good; the people who won, however, were the people who worked the hardest. Gene had a work ethic like mine.

Once I landed a job driving for a taxi company called Metro, based near Queens Plaza, I had money when I needed it but still had near-total flexibility. I drove a big Dodge sedan with a flimsy partition between me and the backseat. The business was at a turning point at the time, with fewer and fewer classic cabbies. The old guys with cigars were being displaced by people like me—actors and musicians, people who needed a source of income and a certain amount of freedom. I quickly figured out what the company looked for as a minimum take for a shift, so I could work to the minimum if I felt like it—basically, how hard I worked determined how much I made. I also figured out where the wires were that lit up the bulb in the rooftop "for hire" sign. I learned how to twist it apart without looking under the dashboard. That meant I could take a fare off the meter without risking being caught by a taxi inspector who might see passengers in a cab with the "for hire" sign still lit up—a giveaway that you didn't have the meter on.

Gene and I rented a rehearsal space on Hester Street in Chinatown, just above Canal Street, in lower Manhattan. The building was what we called "tender wood": if you lit a match, the whole thing would have gone up. But it was great because we could leave our gear there instead of lugging it around all the time. The full band—me, Gene, Steve Coronel, Brooke Ostrander, and drummer Tony Zarrella—rehearsed there three times a week. But Gene and I were there a lot more than that.

Although I hadn't initially been too impressed with Gene's songs, as we gelled, we started to write very effectively together. It was exciting to have a collaborator, someone creative and intelligent to volley ideas with. A writing partner! I didn't feel alone anymore.

Gene was also a terrific bass player. He could play intricate, interesting runs and sing at the same time—something most people couldn't do. And his ability to come up with melodic parts to complement chords was a huge plus. Still, although I valued the partnership, I didn't necessarily value the way he dealt with things. He showed up late to rehearsal a lot of the time and never apologized. It wasn't unusual for me to wait more than an hour beyond our scheduled meeting time at a subway to go together to the rehearsal space. He was very much about himself.

It could be maddening, but I paid him back sometimes. We often ate at a cheap Chinese restaurant on Canal Street where you could get a scoop of whatever dish you selected from the menu over rice or noodles for $1.25. One afternoon Gene and I ordered plates of food and cans of Coke. The place was empty. When Gene went to the bathroom, I grabbed the squeeze bottle of hot mustard and squirted a big dollop into his Coke. When he returned, he put the straw to his lips and took a big swig. I just waited. All of a sudden, his eyes bugged out of his head and started watering, and he screamed, "Oh my God!" He was three years older than I was, and I played pranks on him like a pesky little brother.

Our funds were limited to a few dollars each back then—at most. One day we wanted to get some food while we were practicing but didn't have any money between us. So we took our guitars and went out onto Hester Street in front of the loft and played Beatles songs. The bucket filled up quickly, and we had our meal ticket. We made so much money that day we figured we'd try again. But the next day, almost as soon as we started to play, the cops chased us off. That was the end of our busking career and our dream of unlimited moo shu chicken.

I realized early on that Gene had been taught to value and appreciate money. Sometimes it worked out nicely—I often gave him my old shoes, for instance. Other times, I stirred up shit. I threw pennies into the street in Chinatown because I knew he would run out and retrieve them. I used to just stand on the curb and fling them. And he would run into the gutter to get the coins.

Whatever the disparities in our lives, Gene and I found common ground. We shared some touchstones—we both came from Jewish immigrant families, we both lived in Queens—but I think it had mostly to do with our style of work. He and I both gave 100 percent. The other guys in the band didn't seem driven in the same way. Tony, the drummer, was in the band for one reason only: he was a dead ringer for Geezer Butler of Black Sabbath. He wasn't much of a drummer, but he had a huge set of Ludwig drums and looked the part. He viewed himself as some sort of intellectual. He once came to rehearsal with a drawing that he thought would be perfect as a record cover if we made an album. The image showed the earth and a flower in outer space, crying. He looked at me and said, "You get it?"

"No," I said.

"Yeah, you get it."

"I have no idea what that is. A flower crying on the earth? Okay."

Because Brooke Ostrander played flute as well as keyboards, the band worked out a cover of "Locomotive Breath," a brand-new song by Jethro Tull. But Brooke sometimes had a problem when he sang—saliva would go down the wrong pipe and he would double over coughing. He might be singing one second and then suddenly drop out. I'd turn around and see him choking.

Lead guitarist Steve Coronel and I didn't always get along. After one argument, he started yelling at me. "Do you think you're special or something?" he shouted.

"Yeah, actually I do," I said. "I have an aura."

From the look on Steve's face you would have thought I had just shot his mother. "You think you have an *aura*!?"

Steve was incensed. Then Gene spoke up.

"He's right, Steve," Gene said. "He does."

12.

We played a gig in early 1971 billing ourselves as Rainbow. A community college in Staten Island hosted the gig—and I got crabs for the first time.

You can get crabs from a bed. You can get them directly from a person. But I didn't get them from a bed or a person—which might have helped make it at least a little worthwhile. Instead, I got them from a toilet seat at that community college. Soon after the gig I started itching, but it took a while before I put two and two together. I finally realized I had crabs when I found what looked like bread crumbs in my underpants. Upon closer inspection, the crumbs were crawly things. There must have been a hundred of them. It was revolting thinking they had been living on me, feeding off my body. It was the middle of the night when I figured out what they were, and I woke up my parents and told them I was going to the emergency room. I wasn't going to wait an instant longer to get treated—and it wasn't like there were twenty-four-hour pharmacies back then.

My mom was horrified that I might spread them though the house. "Honestly, Stan," she said, "what kind of dogs are you sleeping with?"

Once I had overcome my revulsion to the critters, I found it all very funny. And the fact that my parents were disgusted and revolted by my lifestyle was a source of pleasure to me. I might never get the approval and support from them that I so desperately sought, but hey, at least I was getting a rise out of them.

In April 1971 the band played another show up in the Catskills, about two hours north of New York City, this time with a new name: Wicked Lester. We played fewer covers and more of the songs Gene and I had written.

Back home in Queens, one day I popped into Middle Earth to say hello. The owner pulled a piece of paper out of the register and handed it to me. "A guy from Electric Lady was here, and we got him to leave his number," he said. "Electric Lady" meant Electric Lady Studios, the facility built by Jimi Hendrix on Eighth Street in Manhattan. To a musician it was like Israel to the Jews. It was hallowed ground.

I examined the note, which had the name "Ron" and a phone number scrawled on it. I couldn't believe they'd gotten this number for me.

I dialed it and said, "Can I speak to Ron, please?"

"Which Ron? Shimon Ron or Ron Johnsen?"

Well, Ron Johnsen sounded more promising somehow. "Ron Johnsen."

"Please hold."

Ron Johnsen was a producer at the studio. I was connected to his secretary and left a message with her about my band, his leaving his number at Middle Earth, the whole spiel.

I called back the next day. Same story: Ron wasn't available. I called back over and over again, day after day, until finally I told his secretary, "You tell him that it's because of people like him that bands like mine break up." That got him to the phone. And he agreed to come to our rehearsal space to listen to the band.

Only later did I learn that the person who had left his number at Middle Earth was actually the other Ron, Shimon Ron, who was head of maintenance at Electric Lady.

When Ron showed up, he liked what he heard. "You guys could be as big as Three Dog Night," he said. There might have been a *tiny* morsel of truth to the comparison. We played a hodgepodge of styles. So, sure, one song might sound like Three Dog Night. But the next sounded completely different. To be honest, Wicked Lester had no real style, no real focus.

Even so, Ron Johnsen said he would record us and then shop the tapes to get us a contract with a label. He presented us with something called a "producer's agreement."

Things were suddenly happening fast.

I took the contract to Matt Rael's dad. He was a businessman and I trusted the family. "This is a completely one-sided contract," Matt's dad told me, "not in your favor."

We signed it anyway. This was a chance to get a record contract, to record at Electric Lady, to put out an album. We were not going to mess it up.

Once we signed the production deal with Ron Johnsen and started to record our songs, he began to line up auditions for record labels. One was with a newly formed label called Metromedia. Afterwards, Ron came to us and said, "They passed." We broke into huge grins and gave big thumbs-up. "Yes! We passed!"

"No," said Ron drily, "*they* passed."

Finally Epic Records told us they would sign Wicked Lester on one condition: we had to get rid of Steve Coronel. It was the first instance when we had to decide whether this was about friendship or about success. We decided to let Steve go. It fell to Gene to tell him.

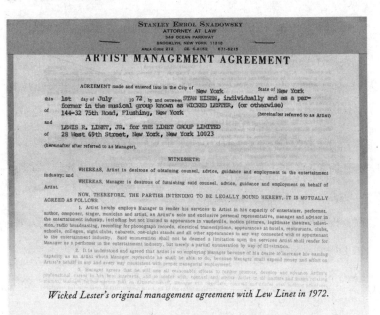

Wicked Lester's original management agreement with Lew Linet in 1972.

The label replaced Steve with a session guy named Ron Lee-jack. And then Epic signed us to a record contract. We were going to put out an album! For a major label! We even got a modest advance. I bought my parents a washer/dryer with my share of it. I was still living at home, after all.

Ron arranged for us to record cheaply, taking advantage of unbooked time at Electric Lady. If a band's session ended at noon and another band wasn't coming in until later in the afternoon, we went in and worked on our record. Often, we waited around late at night, hoping a band might pack it in by one or two in the morning, giving us time to record. It was always a bit of a crapshoot—sometimes we sat around for an entire day before getting a chance to work for a few hours.

The first time I ever saw cocaine was during those sessions. An extremely well-known band was recording in studio A one night when we were in studio B. I managed to talk my way in to hang out while they worked. At some point one of them said, "I need some fresh air." The guy pulled out an Excedrin bottle, poured some powder out of it, and snorted it.

Later the same guy came into our studio to listen to a playback of something we had just put vocals on. Since his band was known for its stellar vocal harmonies, I was hoping for some advice on our track—the harmonies on our song were questionable and clearly needed work. He still had his Excedrin bottle with him. He listened to the song and said, "Man, that sounds good." He came down a few pegs in my mind that night because I *knew* it wasn't good. Maybe it was the blow talking. I don't know.

Then one of his bandmates came in and asked whether any of us could set him up with a girl. I couldn't believe it. These were major stars. One was asking random people at a studio to find him a date, and the other had a vial of coke and couldn't tell that a tune was crap . . . this was the life of a rock star?

Once we started recording—albeit sporadically—we didn't need to rehearse at our own space as often. But one afternoon we all dropped by the Chinatown loft. "Where's the mic stand?" I said. "Where are the amps? Where are the drums? Holy shit, everything's gone!"

We knew people sometimes got into the building. We'd even had a huge, wild-eyed mental patient in a green hospital gown and no shoes barge in on a rehearsal one night after escaping from a local facility. But we didn't expect someone to jimmy open the metal cover over the window leading to the fire escape. A plate steel cover and padlock protected that window. Or so we thought.

The air went out of the room. I don't know what went through the heads of the other guys, but all I could think was, *Okay, how do we get past this?*

Was this a setback? Sure. But I never lost sight of the bigger picture.

We don't really need that stuff anyway—we're in Electric Lady Studios making a record! We're lucky!

We could borrow guitars if we needed to. We could use cardboard boxes as drums. We didn't need to rehearse at the moment anyway. We were at the studio all the time, using equipment that lived there.

I definitely needed more money, though, to replace all that gear. Gene and I also wanted to buy our own PA to be able to play live shows on our own terms. So I started working more taxi shifts. One of my favorite fares had always been dropping people at Madison Square Garden, the legendary arena in midtown Manhattan. As things were going downhill for Wicked Lester, Elvis played four shows there, in June 1972. I picked up a group of people one of those nights. "Where to?" I asked.

"Madison Square Garden," they said. I smiled.

And I'll never forget pulling up to the curb in front of the Garden that night. Because in the midst of all the turmoil, one clear thought rang out in my head as those folks got out to go see the King in all his sequined splendor: *I will be here someday, and people will be taking taxis to come see me.*

13.

By the end of the summer of 1972, we completed the Wicked Lester record. We had recorded some of our own songs but also a lot of songs Ron brought in from publishing companies. Some of the songs had wah-wah pedal, others had horns. We had done what we were told, basically, and the result was awful.

Gene and I both hated the album. We sat down together, just the two of us, and decided we didn't want to release it. In fact, we didn't want to play with this band anymore. It wasn't working as we had hoped. So we decided to scrap the record and part ways with the other guys. That proved more easily said than done. Tony, the drummer, said he wanted to uphold his end of the record contract. So Gene and I quit the band.

At that point, we had no band, no label, and virtually no gear. But what had made us start working together in the first place shined through at that moment, as we both had the same response to the setbacks.

No band, no label, no gear?
No problem.

First off, Gene and I needed a new rehearsal space. We didn't plan on replacing our gear and leaving it to be stolen again. We found a place at 10 East 23rd Street called Jams. We initially rented space on an upper floor by the hour. We didn't have any gear to store there anyway—there was no immediate drawback to taking our acoustic guitars in and out with us. Soon, though, a space a few floors below became available to rent by the month. We took it.

Our new space again had plate steel over the windows. It was a big empty room, and we lined the walls and ceiling with discarded egg cartons, thinking that would help soundproof it. Gene put a mattress in the space so he could sleep over on occasion, and we had a couple of rickety chairs. The overall effect was a bit claustrophobic, though that was also in part because we spent so much time there.

Gene and I talked about the direction we wanted to go, and it became clear very quickly that we both wanted to create a new beast, something cohesive both visually and sonically. In a lot of ways, what we wanted to do was the antithesis of Wicked Lester. That band was all over the place musically, and we wanted to narrow things down. As for the look, Wicked Lester could have been just a bunch of random guys who happened to be waiting in line at the same bus stop.

We knew we needed something like a mission statement in order to create the right kind of cohesiveness. I played him the concept album *S.F. Sorrow,* by the Pretty Things, and records by the Move and Slade. My first thought was to have two drummers, two bass players, and two guitar players—to make a sort of rock orchestra along the lines of what Roy Wood of the Move was trying to do after leaving the Electric Light Orchestra and forming Wizzard, to create a big wall of sound. I wanted to keep things tight, too. Much as I liked Led Zeppelin, I knew we would never be a jam band. We didn't have the ability to stretch a song out for fifteen minutes. You need an extensive musical vocabulary to do that, and we just didn't have it. It would have been pointless and boring for us to try to stretch out at that point.

Much of the time Gene and I sat facing each other on the old wooden chairs, acoustic guitars in our laps. Among the first things we worked on were "100,000 Years," "Deuce," and "Strutter." The chords of "Strutter" were from Gene's old song "Stanley the Parrot." Although the original song was a bit offbeat, I always loved the chords in it. We started trying to recast it in the vein of the Rolling Stones. And the words just came to me.

> *She wears her satins like a lady*
> *She gets her way just like a child*
> *You take her home and she says, "Maybe baby"*
> *She takes you down and drives you wild*

The whole glitter scene was about style, and the girls looked fantastic. Of course, I wasn't doing so well socially—I spent all my time rehearsing or driving a taxi, not hanging out in clubs. God knows, I didn't have a girlfriend in fishnet stockings or satins. But I saw hip women walking around the Village, and I saw other bands with their girlfriends. For me, it was singing about an ideal. I was celebrating something I wasn't really part of. But what the hell, Brian Wilson had never been on a surfboard, either.

My songs tended to be very much chord-based, mainly because my ability to play riffs was fairly limited. So Gene would often supplement some of my songs with riffs. He had a better understanding of how to play notes and runs. On "Black Diamond," for instance, he added a back riff that plays against the chords. The lyrics to "Black Diamond" were another example of creating a romanticized vignette about the life of the city. I mean, I knew about as much about streetwalkers as I did about Lilliputians.

Gene and I fed off each other and filled in blanks for each other—lyrical and musical—as we worked. I remember the words to "100,000 Years" hitting me on 23rd Street: *Sorry to have taken so long / Must have been a bitch while I was gone.* On "Deuce," the guitar figure that starts the song and then reintroduces it after the solo is mine. Even if both of our names didn't appear on any given song, our fingerprints were all over each other's songs.

Gene and I also sparked each other with song titles. I had started a song called "Christine Sixteen," but Gene was the one who ran with the title and came up with a really good song. "Black Diamond" started out as a title of his and I ran with it. There was no animosity or resentment, just the sense that we were working toward our shared goal. Each of us also had a few older songs in complete form that we needed only to slightly re-tweak to make them fit in the new repertoire—"She" was a leftover of Gene's; "Firehouse" and "Let Me Know" were leftovers of mine.

Together we consciously tailored the songs to fit our concept of the band instead of just cranking out whatever struck our fancies on any given day. I was excited. We were doing things that neither of us had been capable of doing on our own up to that point. And we now had built the foundation for success: a rock and roll manifesto in the form of a catalogue of strong, cohesive songs.

Alongside our musical development, we molded ourselves into what we thought we should *be*. For the first time, I knew I was working with someone whose vision was as big as mine. I'd been around kids who could play their instruments before, but Gene seemed to understand the whole *package*, the fact that your music or your musical ability was just one part of making yourself an appealing musician. Like me, he saw the importance of marketing yourself—not in a Madison Avenue way, but in terms of appealing to people, being engaging, promoting yourself. Success wouldn't happen by chance; it would happen by design.

Toward that end, we made a conscious decision to lose weight. Gene started dressing cooler. And we both changed our names. Gene had already changed his name once, from Chaim Weitz to Gene Klein, so one more change, from Klein to Simmons, was no big deal for him. I had always hated my name and even told my parents as a little kid that I was going to change it. They said I could change it when I got older. Little did they know I was going to do it almost as soon as I was legally able.

The chances of a rock star named Stanley Eisen seemed pretty slim. It just didn't sound like Roger Daltrey or Elvis Presley. Stars were supposed to be larger than life. Why was there no Archibald Leach? Because Cary Grant sounded better. Ringo Starr sounded better than Richard Starkey. It wasn't about hiding my ethnicity. I would just rather have been Paul McCartney than Schlomo Ginsberg. But I also didn't want a stupid name like Rock Fury. I wanted a name like the people I aspired to be like, something easily identifiable. The question was, what sort of a name? Ozzy Osbourne's nickname derived from his last name. Eizzy Eisen? Nah. Then it hit me: Paul. That was a comfortable name. There was Paul McCartney, of course, and Paul Rogers of Free, another band I liked. I didn't want to completely give up who I had been, so when I thought about last names, I was happy that my thoughts went Daltrey, Presley . . . Stanley!

Paul Stanley.

Initially I didn't change my name legally because I figured I'd go back to my original name at some point after our career took its course. In those days, bands ran their courses pretty quickly, and nobody then had made it to ten years, though a few—like the Who and the Stones—were closing in on it.

I hoped for five years.

14.

Now that we had the songs and the beginnings of a look and feel, we needed a band. We weren't Simon and Garfunkel; we weren't the Everly Brothers; we weren't Jan and Dean. Our songs were built to rock.

We made finding a lead guitar player our initial priority. I had never aspired to play lead. To be honest, I wasn't sure I was capable of it. When I listened to people sing, I knew I could do something reasonably comparable. But I rarely heard a guitar solo and thought, *I can do something like that.* Unless somebody was playing slowly. Once in a while I heard a solo by Paul Kossoff of Free and thought I might be able to pull it off, but I just wasn't a fast, flashy player. My gut also told me that this was an area where work might *not* pay off for me—that I might get only mediocre results regardless of how much time I put into it.

Fortunately, Gene knew the perfect guy for the job. Unfortunately, the perfect guy for the job lived upstate—and Gene didn't know exactly where. Or even exactly who he was. He had run across somebody when he lived up there, and this person—whoever it was—became our first target. So that fall of 1972 we started hitchhiking up to the Catskills in search of the mythical lead guitar player who apparently played in the bars and ballrooms of the low-rent resort circuit up there. We stood on the side of the Major Deegan Expressway with our thumbs out, me in lime-green high-heel boots and him in an antique woman's fur coat.

Inevitably, we hit the road without a place to stay. One night we met some people from a commune outside one of the towns, and they invited us to stay at their place. It turned out to be a barn, and we slept in the chicken coop. The people we'd met collected the eggs—that was their role in the commune. They offered us warm food, but the place was such a wreck that I was reluctant to eat. Later, in the middle of the night, I woke up famished. I went into the kitchen to see if anything was left in the oven. When I opened it, a mouse scampered out.

Another time, two girls in a VW van pulled over and took us to spend the night at their place at the top of a mountain. It must have taken ten minutes just to get up the winding driveway. Their house was either not yet finished or derelict, and they offered us spots on the subflooring, alongside their dogs. As we were lying on the floor half asleep, one of the girls walked through the room stark naked. Gene opened his eyes, and I watched them follow her. I already knew that Gene tried to screw everybody and anybody. It was part of how he defined himself: possessed by and obsessed with pussy.

"If you make a move on her and she's insulted," I whispered pleadingly, "they're going to throw us out of here in the middle of nowhere. We'll end up freezing to death at the top of this fucking mountain."

He held back. But the next morning he wound up trying it on with her—successfully. It turned out she wore a hearing aid, he told me, and whenever he leaned in close to her, he heard feedback.

Another weekend we ended up in a town that had already rolled up and gone to bed. We stood on a desolate street until finally a car came toward us. We put out our thumbs and the car pulled over. Inside were four tough-looking black guys. "Where you going?" the driver asked.

"Oh, us? We're not going anywhere."

The driver got mad. "You had your thumbs out. Where are you going?"

We told him we were trying to get to Grossinger's, a big Borscht Belt resort. Gene knew somebody there we could crash with.

"Get in." It sounded more like a command than a welcome.

The next thing I knew, we were winding down an unlit dirt road and I was starting to get scared. Then I saw another car pulled off to the side of the road up ahead.

Great, they're waiting for us. Two Jews served up on a stick.

We pulled up and another group of tough-looking guys got out of the other car. My life flashed before my eyes. But it turned out that they just wanted to hang out and drink. When we got back in the car, we said, "You know, you don't have to take us." With a combination of anger and threatening annoyance, the driver hissed, "I said I'd take you."

And he did, all the way to Grossinger's.

We never tracked down that guitar player, but those trips were an affirmation of our commitment. Who else but Gene would have taken those trips?—thumbing rides the way we were dressed, having no place to stay, sleeping on floors, barely having any money in our pockets. Most people would have just put an ad in the newspaper.

Which is what we did next. Or rather, we looked at the ads. Only instead of looking for a lead guitar player, we decided to seek out a drummer. Eventually we found an interesting ad in *Rolling Stone* and rang the number. We had one line of questioning:

"Would you do anything to make it?"

"Yeah," said the guy on the other end of the line.

"Would you wear a dress?"

"Yeah."

We arranged to meet the guy in front of Electric Lady down on Eighth Street. He was dressed very cool. Cooler than us. He looked quite a bit older than I was, and he had about five names—George Peter John Criscuola, blah blah blah—but he went by Peter Criss. We walked to a pizza joint and sat down with our slices. We hadn't been talking for five minutes when Peter blurted out, "I have a nine-inch dick."

I didn't know what to say. *Pass the cheese?*

This guy was very different from us. Peter could barely read or spell, and he wasn't a thinker. Still, we agreed to go see him play a gig he had coming up in a bar in Brooklyn. The place was called the King's Lounge, and the other two guys in his band looked like they should be making pizzas or cement shoes. Peter looked completely different from them, and he exuded an air of confidence. He had swagger.

The crowd was sparse, but something about his performance struck me: he played that bar like it was a packed arena. He was into it. After that, we asked him to come to our rehearsal space the next day to try playing together.

When he played with us the first time at 23rd Street, it didn't sound particularly good. Peter didn't know much about British music. He knew the Beatles. And he liked Charlie Watts of the Stones. But that was probably because he liked to believe he played like Charlie Watts—basic, not showy. As for any other drummers— the ones he couldn't play like—he disliked them all.

Peter also didn't understand the basics of song structure. Verse, chorus, bridge—it all meant nothing to him. If I said, "Let's pick up at the second verse," he just sat there. He had to memorize a song from beginning to end, and if we stopped in the middle or he lost his place, he was fucked. Perhaps as a result, his playing was wild. You could call it unorthodox, but that wouldn't be accurate—it was just plain erratic. His drum parts would change verse to verse. Still, for all he lacked in continuity, he played with fire and vitality. He was scrappy.

We asked him back for another rehearsal.

The next rehearsal went much better. Again, his playing showed personality and a real zest for life. Some of the songs developed a different feel than Gene and I originally might have had in mind— Peter just couldn't play like the drummers we had in our heads as we wrote—but what he delivered still worked as a blueprint for the band we wanted to be. Looking back now, there's no denying that a drummer like John Bonham wouldn't have fit what we were doing, although if we'd had our druthers, Gene and I would certainly have gone in that direction. Back then, Peter was the right guy for the band. His drumming was brash and full of piss and vinegar.

Peter instinctively played ahead. At times we had to catch up to him. In the best-case scenario, a drummer is like the back of a chair: you can lean back on it and know it's there for you. It's a foundation. But Peter ran alongside us, which was a different animal altogether. Even so, things just clicked. Even as a trio, we sounded very promising. So promising, in fact, that we decided to once again play for Epic Records to see whether or not they wanted to keep us under our existing contract.

By this point, Gene and I had scraped together the money to buy new gear. I'd bought two guitars: a tobacco sunburst Gibson Firebird and a guitar I had custom-made by a guy named Charlie Lebeau. I got to know Charlie when he worked at a little second-floor shop on 48th Street—it was the first shop I'd ever seen that specialized in vintage guitars. Dan Armstrong's stocked sunburst Les Pauls from the 1950s—beautiful instruments that were always out of my reach financially. But Charlie, who specialized in repairing the instruments, had struck out on his own and started building guitars. I bought a walnut-colored double-cutaway from him. The Gibson Firebird started off as a standard. I liked it because it reminded me of one Eric Clapton had played in Cream. I sent it to work with my dad one day and asked him to have the guys at the furniture shop paint it black. It didn't end up with the finish you might normally get on a piano or guitar, but it was black.

We had also bought a Peavey sound system, with two big speakers on telescoping stands and a mixing board with huge Frankenstein dials. We needed it for the vocals. In our rehearsal space—and any small clubs we figured we might soon play—we didn't need to mic our guitar amps. They were loud enough on their own.

Don Ellis, who was head of Epic at the time, and some other execs came down to 10 East 23rd to see the band in late November 1972. We referred to ourselves as the new version of Wicked Lester. Of course, we knew this was a completely new entity, but we didn't have a name yet. We played our new repertoire, which was basically the songs that made up KISS's debut album. During "Firehouse" I took a fire bucket full of confetti and threw it over Ellis, who cringed, thinking the bucket was full of water.

In the end, Epic wanted nothing to do with the band. They passed and waived any legal obligations that still might have been lingering from the Wicked Lester contract.

I had never envisioned the band as a power-trio, anyway—I never wanted to try to sustain the band on my guitar alone. Jimi Hendrix could do it, Pete Townsend could do it, Jimmy Page could do it. I could not. And besides, I wanted to swing my arm and pose and leave the acrobatic playing to somebody else.

So it was back to the drawing board. Or rather, back to the newspaper. We really needed a lead guitar player.

15.

GUITAR PLAYER WANTED WITH FLASH AND BALLS.

That was the ad we placed in the *Village Voice*. And when we opened the door to our rehearsal space on the appointed day in December 1972, we had a lot of takers—more than thirty. But becoming a rock star meant *looking* like a rock star, so we had some specific rules: no bald heads, no beards, and no excess weight.

One guy came in a Nehru jacket and beads around his neck. He couldn't speak a word of English. His wife accompanied him as an interpreter. "He's from Italy," she explained. Another guy, named Bob Kulick, was a really good player, but he didn't fit the look we had in mind. After a long and mostly fruitless freak show, a guy walked in wearing one red sneaker and one orange sneaker. He was about my age and kind of goofy and pigeon-toed. While we were still talking to Bob, this other guy plugged in his guitar and started playing.

"Hey, man, shut up and wait your turn," we told him.

Eventually we plugged in with him, and almost from the minute we started playing, something happened that took us to a completely different place. The combination of the four of us was so much bigger than anything we'd done with the other guitar players. We weren't the greatest musicians, but the chemical reaction of the four of us was potent.

One minute we had been one thing, and a minute later—with this guy named Ace Frehley—we became something else, something undeniable. I was absolutely stunned.

This is it.

This is lethal.

This is the goods.

Ace had swagger, that's for sure. His playing reminded me of guys I really liked—Jimmy Page, Jeff Beck. He was also a total oddball. He moved in a rubbery way and barely spoke. He shrugged his shoulders a lot.

We all knew very quickly that this was it. Around Christmas, after our second rehearsal with Ace, we called the guy who had managed Wicked Lester, Lew Linet, to gauge his interest. He was a nice guy but pretty clueless about rock and roll. He managed a band called JF Murphy & Salt that played at the Fillmore East sometimes, as well as an old folkie named Oscar Brand. Lew was more of a beatnik than a rocker, but he agreed to come to the rehearsal space to see the group we had dubbed KISS. Thankfully, all the band members had voted in agreement with the name when I had come up with it. I had been prepared to fight for it because I was so sure the next key to moving forward was coming up with a band name that was classic and timeless. I saw the name as having multiple meanings—there was the kiss of death in addition to kisses of passion. It was easily recognizable. And it was so familiar that I thought people might say, "KISS? Oh yeah, I've heard of them."

When Lew showed up and we launched into our set, he immediately got upset. "If you don't turn down the volume, I'm going to walk out of this room," he shouted angrily.

When we told him about our desire to wear makeup, he whined in exasperation, "Why can't you dress like the Raspberries?" The Raspberries wore matching white suits. Clearly, Lew didn't understand our aim.

Oh well. We could book gigs ourselves. And besides, we still had plenty to work on. We wanted to be a power band with roots in British rock and roll, but we wanted to take it ten steps further. We still didn't know just how that would manifest itself. I had sketch pads full of other ideas. I'd been trying to envision the band I would want to see, as a fan, and in addition to stacks and stacks of amps, that vision included distinct characters—like the four Beatles— and signature looks cribbed from movies like Zorro and the Lone Ranger and from superhero comic books. For now, though, we stuck with the trend of the New York Dolls and all the other local bands and looked glam and feminine, with platform boots and rouge, lipstick, and heavy eye shadow.

Once we had solidified the foursome, we rehearsed seven days a week. While other bands made names for themselves by playing the Mercer Arts Center or hanging out at Max's Kansas City, we ensconced ourselves in our loft on 23rd Street rehearsing. All those bands were far cooler than we were as people, far more socially adept, and they looked the part more than we did, but nobody worked harder than we did. Sometimes when I was driving the taxi, I would even leave my car at the taxi stand on 23rd Street and Fifth Avenue and go up to the loft to practice.

Working with Ace came very organically. We didn't have to coach him the way we had to coach Peter. Ace just fit. And after practicing with him for about a month, we were ready to make our live debut. We booked ourselves three consecutive nights at a place on Queens Boulevard that had just changed its name from Popcorn to Coventry. A lot of the hip New York City bands soon ended up playing out at Coventry, too, including the Dolls, the Brats, the Dictators, Television, and Sniper, which was Joey Ramone's first band.

The first of the three gigs was on January 30, 1973. On the morning of the show, I took the subway to Long Island City, the industrial part of Queens right along the East River. There, I rented a van at Public Service Rentals—it was the cheapest place to get trucks. Then I drove into 23rd Street, where later in the day we loaded our gear from the rehearsal space.

Ace turned up late and refused to carry anything. Not one thing. When we arrived at the club and parked out back, Ace did the same thing. He sat in the back of the van and didn't carry anything. Then, as we were unloading it, Ace pulled out his penis, totally out of the blue, and said, "This is my dick without a hard-on."

Huh?

I didn't know what was up with Ace and Peter and their dick-size obsessions. Though as time went on, I began to suspect that this was the way they defined themselves and what was important to them.

Fewer than ten people showed up for our first gig. The place probably held five hundred. We still tried to blow the roof off the place—we knew we'd always remember this show. And it felt great.

I'll want to remember this.

We played the next two nights at Coventry, and each night the crowd was sparse. After each show we drove back to 23rd Street to stow the gear. Ace sat on his ass and boozed. We were still getting used to his personality. The shows confirmed that he was everything we were looking for musically. But they also confirmed the fact that he was one of the laziest people—no, *the* laziest person—I had ever met.

These first shows made some things clear to me. I had always wanted a big sound, a two-guitar steamroller. Like Humble Pie. And we had achieved elements of that. But at the same time, we lacked a sense of heft, of magnitude. I almost felt as if the other guys had jeopardized the band—they acted small-time. Ace had babbled into the mic during one of the shows. Peter had said, "I want to thank my friends from Canarsie for coming out tonight." That did *not* sound big league. It detracted from the image I wanted to project. Perception was reality. I realized there were three guys on that stage in Queens who were clueless about how to relate to an audience. You want to be small-time? Give a shout out to Tony and Guido. You want to be huge? Make the right impression, no matter how many people are there. Interact with the audience as if you're all at Madison Square Garden.

From that point on I was adamant that I would be the one leading the charge onstage. I would be the spokesman. Everybody chattering away was just too chaotic.

And even though I had never done it, I knew I could. I *knew* it. I already had the blueprint. The reason I loved Humble Pie was Steve Marriott, the lead singer, who always seemed to be leading a church revival. He never spoke—when he communicated with the audience, he testified and sang, bringing everything to a fever pitch. *Say hallelujah!* That was exactly what I was going to do. *Say hallelujah, people!* I wanted KISS to be church. *That's right!* Rock and roll church. *Can I get an amen!*

Funny thought, for a Jew.

Funny thought, too, for a guy who was in many ways still painfully shy. But I was absolutely confident I could create somebody onstage who *would* be riveting and engage the audience. That's probably why I had an odd accent early on—vaguely British, vaguely Southern preacher. It was a way to pass myself off as something a bit more exotic than a kid from Queens. The onstage character camouflaged the ill-suited kid with an ear deformity from a dysfunctional family.

I would be flamboyant and cocksure. I would project the image that I was coveted and desirable. I would be the guy everyone wanted to know. All the people I perceived as having not been nice to me, as having rejected me as a friend? They would be sorry.

But in truth, I would be the Wizard of Oz: the awkward little man behind the curtain operating this huge persona.

16.

The New York Dolls were the template for most bands coming out of the city at the time. Of course I'd heard of them, but up until then I hadn't seen them live. One night in March 1973, Gene and I went to see them at a ballroom in a sleazy midtown hotel called the Diplomat—the kind of hotel where hookers and junkies crashed.

They were the kings of the New York City rock scene and arrived fashionably late—actually intolerably late. They looked spectacular. And when they took the stage, the camaraderie and chemistry were amazing. Their playing, however, was not.

Still, they looked terrific. Their waists were as big as my wrists. Gene and I looked like linebackers by comparison. We looked at each other. We realized KISS looked more like a bunch of firemen in drag or something. This wasn't going to work. We couldn't beat the Dolls at their own game. Forget being a better Dolls; we had to be a better KISS. We had to win on our own terms. After that show, we decided to ditch all our colorful clothing and remake ourselves in a sinister all-black look.

I used to window-shop at a couple of boutiques where they stocked all the latest rock and roll fashions, particularly the stuff that was hot in London. One day I saw a pair of pants in Jumpin' Jack Flash that would be perfect for our new look, but they cost thirty-five bucks. That was a lot of money. I decided I could buy fabric and make something similar myself. I had never used a sewing machine before, but I took apart my favorite pair of bell-bottom jeans and made a pattern. My mom kept saying I wouldn't be able to put in the zipper.

I can do anything.

It's simply a question of working at it.

The pants, in sleek metallic black satin, came out great and cost next to nothing—and the zipper worked fine. Gene liked them so much that he asked me to make a pair for him, too. Which I did. Ace's mom made him a shirt with an applique of an eagle on it.

Then we went to a pet store and bought dog collars for ourselves. I needed a Great Dane collar—the poodle collar didn't fit. Eventually we worked our way to shops that sold S&M gear. I'll never forget climbing the stairs to a place in the meatpacking district and walking in absolutely wide-eyed—I had *no idea* what I was looking at: leather hoods with zippered eyes and a tube in the mouth—what on earth did you *do* with that? We ended up finding some of our early studded cuffs and collars at another S&M place, the Eagle's Nest, down in the West Village.

Somehow, wearing white face paint went hand-in-hand with our new outfits. Together in our loft on 23rd Street, we all sat around looking at a mirror on the back of the door. We had no idea how to apply makeup. It was as if we were possessed, just smearing makeup on, wiping it off, trying different things.

First I tried out red makeup. Then I tried a ring around my eye like Petey the dog in the *Little Rascals*. But stars had always fascinated me, and now, of course, I also intended to be the frontman of the band, the focal point onstage. No longer would I be the awkward kid, the outcast. I would be *the Starchild*.

I painted a star around my right eye. It was hard work trying to draw a two-dimensional symbol on a three-dimensional object—my face. It looked one way from the front and another from the side. I was tired by the time I finally created one good star. I didn't want to struggle through painting another one on the left side. Done.

It was eye-opening to watch the other guys come up with concepts that suited their personalities. Ace's design was ethereal, spacey. And in the short time I had known him then, that was exactly how I would have described him—the Spaceman. He often joked about coming from a planet called Jendal; he constantly threw out off-the-wall sayings like "one by one I kills 'em" and spoke in made-up languages and gibberish. Sometimes he would shiver and ask, "What was that—did we just have an earthquake?" And we'd say, "That was you—you just had a tremor."

Peter's makeup was elementary—the symbolism was direct, not abstract. He felt that over the course of his life he'd gotten lucky during a few close calls, and thus had nine lives. You know, like a cat. The Catman suited him. Peter was not what you'd call an intellectual.

Gene's makeup was arguably the strongest of all. It was symmetrical and demonic. It was lascivious. It had the drama of Kabuki. It was a striking image, and then when he stuck out his tongue—it just made sense. The Demon. And as we would soon realize, his look and mine—me smiling, him scowling—created a great juxtaposition onstage: light and shadow.

The only measure of whether the images "worked" was the extent to which each guy felt comfortable in his. The images all enhanced or reinforced characteristics in each of us, and in that way, they weren't just costumes. They were outward shows of things inside of us. It made sense. And we all in some way enabled each other to find those personas.

We never sat down and articulated the "why" behind the makeup. We had no real understanding of why. We just wanted to go further than others had, to become a band the likes of which we ourselves had never seen. The makeup allowed us to embody all the qualities of the English bands I idolized; it presented a cohesive look, a united feel, and at the same time offered the possibility of distinct personalities.

From this point on, we began to create a world that we ultimately inhabited and ruled. But at the start, we certainly weren't at the center of anything. We weren't part of the clique of New York bands. We weren't junkies; we didn't hang out at the Chelsea Hotel trying to relive somebody else's past; some of us could carry on at least semi-intelligent conversations, and that wasn't cool. We were the outcasts of the outcasts. The New York Dolls and other cool bands hung out in clubs surrounded by beautiful girls. We had no time for clubs or girls. We were still too busy trying to become the band we wanted to be.

The proof would be in the pudding. And we would eat it like kings.

We booked two more shows, this time out in Amityville, Long Island, at a bar called the Daisy. It was basically a storefront and couldn't have held even one hundred people. They sold watered-down drinks for thirty-five cents.

I rented a vehicle at Public Service Rentals again—this time, a decommissioned milk truck. We loaded in our gear—and by "we" I mean Gene, Peter, and me, as Ace, as usual, refused to help—and drove about twenty miles outside of the city. The staff bristled from the word go—I think we looked too weird and effeminate out there in the suburbs. The guy scheduled to be the bouncer that night said he was going to kick my ass. We ended up locking ourselves in the manager's office, hiding and doing our makeup. Periodically some-one pounded on the door and screamed, "I'm gonna fucking kill you!"

The upside of having to wait in the office was that we could answer the house phone. Several people called and asked, "Who's playing there tonight?"

"This great band called KISS. You've gotta see them!"

When we finally emerged and took the stage, there were about thirty-five people in the house. Ace looked at his makeup in the reflective surface of Peter's bass drum and started cracking up.

Still, we didn't encounter the antagonism from the crowd that we might have expected given the bouncer's reaction to us even in our street clothes. A few people chuckled, but more than anything, people were just curious. And pretty much as soon as we hit the stage, they realized two things. First, we were serious. Second, this was great. We might have lacked technical ability, but we played with undeniable focus and ferocity.

My makeup was a mask that provided distance between me and the crowd. It gave me the shield I needed. Whatever fears I had of being ridiculed—whether for my normal appearance or for wearing makeup—disappeared. The makeup was armor. It pro-tected me.

It was also freeing.

Some people were born with it all. I certainly hadn't been. But now I had it.

And I was on a mission. Out came the persona I had in mind. Out came Jimmy Swaggart and Billy Graham. Out came the rock and roll evangelist. I sang the praises of mighty rock and roll and all the things I aspired to when I saw the bands I loved.

This is my calling.

I knew I still had a lot of work to do—fronting a band is a craft—but I managed to engage the crowd. I was able to communicate with the audience and elicit a response. I preached rock and roll.

"Hi! I mean, are you high? Everybody having a good time?"

More people showed up the next night, and we killed it again.

After the second night, we got paid. Once the truck rental and our other expenses were taken care of, we each walked away with thirteen dollars. It was the first time I'd ever ended up on the plus side after a show. I had actually earned money playing rock and roll. What a feeling. And everyone seemed to share that feeling.

With these shows under our belts, we felt confident in our songs. Sure, we still had tinkering to do on our look and stagecraft, but musically, we had gelled extremely quickly, and our set already sounded the way we wanted it to. The next step, we figured, was to make a demo to shop to labels.

Ron Johnsen from Electric Lady had stayed in touch with me and Gene. We had even provided some background vocals for projects he had recorded there. Since we hadn't been paid for those sessions, we approached him with a deal. "Instead of paying us," we suggested, "get Eddie Kramer to do a demo with us at Electric Lady."

Eddie Kramer was a legendary audio engineer and producer who had worked with the Kinks, the Small Faces, Jimi Hendrix, and Led Zeppelin. We'd seen him at the studio, and he was a striking character. He sometimes walked around Electric Lady in a cape, carrying a cane. He elicited both fear and awe.

Ron set it up. Well, sort of. Eddie oversaw the sessions, but his assistant Dave Wittman did the actual recording. We cut demos of "Black Diamond," "Strutter," "Deuce," and "Watchin' You." The other track we cut, "Cold Gin," was a song Ace brought to the table and Gene and I tweaked.

Gene and I knew we would be depended on to bring in the songs for KISS because Peter and Ace never showed much ambition in that department. I didn't begrudge them their limitations, but when Ace showed up with the framework of a song, I was thrilled. After all, we wanted to be like the Beatles—four identifiable characters. People liked the Beatles, but they also had their favorite Beatle. George Harrison had a song or two on Beatles albums, and even Ringo got to sing a novelty song now and then. It made the band—any band—more interesting. Toward that end we had Peter sing my song "Black Diamond." We wanted Ace to sing "Cold Gin," too. But he refused.

We figured the more fully realized the individual members of the band were, the stronger the group would be—adding more ingredients would only make the soup better. I wanted KISS to be a club where every member was represented. I wanted it to be multidimensional, with four formidable personalities. The fact that one of the other guys in our band actually contributed to that illusion—by bringing in a song idea—was a bonus.

Now, with a demo in hand, we knew we couldn't be stopped. If you stood in front of us, we were going to crush you.

17.

I think in some ways all bands are dysfunctional. Often, part of the reason people get involved in rock and roll in the first place is because they themselves are dysfunctional. If you get lucky, you find camaraderie and some sort of chemistry—the fact that you each feel different brings you together. And certainly it's nice to be part of a club of misfits. Life is easier with a support system.

From the very beginning, I felt part of something with KISS. We were all oddballs—quirky, idiosyncratic, neurotic—but we had each other now. I can't speak for anybody else, because I don't know what made them tick or what the appeal was for them at the onset, but for me, KISS gave me a feeling of finally belonging—an us-against-the-world kind of mentality, and I was part of that sense of "us." It was empowering.

In KISS, I had a gang. I wasn't as lonely as I'd always been.

But despite our shared sense of purpose, I think the four of us all saw the others as odd. We *were* all odd. And not necessarily in a way that made us gel. In KISS, we had a collective reason for being, but outside of that, we didn't have a lot in common. So we didn't socialize together outside of the band. Ace and Peter had a lot of friends, and Peter was already married. Gene had a girlfriend. I was still pretty isolated outside of the band.

Even within the band, I never let my guard down. I remained remote around my bandmates. I maintained a wall that made it difficult to get to know me at all and impossible to get to know me well. When the other guys joked around with each other, I chimed in. When they made fun of me, however, I didn't take it well. I never betrayed why I was sensitive. I sure as hell wasn't going to expose myself to potential ridicule by telling them about how shattering my experiences as a child had been as a result of my ear and deafness. I wasn't going to bring up painful things with people who might use those things against me.

"You can dish it out but you can't take it," the guys would say. And it was true. It was an instinctive reaction on my part. They didn't understand how I had spent my childhood being scrutinized and ridiculed. How could they? I didn't tell them.

Still, it took a lot of effort to cover something like that all the time, and it certainly affected my behavior. But I wasn't comfortable enough with myself to handle it any other way.

Peter, it quickly became apparent, was also a very troubled person. He seemed to get off on causing problems within the band. One night after rehearsal, we all went down to the Chinese restaurant where Gene and I used to eat back when Wicked Lester practiced in Chinatown. Peter started making fun of the waiter—in a really derogatory way. We found his behavior embarrassing, and told him that if he didn't stop, we would leave the restaurant. Peter said, "If you leave the restaurant, I'm quitting the band." He kept it up. We got up and left. And sure enough, he quit the band for a few days. This type of needless drama became part of the way he operated.

Ace didn't do things to sabotage the band at that point. Though lazy, he was smart and funny. He constantly told jokes. He liked to drink, but it didn't affect our work—at least in the beginning. Only later would he start to forget the punch lines to his own jokes and have to ask us how they ended. In the early days, when we practiced or played live, he stayed focused and bore down.

Once Peter was back in the fold, we booked two more gigs at the Daisy in April. Quite a few more people showed up than the month before.

I was still learning to control an audience. I felt like a lion tamer. The only way to avoid being destroyed was to put yourself in charge. "It's really great to be back," I said, pretending we'd been out on the road. "We haven't been here because we've been so busy playing."

Yeah, in our egg-carton-lined rehearsal space.

We continued to set up onstage the same way we had from the very start at Coventry and even in our rehearsal space: two vocal microphones, with one on either side of the drum kit. I may have seen myself as the frontman, but my mic was never center stage. We were a combination of elements, and so, like the Beatles, we never wanted anyone in the middle. Either person could be the singer, depending on the song. The odd thing was that because I stood "stage left" (which is the right side from the audience's perspective), my deaf side faced the rest of the band. But it never occurred to me to set up on the other side.

Before and after the shows, Ace continued to say, "I don't want to carry shit." That took colossal balls. But I realized that was who he was, and that together we had something special. I had to weigh things in terms of what was important; I had to prioritize. Was it more important to get some guy off his ass to carry amplifiers— "carry shit or leave"—than to keep moving forward with the band? No. When I carried the gear, I wasn't doing it to be kind or to help *him* out. I was doing the right thing *for me*. I wasn't being charitable to his lazy ass. I knew in the end it would benefit me. It reminded me of my initial reaction to Gene. I put up with crap from him because I stood to gain more by accepting some of his behavior than I would lose by telling him to take a hike.

In May we played our first show in New York City proper, on the eighth floor of a factory building on Bleecker Street. The loft served as the rehearsal space for a new band called the Brats, whose founder, Rick Rivets, had originally been in the New York Dolls. We had seen their debut show a few months before, when they opened for the Dolls.

We agreed to play at their loft for free and provide our PA to the other bands—the Brats and Wayne County, a transvestite and eventually transsexual who fronted a band called Queen Elizabeth. When we loaded our gear in that afternoon, the members of the Brats were not too friendly. They wanted to look like the Yardbirds and pulled it off pretty well. They all wore shag haircuts and the best rock and roll clothing—tailored velvet jackets, satin bell-bottom pants, platform boots—all the latest things from England that I recognized from the windows of Jumpin' Jack Flash and Granny Takes a Trip. And they had rock star names: in addition to Rick Rivets there was Keith Ambrose, Sparky Donovan, and David Leeds.

We plugged in to do a sound check and ran through "Deuce." The atmosphere changed. The Brats suddenly became our buddies. Once again, we had found that our music broke down indifference, and even hostility.

We opened the show that night and then stuck around to hear Wayne County, dressed in drag, looking like a spoof of Phyllis Diller, and backed by twin brothers no bigger than Oompa-Loompas. Wayne's anthem was "It Takes a Man Like Me to Be a Woman Like Me," and the high point of the show came when he/she ate dog food out of a toilet. Not the prettiest sight.

All the cool people came to that party, though I don't think they could make heads or tails of us. I talked to Sylvain Sylvain of the Dolls there. They had just signed a two-record deal with Mercury and were in the process of recording. "Hey," I cajoled him, "why don't *we* do a show together?"

"You guys would kill us," he said.

By the time we went to pack up after the Brats' set, my guitar—the walnut-colored one that Charlie LeBeau had made for me—had been stolen. I had to start using a black Les Paul reissue while LeBeau made me a new guitar: an asymmetrical Flying V, based on one Albert King used to play. I came to be closely associated with that Flying V until, many years down the road, I began to design my own line of signature guitars.

We played the same Bleecker Street loft a month later, followed by another batch of shows at the Daisy. By that point people literally broke the windows trying to get into the Daisy—it was total bedlam. But we began to encounter a Catch-22 when we tried to capitalize on what to us seemed like increasing buzz. Every time we called a booking agent to help get us more gigs, we got the same response: we couldn't get a booking agent unless we had a record label. But whenever we sent demos to labels to try to get a label deal, they wanted to know who our booking agent was.

So we figured we'd just have to continue booking our own shows and hope for the best. But outside of the Daisy, we seemed to run up against a wall on that front, too. "Who's your manager?" club owners asked when we rang them.

"We don't have a manager."

"Well, we need to talk to a manager."

"Unless we play at your club, we can't get a manager."

"Sorry."

Something had to give. Then we had an idea. What about the Hotel Diplomat, where the Dolls had played? It wasn't a club, so we wouldn't need to persuade a booker or manager to hire us. We just needed to rent the place out. It could be our way to bypass the road-blocks we kept running up against. Everything would be in our own hands.

I went to the hotel to inquire about renting the ballroom. It was five hundred bucks. That was a lot of money, but we decided to bite the bullet. We knew we couldn't fill the place on our own, so we asked the Brats to headline the show. We agreed to pay them a few hundred bucks. We even wrote out a contract, like concert promoters. We were up to our necks now.

In order to draw a crowd and have any chance of recouping our outlay, we realized we had to advertise. We needed handbills we could post around town, and we needed to take out an ad in some of the local papers, like the *Village Voice*. This would all take money, too, but Gene and I were still working, and I had gotten Ace a job driving for the same taxi company I drove for.

We also wanted a band logo to make the ads and posters look good. Ace had jotted down a logo for the flyer for our Bleecker Street loft shows. He was a pretty decent artist. I took his sketch and used it as the basis for a series of KISS logos I designed, ultimately arriving at the one that has adorned all things KISS for the past forty years. I vividly remember sitting on my parents' sofa while they were out of town and drawing up the final version on thick white stock using a straightedge and a drafting pen. The SS in the logo actually consists of one S that is thicker than the other, with different proportions, and they aren't exactly parallel—because I just eyeballed it. Ace's concept was closer to the Nazi SS. I certainly suspected that was his inspiration, and the fact that a few years later he bought Nazi memorabilia on our first European tour confirmed this in my mind. As a Jew, I was sensitive about the SS, and Gene's family had survived the Holocaust. My father never liked our logo because he thought my version was still too close to the Nazi lightning bolts, but for me, it didn't hit home until years later, when I learned our logo was banned in Germany because Nazi imagery was illegal there. When I drafted the logo, I certainly never intended to court controversy at the expense of victims of history. I didn't want that on my conscience.

Once we'd taken care of the ads, we put posters up all over the city. We did it ourselves, at night. We'd take two posters, wrap them around something—like a signpost—and staple both sides together.

I also made logo T-shirts, cutting stencils of the logo from cardboard, laying them on black T-shirts, and then painting rubber cement on the fabric and pouring glitter onto it. Take off the stencil, and there was a sparkling metallic KISS logo on black. Peter's sister made some, too, and we passed them out to friends of the band for the show.

We also made up rough-and-ready media kits and sent them out to people whose names we found in magazines and the credits of record sleeves—managers and producers and booking agents. You could find all sorts of information if you scoured publications like *Billboard*. Each kit had a folder with a bio featuring the logo, an eight-by-ten photo, and complementary passes to the Diplomat. Nobody was hustling like that back then. The show passes listed the set time for our show, not the Brats' show, even though they were more the draw. We hoped that the industry types would show up, see a packed ballroom, and assume we had brought the crowd.

We had some additional ideas about our stage show, too. In June I saw Alice Cooper's *Billion Dollar Babies* tour and the theatricality made a huge impression on me. He really opened my eyes to the possibilities of a rock and roll show. Although it was more staged than anything I wanted to do—it seemed quite choreographed, and the whole thing had a scripted feel to it—I liked the atmosphere and environment he created. I wanted KISS to do things as visually arresting as that, but I wanted the *band* to be the show, by itself, as opposed to something that was providing a soundtrack for a separate drama. I wanted KISS to command the same kind of attention without the use of dancers or giant toothbrushes. The question was, *how?*

It would be a while before we fleshed out anything along those lines, but one thing we did immediately was buy a truckload of empty speaker cabinets. They cost next to nothing and looked like Marshall amps. We figured we could stack the empty speaker cabinets onstage to give our set-up the right image. We just had to warn the spotlight operator not to hit them with the light, because then people would be able to see that they were empty.

Early on the day of the show, July 13, 1973, I rented a van and we loaded in and inconspicuously set up all our gear before anyone else arrived. This was a ruse to make people think we had a road crew. When people eventually showed up, we wanted them to see everything ready for us to walk on to the stage, as if somebody had taken care of it all before we even arrived at the venue. Nobody would realize we had humped it all ourselves. In actuality, we had just one guy, a friend of Ace's named Eddie Solon, who handled the sound on our PA.

After we had set everything up at the hotel, we went back to our loft on 23rd Street and got ready for the show, doing our makeup and putting on our outfits. Peter was up to his usual shenanigans, threatening to quit the band just as we thought we were on the verge of taking a step forward. In order to make him feel better, Gene and I arranged a special treat. When we all went downstairs to go to the hotel, a limo was waiting at the curb. It made all of us, not just Peter, feel special to show up in that car. I can't imagine a limo had ever pulled up in front of that place.

The ballroom was nearly full. We realized immediately that we must have covered our expenses—there were probably four hundred people there, and at three bucks a ticket we would be in the black. We stomped through the audience in full regalia and took the stage.

At least one A&R exec showed up for the show, as we had hoped. His name was Rich Totoian, and he worked for Windfall Records, which was the home of the band Mountain—who'd had a massive hit with "Mississippi Queen" a few years before. "Listen," he said. "You guys are great. But honestly, I don't know what to do with you."

It didn't seem like a big mystery to me. If you thought we were good live, just put out a record. I didn't think people needed to think about packaging us or marketing us. Just put it out. Of course, it wasn't the last time somebody was taken aback by our makeup. But by this time, we had confidence—conviction, even—in what we were doing. And since we hadn't lost money on the show, we also knew we could do this again and get more people to check us out. Maybe somebody would figure us out.

"This is who we are," we told the guy. "We are KISS."

18.

We decided to stage another rock and roll ball at the Hotel Diplomat on Friday, August 10, 1973. This time we took a leap of faith and headlined it ourselves. We felt we'd done our apprenticeship and were ready to make a bombastic entrance onto the next level.

Yet, in many ways, KISS was still an unknown commodity. One day I ran into a girl I'd known at school and showed her the poster for our upcoming Diplomat show. "We'll have three or four hundred people there," I told her.

"What? No way." She wasn't joking. She really didn't believe me.

In the grand scheme of things, KISS still didn't really exist. We knew we had a small following, but filling the Daisy or even the Diplomat—what did it mean? Then again, did the Dolls have a much bigger following? They had a record deal, but they were still basically a local act. Did anyone know the Dolls in Portland, Oregon? No. And for that matter, did the people I grew up with in Queens know the Dolls? Doubtful.

Just to be safe, we still pulled in a couple of the "cool" bands to open—Street Punk and Luger, who, like the Brats, had shared bills with the Dolls. Again we took out ads in the paper, put up posters all over town, and sent out media kits to anyone in the industry we could identify and track down.

And again, mercifully, the same result: a full house.

But again we failed to land a deal for a booker, a manager, or a record label. There was, however, one person waiting to talk to us after the show. His name was Bill Aucoin. He mentioned that he had worked on something called *Flipside*, which didn't ring a bell for me. I assumed it was a teen magazine, like *Tigerbeat* or *16*. Bill didn't come from a management background, obviously, but here he was talking about how he wanted to manage us. He seemed to get us. Not only that, he seemed really into us. He'd heard us, he'd seen us, and he seemed to believe in us.

We agreed to meet him.

A few days later, Gene and I went to his office at 75 East 55th Street, just off Madison Avenue. He shared space with an ad agency called Howard Marks Advertising. It seemed like a friendly place all around. "Listen," he said right off the bat, "unless you want to be the biggest band in the world, I'm not interested in managing you."

That was quite a statement from a guy who had never managed a band. But as Bill talked, he struck me as the missing piece of the puzzle. I had the same feeling I'd had when Ace plugged in. Bill was a kindred spirit.

It turned out that *Flipside* was a TV show that took viewers into the studio with bands as they recorded. Bill had also been the director of photography for a Barbra Streisand TV special. Somehow, it seemed logical that an unconventional band would hook up with a manager who wasn't a manager. What Bill did have was contacts that could take us to the next level. We weren't going to find that in a rock club even if we landed a booking agent.

Maybe it wasn't surprising, given his background in TV, that Bill had a lot of ideas about theatricality, too. One thing he suggested was that we never be seen without our makeup. I would never have thought of that. We would exist only as KISS. He thought beyond what any of us was thinking at that point—he saw a much bigger picture. He was definitely tuned in to what we were doing and what we could yet do. And his belief in KISS was striking. Maybe he wasn't jaded because he'd never been a manager.

Bill made one other claim: "If you decide to sign with me and I can't get you a record contract within two weeks, I'll void the contract. You'll be free."

Two weeks. Wow.

At that point, the only sniff we'd had from a label was the guy from Windfall. We said we'd think it over.

Outside his office, Gene and I agreed that we liked Bill and his ideas. But I asked Gene, "Do you care if our manager's gay?"

"Why?"

Bill was fastidious and very well manicured. I read him as gay. But since Bill wasn't overtly effeminate, it had gone right over Gene's head, apparently. "Because this guy's gay."

"How can you tell?" Gene asked.

"Well, he was impeccable, too studied for a heterosexual. Everything was right—the tie, the jacket, the haircut. Even his shoes. You and I would never bother with all that."

Gene shrugged his shoulders. Good. It wasn't an issue for either of us.

Next we called Peter. "We met the guy who should be our manager," we told him. We explained that Bill really understood KISS, he really got it. We talked about all the things Bill had said he could do for us. Peter was skeptical, as he should have been. When I told him that Bill didn't want to work with us unless we wanted to be the biggest band in the world, Peter said, "Bullshit. People say shit like that all the time."

"No, this guy is the real deal," I said. "Get this. If he doesn't get us a record deal within two weeks, we can leave." That did the trick.

After chatting with Ace, who also got on board, we called Bill and said we wanted him to manage us. "Just one last thing," he said. "You guys don't have any contracts with anyone else, right?"

We told him that we had signed something with Ron Johnsen but that it was no big deal.

Bill needed to see the agreement anyway. We took a copy to him.

We were crushed when he told us, "I'm really sorry, guys, but I can't do anything. You can't piss without Ron Johnsen's permission. You're signed lock, stock, and barrel. I can't manage you. There's nothing to manage."

A few days after that conversation with Bill, Ron called me out of the blue. "There's a minor complication with your contract with me," he said. "It's run out, so we have to get together and re-sign it." Apparently the production deal Gene and I had signed with Ron while still in Wicked Lester had expired unnoticed.

That was fate. I called the other guys and then we called Bill to tell him that we were free.

Bill Aucoin became our manager. And soon, we came to consider him the fifth member of KISS.

19.

We can argue about whether beggars can be choosers, but when Bill told us Neil Bogart wanted to sign KISS to a record deal, I thought it was our shot. Neil had turned Buddha Records into the number one singles label in the country by cranking out what some in the rock community might have regarded as prefab crap. He basically invented bubblegum music, with acts like the Ohio Express, 1910 Fruitgum Company, and the Lemon Pipers. *Yummy, yummy, yummy, chewy, chewy, chewy*.

Neil had recently left Buddha to start his own venture, which was originally going to be called Emerald City Records but eventually became known as Casablanca. He agreed to sign us after he heard our demo and a couple of producers he knew told him how good they thought the demos were, too. Neil told Bill, "I'm leaving Buddha and want your guys to be my first act."

But Neil had never seen us live at that point. When he finally saw the makeup, he asked us to take it off. That was a deal breaker.

Soon, though, Neil realized it was our calling card—the visual embodiment of our mentality. He acquiesced and made us the very first act on his new label.

Neil and Bill set up a private concert for the press in early September 1973, and, for dramatic effect, we signed the contract in makeup at that event. Now at first blush, I would certainly rather have signed to a label like Atlantic. Neil had made his career flogging singles, and though he said he wanted to launch Casablanca with a credible rock band—which almost by definition meant marketing albums, not singles—I had my doubts. After all, singles sold by getting airplay on Top 40 radio on the AM dial; rock was played on progressive FM radio stations. But nothing in KISS world ever went according to plan. In retrospect, that's part of the beauty of it. Throughout the band's career we've ignored the rules, either deliberately or by circumstance. In this case we didn't seem to have any choice. It wasn't as if other labels were beating down our door.

Once fully on board, Neil got excited. He began to chip in with ideas on how to make our show even bigger. It was Neil who suggested the elevating drum riser. His original concept was basically a forklift—two prongs beneath the drum riser to lift it. Neil, it was clear, got it.

Bill, however, proved the critical visionary able to take what was still a rough diamond and polish it. Once we had secured our deal with Casablanca, Bill quickly unveiled some of his ideas for the band. The first thing he did was introduce us to his boyfriend, Sean Delaney, who unified our look by dying all of our hair blue-black. We all had dark hair already, but he wanted us to match. We went to an apartment on 11th Street and Sixth Avenue and dunked our heads in a bathtub to give us what Sean wanted to be the jet-black hair of Elvis or Roy Orbison.

Bill also rented a new rehearsal space for us—a cramped, rat-infested basement in the Village. And in there he set up a video camera. Again, this was something that never would have occurred to me. We could see ourselves. Great idea. Even bands like KISS, that prided themselves on being visually arresting, rarely had a chance to see what they really looked like. Together with Sean, who was himself a performer, singer, and songwriter, Bill wanted to analyze the way we moved. This was the TV guy thinking, obviously.

When I performed, I thought of myself as moving all around, swinging my arms, and embodying the rock and roll guitar hero thing. But when we went to the videotape, I could see how small everything was. You could barely make out my gestures. I had to modify my moves if I really wanted to grab the audience. Sean served as coach and cheerleader, helping me develop dynamic, effective moves.

Like everyone else in our haphazardly assembled team, Sean became devoted to fleshing out the KISS concept and helping us be as good as we could possibly be. Once during rehearsal he noticed us kind of swaying in unison for a second. He found the spot on tape and played it back for us. "See this moment when you move together?" he said. "That should be part of the show. That should be something you do—a signature move."

I think initially we all thought it was kind of corny. We were going to be choreographed? But we decided to give Sean's idea a go, and the three of us—Gene, Ace, and me—stood close together at the front of the stage moving our guitars and swaying. Looking at the videos, we realized that it worked. Sean was right. And sure enough, when we first did it in front of an audience, people went crazy. Sean's move killed. We didn't know we needed a Sean until we had Sean. He really upped the theatricality of our act—and later he co-wrote songs with almost all of us.

Another day Bill had us into his office. He introduced us to a guy named the Amazing Amazo or something corny like that. A magician, he said. The guy breathed a ball of fire and scorched the ceiling of Bill's office. "Okay," said Bill. "Who wants to do this onstage?"

Not me!

Gene agreed to give it a try, and the rest is history.

All of this reinforced my initial thoughts about Bill: his ideas were miles away from those of other people, including the members of the band—or any other band, for that matter. Bill understood as much as we did that we didn't have to play by anyone else's rules. He approached things without preconceptions. And he was energetically delivering on everything he had said at our first meeting.

Near the end of September, almost nine months to the day since our first-ever gig together at Coventry, and only a few weeks beyond Bill's self-imposed two-week deadline, we went into Bell Sound to record our debut album. Our debut album!

We requested Eddie Kramer as the producer, since we were pretty pleased with the demo he had supervised. But Neil had something against him—Eddie had worked on an album, by the band Stories, for Buddha Records that hadn't spawned any hits and might also have cost more than Neil expected. So Neil paired us with Richie Wise and Kenny Kerner—who had actually gone into the studio with Stories after Eddie and cut their big hit, "Brother Louie."

Opening that door on 54th Street, walking up the stairs, and entering Bell Sound the first day was terrific and terrifying. We set up all our gear, and the technicians placed all the microphones. I was afraid that if anything moved, the results would be cataclysmic. I ran around telling the guys, "Don't touch anything! It's exactly where it needs to be!"

We were totally green. But this could not have been more different from Wicked Lester going into the studio on spec time. This time, we had producers who led us and told us what to do. We recorded quickly, all in the same room, with virtually no overdubs. We had the songs down, and they changed very little from the demos we had cut back in March. We didn't understand anything. We just waited to be told what was next.

At first, I was self-conscious in the studio. I knew the songs so well, but when the tape was rolling, I started watching my fingers on the guitar and fouled up. Something that came so naturally

became stilted. I saw the microphone as an intimidating obstacle in front of my face instead of seeing it as an ear—just a way to speak to the public, like onstage. I had to stop thinking about the surroundings. I had to recognize that all the studio gadgetry was a vehicle to get to the public, not an obstacle.

It took some time, but I settled down.

I still had a lot to learn— how to sing into the mic, when to sing away from it. But part of what makes a first album so vibrant and alive is

Recording the first KISS album in 1973 at Bell Sound Studios on 54th Street.

the fact that the musicians are typically just pups. That was certainly true for us. I was only twenty-one years old.

When it came to listening back to our music on studio equipment, the fact that I was deaf on one side had no effect—it was the way I had always heard music, and my inability to hear stereo had no bearing on what I did or thought because it was the way I had always heard things. The one thing I noticed was that when we listened to the mixes, I found myself sitting a few feet to the right of center. I just scooted over to compensate, without even thinking about it. That didn't mean I was hearing stereo, but it created a balance. Whenever I was between two speakers, I would move to where the sound was optimal for me; if I looked up, I was always toward the right side.

At lunchtime, sandwiches magically appeared. It was incredible. All this and free food, too? We had no idea at the time that all those sorts of perks were tacked on to the recording bill, which went onto the tab we owed the record company. All I could think was, *We're in a studio, recording songs we wrote, living the dream, and being fed—how much better can it get?*

We talked Peter through the songs as we recorded them. I had a microphone into which I had to say things like, "Okay, here comes the dat-dat-dat" or "now the rat-a-tat-tat." It was the only thing that worked.

I didn't think the drums had the same power I heard on records by a lot of British bands I listened to at the time. But that was mostly because of the way our album was engineered. Old-school engineers didn't believe in pushing the meters into the red. They thought it was wrong—you didn't want distortion, you didn't want to overdrive things. Kenny and Richie's engineer definitely fell into that school, and it affected the recordings. I wished we had somebody who was aware of what was being done in the contemporary world of the genre we worked in. But we didn't, so our record came out a bit flat. The guitars sounded plinky and piano-like instead of big; Gene's bass runs—he wasn't a bass player who stuck to peddling on the root note—got lost; the vocals had more of an ambient quality; the overall sound lacked breadth. Pushing the limits on the recording console gave a lot of our contemporaries a pulsating urgency that our record lacked.

It was another case of things not going to plan. Sure, it was a bit rinky-dink sounding, but based on the way the album has since been received, I suppose it might have been a blessing in disguise that the recordings didn't sound as bombastic as I thought we sounded live. And anyway, just making a record far outweighed any critiques I might have had about the sonic qualities of the recordings.

Each night we left the studio with a great sense of accomplishment. We said goodnight, see you tomorrow, and then we each went to our parents' places—except Peter, who was married and living with his wife. Before long we had finished all nine songs. We had our debut album in the can.

The art department at Casablanca asked whether they should redraft the logo for the album cover to make each S the same width and ensure they were perfectly parallel. "It got us this far," I said. "Don't touch it."

Next we needed a band photo for the album cover. In those days people still misunderstood us—even people hired to work with us. The photographer who shot our first album cover, Joel Brodsky, had done the *Strange Days* cover for the Doors. When we showed up at his studio, he was very friendly and seemed genuinely excited. "Look what I've got for you!" he said.

He brought out a carton filled with all sorts of straw hats and red rubber noses.

What the hell?

"You know, for your pictures," Joel said.

"No, I don't think you understand," we told him. "We're *serious*. We're not clowns. This is what we do."

He was stunned. "You mean, you guys aren't meant to be funny?"

"No, this is us." He could keep the straw hats and red noses.

A lot of people didn't understand that this wasn't fun and games to us. It wasn't frivolous. It was a religion. It was a crusade.

Joel told us there was a makeup person on hand for the shoot.

We all did our own makeup anyway. Except Peter. He had the makeup person do it, who decided to make his face look like some sort of tribal lion mask. We had never seen that makeup before, and we were glad not to see it again.

So maybe our record cover didn't look the way I had expected. And maybe the record didn't sound the way I had expected. But by God we had an album. That trumped everything else. I was so excited. For all the minuses I may have felt—about the sound or the cover—we now had a finished album, which was the prerequisite for all the other things we wanted to do. We were in the game now.

With everything done, Bill told us we were going to go out and start playing. I had no concept of the country we lived in, let alone the world. The idea that we were going to travel to other cities . . . I didn't have the slightest idea what these places were like. I just assumed every new city would be like New York.

We had our revamped show nearly ready to go. The forklift contraption would lift Peter's drum kit up about seven feet. We had Gene fire breathing and the three of us swaying in unison. Just one last piece of the puzzle remained as far as our show was concerned: pyro.

Pyro had not yet become a science. We just "auditioned" a few maniacs who liked to blow shit up. We needed somebody who could make big booms. Bill eventually found our guy. God knows where. I don't really know if there were any credentials at all for early pyrotechnicians. All they needed was a fascination with fire and explosives.

We probably saved lives and property by hiring these guys and keeping some arsonists and pyromaniacs off the streets.

20.

On December 31, 1973, we glimpsed the future.

Bill somehow got us added to a New Year's Eve bill at the Academy of Music featuring Blue Öyster Cult and Iggy and the Stooges. We were fourth on the bill under a local New York band called Teenage Lust. Now, I *knew* it was just a matter of time before we started blowing everybody away. And that night, we certainly made an impression.

When we walked out on the stage in front of four thousand people, I was stunned. It might as well have been four *hundred* thousand. Not long into the set, I popped the button on my homemade pants and struggled to keep them up for the rest of the set, pressing my guitar awkwardly against my crotch to keep them from slipping down. Then Gene lit his hair on fire when he tried the fire breathing that the Amazing Amazo had taught him.

We were dangerous, alright—to ourselves.

Still, even before the end of the night, I realized I didn't need to feel too bad. When it was time for the Stooges to play, the band took the stage and started playing—without Iggy. Crew members had to carry Iggy down a flight of steps, drag him to the side of the stage, prop him up behind the curtains dangling there beside the stage, and then basically throw him out onstage. Iggy could barely stand up, much less walk or jump. I suddenly realized why he did all those crazy contortions. Despite the hype and legend, I thought the Stooges were awful.

Even so, we now knew we weren't ready to be headliners. Not yet.

Fortunately, we had one more small-scale tune-up show scheduled before we headed off to Canada to kick off our promotional tour. Unfortunately, Neil chose that moment to approach me about something bugging him about my Starchild character. "I was wondering if we could tweak your makeup a little," he said.

"What? Why?"

"Your makeup is . . . well, it's a little . . . effeminate. Maybe you can ditch the star and try something else?"

To be a good sport, I agreed to experiment with a mask, something closer to Zorro or the Lone Ranger. After the show Neil said, "Can you also maybe lumber around onstage? You know, like a caveman or something?"

Fuck this.

"Why would I do that? It's not what I'm about."

I just didn't understand his objections. I was proud to be the Starchild, and I didn't see how any of what I did had the slightest thing to do with my sexuality, or my perceived sexuality. If anything, I thought hints of androgyny demonstrated confidence and comfort with my sexuality. And besides, people were drawn to it, so who cared what they read into it? It was just the way of the world back then—a lot more people were afraid of anything that might be taken for gay. In fact, that would become more clear in the following years. In that regard, Neil was right about how my character might be interpreted. It's just that I didn't care. We didn't play by

the rules. And I wasn't going to yield to received wisdom or irrational fear. My idealized vision of a frontman was definitely not a
Neanderthal.

I went back to the star after that single show in January 1974.

I was still living at home, and my parents were raising my niece,
Ericka. I didn't have much money and sure as hell wasn't going to
spend what little I did have to rent a place of my own. I knew from
this point on I wouldn't be around much, but I loved the increasingly deep bond I shared with Ericka and loved serving as a big
brother to her now that she was walking and talking.

Next thing I knew, my parents were driving me to the airport to
catch a flight to Edmonton, Canada. Our album had yet to come
out, but a musician I wasn't aware of, Mike Quatro—whose sister
Suzi was very popular in England—had canceled some dates in
Canada, and Bill snagged them for us. Sitting in the back seat of my
parents' car on the way to the airport, I felt like I was being driven
to summer camp. Little did my parents know, they were actually
driving me to a residency in a traveling whorehouse. Almost as
soon as we landed in Canada, I realized that girls wanted to sleep
with me—though the sleeping part was not a priority and was definitely secondary to more strenuous bedroom activity—based on
only one criterion: I was in a band.

I was *desirable*, and I could hardly believe it.

In addition to easy, random, nonstop sex, there were concerts to
be played. The venues for those three shows were college cafeterias,
and we didn't have our full arsenal of tricks along for the ride.
Peter's drum riser stayed in New York, though Gene still breathed
fire, and the stage—which on these dates was hardly more than
some folding tables pushed together—was wreathed in dry ice fog.

Mike Quatro obviously had enough of a following to have those
shows booked for him. And even though he couldn't have been that
big, given the venues, people were confused when we took the stage

each night. They had no idea who we were. Hard to blame them, since our album hadn't been released yet.

We had a few interviews on that first trip. We had no idea how to do an interview. We had no strategy on how to come across cohesively. The only thing we had discussed with Bill was the fact that we would never be photographed without the makeup. That strategy—while great in concept—turned out to be a bit of a bummer in practice when we were first faced with the possibility of at least the minor fame that could be said to go along with having your picture in a local newspaper.

Since we were to exist only onstage and in photos of us in full regalia, the journalists came to the venues and talked to us all together, after we were already made up. It became clear that the four of us had no idea how to discuss the particulars about things like how the band got together or what we were trying to accomplish. We hadn't conceptualized those things individually, much less as a group. We tried to sound interesting or controversial but just came off like a bunch of idiots. We'd been thrown into the deep end of the pool and had no idea how to swim.

One thing that struck me, though, was that for a guy with a great vocabulary, Gene sure used the word "I" a lot. Whenever I tried to answer questions about the band, I naturally answered using "we." But when Gene answered similar questions, he always cast it as "I." That really threw me. The questions were about the *band*. This wasn't supposed to be about him, it was about all of us—KISS.

Our idea had always been to present ourselves like the Beatles— the four guys all living in the same house, skiing down the hill in *Help!* or whatever. As an only child, Gene apparently didn't feel he had to answer to anybody or explain himself. It pissed me off, but I said nothing.

Back in New York after about a week in Canada, Neil tipped us off that "Nothing to Lose," which he had released as a single, was going to be played at 2 P.M. one day on WNEW, the big local FM rock station. My parents and I crowded around their Harmon Kardon console and waited. Then Alison Steele said, "There's a new band called KISS, and here's their first song." Then "Nothing to Lose" played in our living room. That moment—hearing my band on the same station that played Led Zeppelin and the Who—was monumental. I'd spent hours listening to my heroes on that station.

There had been a sense of unreality about the album until other people heard it. Even when I'd seen the finished cover in Bill's office, it hadn't seemed real. *Now* it was real. And the following week, when the album would be available in record shops and maybe even displayed in shop windows, and we would play a launch party in Los Angeles, it would be even more real.

We flew to Los Angeles in mid-February for the party, which Neil had organized at the Century Plaza Hotel. It was a coming-out party to introduce us to the industry—including Neil's partners at Warner Bros. Records—and whatever celebrities Casablanca could rope into coming.

I immediately loved L.A. It was a different country—a world apart from the one I knew. Driving down Sunset Boulevard I saw billboards touting *bands* instead of cigarettes or beer. *Wow.* I hoped to see KISS up there one day. The city embraced music in a way New York didn't. It seemed to revolve around music and movies. It also felt somehow healthier—the combination of the sunny weather and the way people took care of themselves struck me.

Casablanca put us up in the Chateau Marmont and rented two Chevys for us to drive around town. We would pile into the cars and go to Denny's or McDonald's. I roomed with Ace in a two-story bungalow off in a private section of the grounds. Gene roomed with Peter. Each bungalow had two levels and several bedrooms and bathrooms. The first day Ace went out for a walk, and I decided to take a shower. While I was in there, the bathroom started to smell horrible. I pulled open the curtain to see what it could be— and there was Ace sitting on the toilet taking a dump. He looked up. "What are you doing in here?" I yelled. There were other bathrooms in the place, after all. He just shrugged. Ace was odd.

Early in our L.A. visit, I asked a few people, "What do you do here? Where do you go at night?" One of the first places mentioned was the Rainbow, a bar and restaurant on Sunset Boulevard in West Hollywood. I had never heard of it, but as soon as I walked in, I knew I had found my synagogue. A new house of worship.

The people in there weren't looking for anything more than a promise of tonight. It seemed to be a system of friends-with-benefits, or strangers-with-benefits for a newcomer like me. The very first night I met a great-looking blonde whose only criterion for going back to my room at the Chateau Marmont was that I was in a band that had a record deal. Being a musician and looking the part—I was in platform boots and rock star chic, as usual—got you pretty far on Sunset Boulevard. Which was fine with me. It was all so uncomplicated. In a way, she and I were both celebrating the same thing: the exaltation of rock and roll.

I had just gotten Led Zeppelin's *Houses of the Holy* on cassette, and I put that in a cassette player next to my bed in the hotel room. That album will always be synonymous with my first foray into the appreciation society of the Rainbow.

When the woman left the next morning, I realized the scene in L.A. had no false expectations—in either direction. There was no judgment, no sense of condescension. We appreciated each other in a kind of wholesome way, as odd as it may sound.

That night—and the subsequent nights, all of which I spent at the Rainbow—was my rite of passage into rock and roll at a level I didn't know existed. I had heard about a rock and roll lifestyle, but I didn't have a sufficient idea of what it was like to even fantasize about it. My concepts of fame and rock and roll had been hampered by my limited experience. I expected the payoff to come in the form of a hot girlfriend; instead, it came in the form of being with a different hot girl every day, sometimes several in the space of one day. It was incredible. L.A. seemed like the Land of Oz.

On February 18, 1974, Casablanca officially unveiled us at a party that was a bit like a cross between a bar mitzvah and a C-list celebrity gathering. Neil got up onstage and introduced us and we started playing. Before we finished our first song, everybody cleared out of the ballroom. Too loud and too garish, they complained. Hey, we weren't the Eagles. No comfortable volume or songs about being desperate in the desert. We were East Coast, proud of it, and thought the whole West Coast cowboy thing was a bit of a joke. I felt an odd sense of pride at having scared off these people. What did we care if they didn't like us? They weren't our type, either.

Alice Cooper came to the event that night, too. Afterwards he joked, "What you guys need is a gimmick."

A few nights later we drove down to the Aquarius Theater, also on Sunset, to make our first-ever TV appearance. Dick Clark had expanded beyond *American Bandstand* and had a show called *In Concert* that featured three different bands playing a few songs live on each episode. The format suited us—just us doing what we did. And it felt like another milestone—a network television show, hosted by Dick Clark no less. Dick came to our dressing room when we arrived to get ready for the performance. I learned over time that a lot of people in similar positions weren't nearly as cordial as he was. Bill Graham, for instance, a highly respected promoter who ran the Fillmore and Winterland, was anything but nice to us when we first met him a few months later. But Dick was special, and when I shook his hand, all I could think was, *That's Dick fucking Clark!* For all those years he had been an inspiration to me as a kid, he had seemed as fantastical as Superman—but, no, Dick Clark really existed.

We set up on a revolving stage, and a band called Redbone played before us. Then the stage turned and the dim lighting suddenly became bright stage lighting. There we were in front of the cameras. But we were a machine by that point, and we played ferociously wherever we were. We felt good about the performance. We didn't see it until six weeks later, when we hurried back to a motel after a concert in Asbury Park, New Jersey, to watch the broadcast on a crappy TV.

After taping *In Concert*, we flew back to New York to cool our boots for a few weeks before setting out on our first real tour in mid-March. I remember lying in bed in my parents' apartment, thinking about my time in Los Angeles—women, restaurants, TV shows, fancy hotels, and all the perks and amenities that went along with success.

And I prayed.

God, please don't take this away from me now.

That small modicum of recognition was so addictive—the fact that the chubby unpopular kid was being chased by women, purely because of how I was perceived differently now. And I was now being *paid* to do what I loved doing anyway. It had been okay before I knew it existed, but now that I had tasted it, I couldn't bear the thought of having it taken away. I was fine before I had tasted the cake. Everything was different now. I prayed, fearful that it would be pulled off the table before I had made the most of it. The crumbs were so exhilarating. I wanted more. And I was terrified it would end too soon.

God, don't take this away from me yet.

Please, God. Not now, not yet.

21.

Now that we had a record, we secured a national booking agency, ATI, to keep us on the road. ATI added us to bills as the opener and got us into clubs on our own. Our first show, on March 22, 1974, in Pennsylvania, we opened again for Redbone, the same band we had shared Dick Clark's rotating stage with the month before. Then we did a couple of shows with the British band Argent, and we were on our way. During the course of the year we opened for ZZ Top, Blue Öyster Cult, Manfred Mann, and many other bands—even the New York Dolls.

When you went to a concert in a theater or arena in the early 1970s, you typically saw three bands. First, an unknown act— KISS, in this case—then a somewhat bigger band, often billed as "special guests," and then the headliner. The goal was to work your way up the ladder.

The three-tiered system gave you a chance to hone your craft. And while we understood the need to hone our craft, we also took our full arsenal of explosives, smoke, and fire with us wherever we played, whether we headlined a tiny club or played to a half-empty ballroom before two other bands. A KISS show would always be a KISS show—breathing fire, waving our guitars in unison, blowing shit up. If we sometimes ended up getting Peter pinned to the ceiling when his drums elevated or we offended a headliner because our pyro filled the venue with smoke, then so be it.

We didn't compromise, and fortunately, Bill Aucoin seemingly had no credit limit on his American Express card, because he funded the expenses of transporting and staging our show at a time when what we earned each night didn't come close to covering those costs. We drove a station wagon from town to town, staying in fleabag motels. Sean Delaney served as tour manager and did the driving. He was like a den mother, making sure nobody got lost on the field trip and managing the personalities. Bill came along for parts of the tour as well—and when he wasn't around, we each talked to him on the phone every day. He had a knack for making each of us feel like his favorite member of the band.

And, of course, we had a road crew to set up and tear down our stage and effects, to maintain our instruments, and, it often turned out, to fight with the headliners' road crews when they demanded we tone down our act since we were just the opening band. The road crew drove a big truck with all the gear—except for the four Samsonite makeup cases, complete with mirrors. Those stayed with us in the station wagon.

When we played a few dates with the band Argent, their crew kept cutting our set short, pulling the power before we finished. They also fought us tooth and nail on all of our effects—it's tough to follow a band that leaves the place filled with smoke to remind everyone throughout the rest of the concert that World War III had just been fought and won by four guys in eight-inch heels, black leather, and makeup. Then on the last night of our tour leg with them, we miraculously had a trouble-free show. Afterwards we found out why: our crew had locked the guy in charge of their production in one of the huge road cases we carted our gear in. Our road crew believed in the cause.

Another time, when we opened for Aerosmith—who were also an up-and-coming band at the time, but somewhat ahead of us—our crew showed up and found their crew had set up in a way that left us only a few feet of depth. We would have to have crab-walked onto the stage. Our crew told the Aerosmith crew, "You have five minutes to move your amp line back, or we throw everything into the pit," and one of our guys pulled a knife, just to emphasize how serious they were. They quickly made room for us.

Of the initial few shows, one at the Bayou in Washington, D.C., on March 25, stands out. Everything was magical at that point—we were barnstorming around the country getting paid to do what we loved most. I didn't really have any bills to pay back then, but the idea that in theory I could pay them by playing rock and roll was a terrific feeling. This was my occupation. This was how I made my livelihood.

The night of the show at the Bayou, I saw my first gang bang. I walked into a motel room where the crew was staying, and there was a young woman on the bed and a line of guys—our roadies and various other people—waiting their turn to mount her. I had never seen anything like that. It was as if they were waiting for the bus. And it was not something for me.

I did meet a woman that night, though. She was strikingly beautiful—she'd have been far out of my league a few weeks earlier. Somehow it made me feel a little paranoid. What if she had a boyfriend or husband who would want to kick my ass? Suddenly there was more to it than just whether she and I wanted to consummate and celebrate all things rock and roll. Other people might be connected to her decisions, people who might not be happy about her indulgences. To make things worse, I eventually connected the dots based on the things she told me and realized that her dad was a mobster. At some stage, as we lay in bed naked, I turned to her and said, "Are you here because you want to be here, or are you here because you're drunk?"

"I'm here because I'm drunk!" she laughed.

Sometimes I felt like a bull in a china shop; other times I heard a voice telling me that sex went hand in hand with fear and consequences. *If you get somebody pregnant, you're on your own.* In other words, if you fuck the wrong woman, you're dead.

No matter the fear, anxiety, or inner conflicts, sex was my drug of choice. And I always went back for more.

I had a few drinks now and then, but I didn't need booze to screw up the courage to talk to women. I had no trouble making advances or starting a conversation. And anyway, I quickly learned that it didn't take a lot of witty banter to interest a woman—I was in a band, and that was enough to make me desirable.

Drinking more heavily or doing drugs didn't appeal to me. I never wanted to lose control. I was dealing with newfound freedoms and opportunities, and I wanted to remain lucid and remember it all. But drugs were around from the earliest days of the band. People showed up at the venues, at the motels, and at the radio stations and record shops where we did promo appearances and wanted to befriend us. The guys threw drugs at us, and the women threw their bodies; I had use for only one.

The road crew, on the other hand, picked up the various colored pills that fans threw on the stage and gobbled them down like Skittles. It freaked me out. "You don't even know what you just ate!"

One morning I went to our pyro guy's room and there was no answer. I pushed the door open, and he was huddled in the corner with a blanket over his head, looking green and unable to move. I didn't see the fun in that.

The fact that nearly everyone in the rock world was high definitely contributed to my socializing less. Drugs were part of the culture, and not doing drugs set me apart. The fact that I wasn't doing blow or taking pills made other people uncomfortable; the fact that they were uncomfortable made me uncomfortable. My interactions with groupies and other women, on the other hand, were purely sexual, and drug use rarely came up. I couldn't imagine a better rush than having a woman want to go back to my room with me.

Ace was an alcoholic, but in the beginning he stayed sober until after the show—at which point it was normal for him to drink until he was unable to stand. It was still funny then. For me, the ultimate gauge of whether his drinking was a problem was whether he was doing his job—and he was. What he wanted to do offstage was his business.

One night I found him crawling down the hall of a motel on all fours, talking to himself. "What are you doing, man?" I asked him.

"I've got my little people with me," he said, gesturing around himself.

As I tried to get past him, he said, "Oh! You just stepped on one!"

In some ways it was pathetic, but in other ways, I have to say, it was funny. We laughed at Ace a lot—and not in a demeaning way. He was amusing. He was an oddball. He constantly told jokes. Only later did it become ugly. Once he mixed in Valium and cocaine, it wasn't as funny anymore. Initially, though, he was just a likable kook.

At one point, Ace got the nickname "the chef." With the exception of Gene, who never took his clothes off or showered in front of anyone else, we often didn't wear a lot in the dressing room before or after a concert. One night while we were sitting in front of our mirrors putting on our makeup, Peter walked up behind Ace and put his dick on his shoulder. Ace very nonchalantly turned to the side and gave it a kiss. So he became the chef, because he had to taste everything.

We also called Ace "Scraps" back then because he often reached across the table and took stuff off our plates. "Are you eating that?" he'd ask, and then grab.

We all had breakfast and dinner together on the road. The breakfasts at cheap motels were pretty much the same: scrambled eggs and toast and those little cups of grape jelly you peeled the top off of. Dinner varied. If someone had shrimp, Ace would eat the tails you left on the plate. Sometimes in motels he would rummage through discarded room service trays as we walked down the hallways.

It wasn't unusual to spend ten or more hours a day in the station wagon together. Ace kept us laughing. One time Peter, who was older than all of us and had a long, mopey face, said, "I have the baby face in the band."

Ace said, "Yeah, maybe a baby walrus."

Another time in the car Ace said, "I could really use a drink." This was not unusual for Ace.

"You can drink my cologne," I said.

"Really?"

"Sure," I said, "cologne is alcohol."

So he screwed off the spray cap and took a swig of my Aramis. He spit it right out. We all laughed, including Ace.

I thought of us as the four musketeers and figured we'd be together forever. We were the Vikings, the Huns, the Mongols, wreaking havoc in every town we invaded. We were the Beatles skiing down the hill in *Help!*

We were KISS.

There was a genuine sense of camaraderie as we ate together, traveled together, got dressed for a show together, and played together—and onstage we were a unified force. It wasn't real life, of course, and when we occasionally went home for brief stretches, we didn't see each other at all. On the road, though, we were KISS. And it was fun to be KISS.

I knew we would work through and beyond this phase. There was almost a wistfulness—I was conscious that we were living this quaint rock and roll existence on the way to stardom. Because stardom was never a question in my mind.

We are going to make it.

Bill set up promotional appearances at local papers, radio stations, and record shops at every possible opportunity. After a few months, we began to get a little big for our britches, moaning about having to do appearances. One afternoon when we were supposed to get dressed and go to a record store, we decided we weren't going to show up. Fuck it. Bill was out with us at the time, and he came storming to our motel rooms, gathered us together, and yelled, "Are you kidding me?"

We told him we didn't feel like doing it—we felt it was a waste of time, and maybe even beneath us.

"You guys are acting like you've qualified for the Olympics or something," he scolded. "You're not even *contenders* yet."

We looked at each other and said, "Oh."

We put on our makeup. We went to the record store. We listened to Bill and he was almost always right.

Neil, on the other hand, approached things from an entirely different philosophy—learned during his Buddha days—and seemed to find nothing wrong with jeopardizing an act's potential career longevity for the chance of a hit single today, no matter how trite or substandard. He got us into a recording studio in early spring of 1974 to do a cover of an old Bobby Rydell song called "Kissin' Time." He told us it was "promotional music" for a kissing contest—an idea that was contrary to everything I envisioned for the band. I thought it was tacky. The bands I looked up to wouldn't do something like that. But Neil assured us our recording would be used for background music in a radio spot for the contest, nothing more. Of course, no sooner had we cut the not-particularly-great rendition of the song than Neil issued it as a single. He had a unique way of dealing with things sometimes.

After the single was released and the kissing contest was rolled out on some radio stations around the country, Neil scheduled us to appear at one of the contests being held at a record store. I walked in there, in full makeup, feeling very full of myself, and strolled over to a couple who had their lips locked. I bent down—we had our platform boots on—and the guy, while keeping his lips in contact with the girl's, looked out of the side of his eyes and said, "Who the hell are you?"

They were just two kids in a kissing contest. They had no idea it had anything to do with us.

"Never mind," I said, and made for the door as quickly as my studded heels would carry me.

22.

We averaged a little better than one concert every two days. At the end of April, Bill landed us another national TV appearance, this time on *The Mike Douglas Show*.

I could tell this one would be different. It was a variety show, not a music show. We could just as easily have been monkeys on unicycles or spinning dishes on sticks. Ed Sullivan's show was like that, too: "We've got Topo Gigio and the dancing bears, and for the kids . . . the Beatles." Only on Mike Douglas's show, the audience was just like Mike Douglas—older, to put it mildly. The crowd looked like moms and pops out of a Norman Rockwell painting, and we looked like aliens to them. We were clearly out of our element, and I had a feeling we would be not only treated as a novelty, but milked for laughs.

We had to win over audiences when we opened for other bands, and we relished the challenge. This, however, did not look like fun. This wasn't an audience I thought I could win over, and I had no desire to go out and get ridiculed.

Bill asked, "Who wants to sit in the chair and do the talking during the panel discussion portion of the show?"

I said, "Not me, I'm staying backstage."

Gene went out. He didn't know what to say and described himself as "evil incarnate" and stuck out his tongue. Totie Fields, a comedienne who was also a guest that night, dismissed him as a nice Jewish boy, despite the demon getup. He came off pretty goofy. But his being the default spokesman of the band would lead to countless more episodes of him using "I" instead of "we," subtly and not so subtly implying that he was the frontman, lead singer, and mastermind all wrapped up in one. He never attempted to clarify his role or refute media assumptions. Why would he? Those false assumptions were based on Gene's own statements. Once again I found myself scratching my head at his refusal to be honest and his insistence on using every opportunity to discuss things from his own perspective rather than the band's collective perspective. He was cheating.

Earlier that month we'd opened a show at the Agora in Cleveland for Rory Gallagher. When we walked out onto the stage, a girl in the front started elbowing her boyfriend and laughing.

You won't be laughing for long.

We blew the place up. Smoke filled the entire venue. These places were not ventilated well. Back then our pyro guys had to make their own flashpots. Each day they built enclosures and filled them with explosives. One night the flashpots could be like kernels of popcorn being popped, and the next night they might blow a hole in the stage. We didn't have to apply for permits or have a fire marshal inspect what we were doing—nobody knew what we were doing, and nobody had done it before. We just blew crap up and set off explosions with no oversight or expertise. It was intense.

On nights like that I might as well have turned over an hourglass and waited for the sand to trickle down. It was like clockwork. We always won over even the most skeptical people. We never failed to get a crowd on its feet. Of course, no show, no matter how big, could mask a crappy band. And KISS started with the four of us *bringing it*. You can have a beautiful car, with a sparkling paint job and loads of chrome trim, but if it doesn't have a great engine, it isn't going anywhere. We provided the engine, and we won audiences because of the power of the four characters and the music we made.

Another night we opened for a midlevel British blues band called Savoy Brown at a jam-packed ice-skating rink in Michigan. Some of the guys in the band had never seen us, and they came to the side of the stage as we started playing and laughed in full view of us. I was laughing inside, though, because I knew how tough it was to follow KISS. And sure enough, they may have been laughing during our set, but they were crying when half the audience left during theirs. They changed their tune after that.

Some of the musicians we met I liked as people, and we played with a lot of bands whose music I liked and respected, but our attitude as a band was always the same: *We will annihilate you*. When I reached the stage steps, it was no longer a Kumbaya moment. Even though it wasn't conceived in hatred or animosity, we were deadly serious about the fact that we wanted to *kill* other bands when we hit that stage. Not the audience, the other band. We took huge pride in what we were doing, we were focused, we were driven, and we wanted to decimate them.

We are KISS!

We were missionaries for KISS's brand of rock and roll, and we would not stop until we converted everyone.

Sometimes our missionary fervor took on biblical proportions. One night in Fayetteville, North Carolina, our bombs set the curtain on fire—the curtain owned by the headliners, Black Oak Arkansas. We got thrown off that tour.

In the Deep South, people loved us when we were onstage. We

had a license to be freaks onstage and were welcomed as entertainers. But offstage, people wanted to kill us. As soon as we left the venues and were just guys in platform boots with big hair, wearing scarves, jewelry, and women's blouses, we felt hunted. Outside of rock clubs, people had zero tolerance for guys who looked to them like "fags," which people constantly shouted at us. I kept worrying we might end up squealing like pigs, like in the scene from the movie *Deliverance*, which I had seen the year before.

I realized I'd grown up pretty insulated in New York City, not understanding the kind of anger that looking different could elicit in other places. Still, I sensed the discrimination more than I saw it. That couldn't be said for some of our crew members, like our road manager J.R. Smalling—the guy who came up with our stage introduction, "You wanted the best, you got the best." J.R. was black, and for several days when we had a local driver in the South, the white driver kept referring to J.R. as "Leroy." I also heard the N-word hurled around a lot.

We didn't attract hecklers, though. For one thing, I think people who came to shows found us somewhat intimidating. And our willfulness was obvious, too, our commitment to what we were doing. When we ran into people outside the show calling us names, I wanted to say, "Hang on a minute—I'm the same guy you were clapping for. I put down my guitar and you want to lynch me?"

We stuck close to our motels in places where we didn't feel safe. We ate at the motels, got in our car, and hit the road. We weren't big on stopping at Billy Bob's Diner or Bubba's Barbeque. We got our asses from point A to point B.

We passed Graceland at some point along the road, and I was very disappointed. It just looked like an anonymous doctor's house in the suburbs. I had expected a massive mansion. I opted to go off with a couple of women who owned a clothing store in Memphis instead of taking the tour of Elvis's place.

Even in the South or in other conservative places like Salt Lake City, we found our fans or they found us. And, always, women. Girls waited in the lobby or out front of our hotel rooms until we were available. We could have had one of those machines you see at the motor vehicles department—take a number and wait for it to be called. Most of the time, I didn't even know the girls' names.

It still amazed me that the women I met on the road came to my room with barely so much as an introduction when I figured there were probably guys in town who had to date them for months to get anywhere. It all quickly became normal. And what a relief. I was now getting laid and felt desired without any fear of emotional connection, which was the last thing I wanted. I got what I craved without any of the dangers, as I saw it. Because of my insecurities, my ear, my hearing, and the defenses I had built up over the course of my life, emotional connection continued to frighten me. It meant having to open up and give something of myself, which I didn't want to do.

We couldn't afford individual rooms yet. I roomed with Peter, and we both hoped we wouldn't be alone in bed when the other guy had someone there. We never had any privacy. But it was certainly nicer when both beds were filled rather than one of us having to put a pillow over his head. In those cases I hoped for a quick few minutes with Peter's guest if he left the room. It made sleeping easier. Eventually Sean Delaney began to see it as his job to kick girls out of our rooms under the pretense that we needed sleep. Sean wasn't fond of the girls, whom he often called "breeders."

That first six months of touring in 1974 was a bit of a blur: long drives punctuated by stops in venues with names like Thunderchicken, Mother's, and Flash's. We played college auditoriums, gymnasiums, and even a jai alai stadium in Florida; we made it as far as Alaska, where we played outdoors at a drive-in cinema and the space heaters at the front of the stage kept throwing the metal strings on our guitars out of tune. Even during that first blurred year, however, we found places that became favorites—like the

Electric Ballroom in Atlanta. Somehow we headlined blocks of shows there. We played four nights in a row in June; after we drew crowds for several more nights in July, they booked us for four additional nights in September. The parties and hospitality on all levels were never ending, and we got excited whenever we saw it on the itinerary. Any girlfriend or wife in New York didn't.

KISS also clearly connected with Detroit from the get-go. People there got us. It was such a fertile area for rock that we loved, too—from Mitch Ryder to Bob Seger to Alice Cooper. Ann Arbor had the MC5 and the Stooges, Flint had Grand Funk Railroad. Michigan embraced us, and before the end of 1974, Detroit became the first place we could headline a theater. I would always recall it as the first city to open its arms, and its legs, to us.

Through all of this touring we didn't have multiple sets of stage clothes, so we could always find the dressing room at a venue by following the stench; as the smell got stronger, I knew I was getting closer. Some days we did two sets, an early show and a late show, but even on days with just one, the clothes never dried. Putting on damp, fetid clothing made my skin crawl. Whenever possible, I took a hair dryer to my jumpsuit—at least then it was warm damp clothing. After my wardrobe malfunction at the Academy of Music, with the button popping on my homemade pants, I had bought a pair of Danskin tights. I took a lot of flak for them at first, but they turned out to be really practical and the other guys ultimately made the switch, too. Leather and satin got crisp and mossy after they soaked up enough sweat.

Damp boots were another problem: mold or algae grew in them. The inside of each boot looked like its own little ecosystem—the only thing missing was frogs jumping around in there. We often had to scrape green crud off the outside of the boots, too. Still, nobody ever complained.

In my case it was because there was nothing that compared to the rush I got when the curtain dropped and the audience went crazy. The curtain might as well have been a fifteen-foot-thick concrete wall, and when that barrier was removed: *utter chaos*. I could be on one side of the curtain with a 102-degree fever and a sore throat struggling to sing the first notes of "Strutter" or "Firehouse" with some effort. But when the curtain dropped, I sang like a bird because the adrenaline kicked in. It didn't matter how tired or sore or sick I was—when I got up onstage, I felt supernatural.

People wanted to surrender to us. Part of what made me feel powerful onstage was taking that license and knowing how far I could push it. That took time to learn. I realized that if I asked people to do things they already wanted to do, I came across as omnipotent. I was in control. People responded to that. People wanted to be told, "Get up!" or "Raise your hands!"

Did putting their hands up have anything to do with a song? Only in the same way that a church congregation raises its hands skyward to try to touch something holy. It was also fun—like riding a roller coaster without holding the bar.

It was all about what we could create together. It was all in the back and forth. Most of the people were willing to go, they just needed somebody to guide them. They needed *me*. I had to connect. I wasn't just playing to the back row of a theater—I was playing to people. I had to make that person in the last row feel as important as the one up in the front. I wasn't playing to a mass but to each and every one of those people.

I am talking to you. You, *right there!*

That was my job—to take us all to the rock and roll promised land, individually and collectively. "Some of you people are sitting down. If you want to sit down, go home and watch television. But if you believe in rock and roll, stand up for what you believe in!"

Each night we created something magical with the audience— and it was every bit as magical for me as for them.

23.

I learned a lesson early on. Bill Aucoin said at one point in the summer of 1974 that we needed to make another album. "But I don't have any inspiration," I said.

"I'll show you the bills, and you'll get inspired," he said.

That may sound cold, but it rang true. Anybody could sit around and wait for inspiration. Talent was being able to conjure it up—to *get* inspired. Our first album, *KISS*, had leveled out at sales of about sixty thousand, and we needed new product.

We set up camp at the Ramada Inn in L.A. for a month in August to make *Hotter Than Hell*. We each got our own room this time. We felt like stars. Walking around one morning after breakfast, I noticed Lyle Tuttle's tattoo parlor on Sunset Boulevard. I walked in. I decided I would get one tattoo—I swore to myself that it would be one, just one, for life. I knew I didn't want a skull with a top hat or a battleship or "Mom," so I settled on a rose on my shoulder.

Back at the hotel with my new ink, I called home. I was excited and also wanted to ruffle my parents' feathers, I guess. "Guess what, Mom? I just got a tattoo!"

"Oh, Stan," my mother said, referring to a Jewish cultural taboo, "now you can't be buried in a Jewish cemetery!"

"Cut my arm off, mom. It's not going to matter to me."

Again I found L.A. inspiring. The city revolved around music and the entertainment industry. I rarely met people who had grown up there. It was a place people went with a sense of purpose. Lots of New Yorkers lived there, having migrated to California and taken over businesses. The locals were so laid-back that New Yorkers could devour everything. L.A. was a destination for people with a career plan or an agenda. It was a rootless place where people went to chase dreams and follow their aspirations.

Neil rented Village Recorder out by the beach in Santa Monica and flew out Richie and Kenny. The studio was in a cool old building with a huge mural on one side of it depicting a postapocalyptic cityscape—crumbled buildings, collapsed highway overpasses.

We hoped to remedy some of the problems we heard on the first album. The main thing was to make it heavier. We did end up recording it "hot" this time—meaning, with distortion—but that didn't work well, either. Once again, we didn't get what we were looking for, and the result was an unpleasant distortion on the instruments.

Among the songs we recorded, some were leftovers—like "Watchin' You" and "Let Me Go, Rock 'n' Roll"—and some we wrote in the studio and never even demoed—we didn't have an album's worth of material when we started recording. We didn't travel with acoustic guitars, and little practice amps weren't common, either, so we hadn't written much on the road that first year. Occasionally I would write down lyrics, but the creative key for me was recording the melody on some kind of device.

The title track, "Hotter Than Hell," I wrote in L.A. It was an homage of sorts to "All Right Now" by Free and started with the same basic premise—meeting a woman. Gene brought in "Goin'

Blind," a song he'd written with Steve Coronel. It sounded cool, and I knew what they were going for. I suggested the line, "I'm ninety-three, you're sixteen," which sounded very warped and knocked the whole thing a little sideways. "That's weird," Gene said. "That's a really weird line. Do you think we should?"

"Yeah, absolutely," I said. And with that one line it became a song about an old man in love with a young girl.

"Got to Choose" was based on a song I'd heard at Electric Lady. The facility had two studios, and they were often both in use nearly twenty-four hours a day. It was a round-the-clock fortress of creativity. One evening they had been running off copies on the two-track machine of an album by a band called Boomerang. They were a blue-eyed soul unit made up of Mark Stein from Vanilla Fudge along with a couple other guys. Boomerang had recorded a cover of the Wilson Pickett song "Ninety-Nine and a Half (Won't Do)," and that was the seed for "Got to Choose."

We tried to get Ace to sing "Strange Ways" or "Parasite." Again, he refused to sing on the album. Gene ended up singing "Parasite," and Peter did "Strange Ways." "Comin' Home" was a road song Ace and I built around a damn good riff and some fragments of ideas he had. I wrote "Mainline" in L.A., too, and thought it had a great swagger to it. When we were working on it at Village Recorder, Peter said, "Either I sing that song or I'm quitting the band."

I was astonished. Same shit. Different day.

Right from the beginning, Bill had pushed the idea of pooling the money we made off songs and sharing the revenue so everyone would feel equal. He figured that way nobody would demand to have songs on an album just for the financial reward, and we could determine the song selection based on what worked best in our eyes and the eyes of the producers working with us. We had done that. But with *Hotter Than Hell*, we saw the first signs that this wouldn't always help stave off potential friction.

Maybe everyone in the band was just too different for us to be cohesive. Though I never saw Gene as like-minded, I did see him as a partner. But to me it was clear that Gene continued to see the band as a vehicle for himself as an individual. Gene was in it for Gene. Whatever the reasons, he didn't share the collective mentality I had. I found security in the band—it provided something lacking in my life. I wanted to belong. I needed that sense of family, of camaraderie, of a support group. So for me it was always about the team, and I coveted the band above all else.

Ace was increasingly self-destructive in a way that chipped away at his talent. One night, he repeatedly drove his rental car down a steep winding road to see how fast he could go and still make the turn at the bottom. The ultimate outcome of the experiment would have been obvious to anyone but an inebriated Ace. And sure enough, he finally lost control of the car and wrapped it around a pole. We weren't yet to the point where we had to desperately try to get a solo out of him before he passed out in the studio—although that would soon come—but he certainly wasn't fully realizing his potential and giving his all.

Peter seemed to resent everything he was given. It was a no-win situation. The fact that he was given things further highlighted his inability to contribute. He began to vent his inner turmoil and feelings of insecurity by trying to make everyone else as miserable as he was inside. Peter also resented me for not "paying my dues," as he constantly put it. As far as I saw it, Peter hadn't succeeded before hooking up with us because he had no idea what it took to become successful or to sustain success. Now he was along for the ride and couldn't help trying to hamper things and create strife.

I didn't begrudge anybody's limitations, but I definitely begrudged Peter's attitude—the animosity and conniving.

I couldn't wait to leave the studio each night around 9 P.M. I went straight to the Rainbow. I was a convert from our first visit to

L.A. in February. Now, in town for a month, I went to "mass" every night. We certainly weren't famous, but in there we had rock star status. We had an album out. We were recording another.

I really hit it off with a woman named Karen who worked there as a hostess. She was a bit older than I was, and we instantly took a liking to each other. She befriended me. She had traveled on tours with various band members of Deep Purple and Led Zeppelin—the upper rungs of the rock hierarchy. One of the walls in her apartment could have been in a music shop on 48th Street—rows and rows of signed eight-by-ten photos of bands. We remained good friends, and it never seemed odd to me that our relationship turned physical only later—after KISS took off and we became famous.

There was a purity to the system at the Rainbow. The women were part of the rhythm of rock and roll—they were essential to it. No possessiveness, no judgment.

And each morning, back to Village Recorder. One day I entered the studio and looked around. "Where's my guitar?" I asked. "Wait, where's my amp?"

"Oh," one of the studio employees said, "they already came and picked up all the gear."

"What? What are you talking about?"

"Yeah, they came for it already. They were here, said they had come to pick it up."

Thieves had dispensed with any high-tech scheme and just walked in and said they were a shipping company and made off with all of our gear. The easiest way out was through the front door. We got reimbursed and bought new gear, but some of my guitars—like my Flying V—had been custom-made and could never be replaced.

Another day I was on my way to the studio in a rental car when a police car pulled up behind me and turned on its lights and siren. I pulled over. I was wearing my usual off-duty uniform of hip-hugger jeans—really low rise, with about a three-inch zipper—platform boots, ruffled woman's blouse, and jewelry, with my hair tumbling in long curls over my shoulders. In New York this wasn't a big deal at the time.

The officer walked up to the side of my car. "License and registration, please."

"It's a rental—I have no idea where the registration is," I said, as I reached for my wallet. My wallet wasn't in my pocket. "I left it . . . I . . . I don't have my wallet," I stammered. "I must have left it at the hotel." In New York, not having my license with me had never been a problem.

"Well, then," the cop said, "you're going to jail."

I nearly pissed my pants. I turned as white as a sheet. "JAIL? Look at me! You can't take me to jail looking like this!"

The cop looked at me. He must have seen my terror. "Be sure to carry your license next time," he said, and motioned for me to drive off.

Note to self: always carry wallet.

24

KISS had slowly climbed the touring ladder, and for some of the shows toward the end of 1974, we started to be "special guests," the second band on a bill, rather than the anonymous third. You know, "Tonight in Cedar Rapids: REO Speedwagon and special guest KISS plus surprise third act!"

Part of becoming successful was getting your own hotel room. Part of becoming successful was traveling by plane instead of by station wagon or rental car. Sometimes when I was home for an off-day, still crashing at my parents' place, a limo picked me up to take me to the airport. We had switched to flying commercial flights from gig to gig, getting picked up and driven to and from hotels, while the gear caught up with us by truck and met us at the venue. We had also moved up to Holiday Inns instead of roadside motor lodges. It was easy to think we'd won the lottery as I put another quarter in the vibrating bed each night.

At some point, in addition to having our own rooms, we even began to rent a spare room, dubbed the "Chicken Coop," where we could party and girls could wait their turn instead of loitering in the lobby. After a show, we would retire to our individual hotel rooms to freshen up, and then the phone would ring. "The Chicken Coop is room 917," the tour manager would tell us. We'd go down to a room full of girls, all of whom wanted to go back to our rooms. Some of them came from the concert audience, others were connected to a local radio station or knew somebody who knew somebody on the crew or at our label or whatever.

We had also managed to get additional clothes. We hired a guy named Larry Legaspi, who made clothes for the band Labelle, who had a huge hit at the time with "Lady Marmalade" and had a kind of disco-in-outer-space look. We also gave sketches of the new boots we wanted to the uptown New York bootmaker Frank Anania. An old-world craftsman, he couldn't make heads or tails of the designs, but he made us boots that, unlike the street versions we had used up to then, were both more stable and more sturdy—all the better for all the jumping and running around we did onstage.

I met my first girlfriend in Atlanta in September when we returned to the Electric Ballroom. Or rather, she became my girlfriend at the end of that run in Atlanta. Amanda was a tall curvy blonde from Michigan who was traveling with one of our technicians. She flirted with everybody, and finally one night when the technician wasn't feeling well, she slipped him a couple of Valiums and took off with me.

I took her back to New York since we had a few days off. I was still living with my parents. She and I slept on the fold-out sofa in the living room, which was where I slept when I was home. I didn't have a room anymore because the one I had shared with my sister now was my niece Ericka's room. The sofa-bed sat against the wall to my parents' bedroom. One morning when Amanda and I were staying there, my mom came out and, just making small talk, I asked her, "How'd you sleep last night?"

"Not well," she said. "The sofa kept banging against the wall."

I knew it was time to get a place of my own. To be honest, I had known that for a while, but I hadn't been totally comfortable with the idea of living on my own. Now, conveniently, I had found somebody to move in with.

We grabbed a copy of the *Long Island Press* and paged through the listings for apartment rentals. We found a furnished apartment on Woodhaven Boulevard in Queens, near the Long Island Expressway, that was cheap and available immediately. We took it. It wasn't the Waldorf-Astoria, but it still made my finances very tight.

Our first day there, we sat around listening to *AWB*, the new album by the Average White Band. Then I was off on tour again, gone for weeks at a time. I was always above board when I left and told her not to ask me what happened on tour unless she wanted to hear the truth. She knew that world. But she didn't care. She had worked her way up from a lighting technician to a band member.

Touring came with a certain amount of isolation. We had no contact with other bands at our level. With the exception of Rush, we didn't socialize much with other bands. Even if we wanted to, we had two hours of makeup and wardrobe to deal with before each show. Since we traveled constantly, the only interactions we had with the few musicians we did know were secondhand—news we gleaned from groupies who had seen them when they passed through town the week before. "Oh, Queen's coming through next week?" I remember saying to a female guest in Kentucky. "And you'll be with Roger? Say hi for me."

The demands on the road crew and tour managers were so extreme that they often couldn't hack it for long—road managers in particular we shuffled through constantly. We hung out with those guys, but it was such a revolving door that few became real friends. Wives and girlfriends quickly became abstract realities because there were no cell phones, and hotel phones were expensive—nobody even had answering machines or call-waiting, so the chances of catching somebody were slim. We lived in a bubble.

Still, being back out on the road also meant less conflict within the band. For one thing, we were forced to function as a unit on the road. For another thing, despite whatever issues each of us was dealing with, the availability of women tended to replace the intra-band friction with a much more pleasurable type of friction when we were on tour. And anyway, being onstage playing rock and roll was my dream. Sure, we were making only sixty dollars a week—that's what Bill salaried us—but I was getting paid to rock. *This was my job.* Every week on the road was another week I wasn't driving a taxi or working for the phone company.

Despite all the apparent progress of our career, sales of *Hotter Than Hell* leveled off quickly, selling only a little better than the first album. The situation was more dire than we realized.

One afternoon, back in New York for a day or two off, I went into Manhattan to see Bill at his office. I had decided to ask him for a raise. I thought we should get ten bucks more per week than the sixty dollars we had been earning for about a year now. I walked in and sat down facing Bill, who was sitting with his feet up on his desk. There was a hole in the bottom of his shoe and duct tape stuffed into the hole to keep it somewhat closed. He had a hole in his sweater, too.

On second thought, never mind.

Little did I know, Bill was a quarter million dollars in debt on his credit card from financing our tours, and Casablanca was on the verge of collapse. "What's on your mind, Paul?" he asked.

"Oh, nothing. Just came by to chat," I lied. When I saw Bill, it was obvious we were all in the same boat. He was making sacrifices for something he believed in, too. I stuck with my sixty dollars a week.

Fortunately, as the band began to climb the ladder, Gibson started giving me free guitars. All I had to do was call the company and ask. Then, whenever I was in New York, I would unpack them from their shipping boxes and get on the subway to 48th Street. I took the brand-new Marauders they sent me and unloaded them at music stores to put a little extra money in my pocket or to pay the rent.

When KISS played at the Santa Monica Civic Center as Jo Jo Gunne's special guest on February 1, 1975, Neil Bogart, who had relocated Casablanca to L.A., came to see us. He came backstage and told us, "Your album stopped selling. *Hotter Than Hell* is dead. You have to end the tour and go back to New York to do another album."

We had one song finished that I knew was special. Weeks earlier Neil had said something with a sense of perception that was much clearer than ours. "You need a song that your fans can rally behind—that states your cause. Something like Sly and the Family Stone's 'Dance to the Music.' You want to get people pumping their fists and joining in."

I had taken a guitar back to the Continental Hyatt House that night and went straight to work. Pretty quickly I came up with the chords and a few lines for a chorus: "I want to rock and roll all night and party every day."

I knew this was the perfect battle cry.

I went down the hall and knocked on Gene's door. "What do you think of this?" I asked, playing what I had.

"I have a song called 'Drive Me Wild,' but I only have the verses and no chorus," he said. It went, "You show us everything you got, you drive us wild, we'll drive you crazy." We coupled his verse to my battle cry.

As we got to work and finished the song, I could picture people pumping their fists and singing along.

This could be the rock and roll national anthem.

25.

We flew back almost immediately to New York to record *Dressed to Kill* in early February 1975. Neil came, too, because he had decided to produce the album himself instead of using Richie and Kenny for a third time.

Some songs Gene and I wrote in the morning, and Peter and Ace came in the afternoon to record. We had very few leftovers—just "She" and "Love Her All I Can"—so we had little choice. We also hadn't written anything on the road. When faced with the choice of noodling on our guitars or nailing a woman from the Chicken Coop, it was no contest.

When I wrote a song like "Room Service," it was a musical diary—I was totally immersed in that life now. The cocksmanship was no longer just a fantasy the way it had been on our debut album. Life on the road was everything I had conceived of and more—hot and cold running women. Everybody and anybody, willingly, gladly, take no names. The joy in the vocal on "Room Service" is real—I was celebrating this life we were living. I was reveling in it.

"C'mon and Love Me" came to me quickly in my apartment—
very organically, just stream of consciousness.

> *She's a dancer, a romancer*
> *I'm a Capricorn and she's a Cancer*
> *She saw my picture in a music magazine*
> *When she met me, said she'd get me*
> *Touched her hips and told me that she'd let me . . .*

To be able to write something like that without laboring over it
is a place you just can't get back to. It's writing without rules, without any thoughts of justifying or answering to anybody. I think that
over time you can become a more technically proficient songwriter,
but that doesn't mean you write better songs. This was our third
album, yes, but all three within barely a year, so we still had the
freedom of not really knowing the rules, of not analyzing the lyrics
under a microscope. The lyrics in "C'mon and Love Me" created
such a fluid rhythmic effect. Later in life, I couldn't write lyrics like
that even if you put a gun to my head.

A guy in the studio who had worked with Bachman-Turner
Overdrive told me that BTO used acoustic guitars in the mix to
help sonically define the guitar sound. We tried that on "Room Service" and "Anything for My Baby." We used acoustic guitar to pad
things—to give additional clarity and definition. We were really
grasping at straws at that point—anything to try to get something
of the sound we wanted. It didn't seem like it should be so difficult
to get the sound we heard in our heads and onstage.

All we want is to sound the way we do live!

Neil didn't do much. He sat in the room and tried to keep us
from doing too many takes. Not because he thought he could capture something special in an early take—just to save money by getting the album done more quickly. I remember doing a sloppy take
and Neil saying, "Well, that should do it."

"No," I told him, "we need to do that again."

We recorded the whole thing in about ten days, and the entire album clocked in at something like twenty-eight minutes. Most of the songs were well under three minutes long. On the original vinyl version, the space between the songs was quite wide to try to make the album seem longer.

Casablanca pressed and released the record about two weeks after we finished recording it—the company's situation was clearly getting desperate. A few days after the release of *Dressed to Kill*—on March 21, 1975—we had a homecoming show booked at the Beacon Theatre in Manhattan. Fewer than two months after we had opened for Jo Jo Gunne in Santa Monica and were told to come up with another album, Jo Jo Gunne opened for us at the Beacon.

The Beacon represented a step up. A lot of the places we played during our first year of touring were converted movie theaters or vaudeville theaters—places like the Tower Theater in Philadelphia, the Paramount in Portland, and the Orpheum in Boston. (My old haunt, the Fillmore East, which had already closed by then, started life as a Yiddish theater, too.) They were grand theaters with terrific acoustics, but they were about half the size of the Beacon. The Beacon was so big that the New York promoter Ron Delsener agreed to do the show only if he didn't have to put up any money in advance. He didn't think he'd sell enough tickets to cover a guarantee. But when the tickets went on sale, they sold so quickly that the only way to meet the demand was to do two shows in one night.

We felt like returning heroes when we came back to the city to headline two shows. We'd gone off boys and come back men. We were a different band—with a lot more experience, and a following that a lot of people, including the New York promoter, didn't realize we had. It felt like a victory parade.

Except in Queens. When I ran into people I knew out there, they often still had no idea about the band. With the Beacon shows,

I thought of us as the biggest New York band, but that didn't make us a household name by any means. We had a cult following, that was all. I was proud that many local celebrities and members of other bands came to the show—we were the big band in town now. They all came to see us now.

But the world still beckoned. I knew we had reached only one of the base camps on the way up the mountain. I never thought that was the peak. I planned for us to be superstars. But this was a chance for us to take stock and see how far we'd come.

I was so tired after the first show. I went up to the dressing room to retouch my makeup. I figured it would be easier to touch it up and dry my hair and outfit with a hair dryer than to start over. We didn't have much time for reflection after the shows, as we left the next day for Ohio.

As the tour continued, we flipped the script on a lot of the bands we'd worked with the year before. Slade, Uriah Heep, and the James Gang were *our* special guests now, and we took out baby bands like Styx, Journey, and Montrose.

There was no consistency. One night in Wilkes-Barre, Pennsylvania, our opening act was a circus juggler. He rode a unicycle and people in the audience tried to knock him off by throwing coins at him. Now, I had seen strange bills in the late 1960s and early 1970s—things like Led Zeppelin and Woody Herman's orchestra. That sort of thing was considered hip. But putting some poor soul onstage on a unicycle before KISS? It was tough enough for a regular band to open for us.

In the summer of 1975 we still opened some shows, too. We played as a support act for Black Sabbath and for Rare Earth. But in those cases the venues were massive. The first show we played with Sabbath was at the Baltimore Civic Center for ten thousand people. And again, just as the year before, whether or not we opened, we did a full-on KISS show. We had pyro and the big KISS logo sign behind us. That night in Baltimore, nobody took down or covered our sign—so Sabbath played in front of a huge KISS logo.

The next night we were scheduled to open for Sabbath again, this time in Providence, Rhode Island. Their people told us, "No pyro tonight."

"Fine," we said. "We're going back to the hotel. We're not playing. You know where to reach us if you change your mind."

It was our way or no way. We felt committed to doing a KISS show, and we really were prepared not to do the show.

A little while later the phone rang at the hotel. "Okay, come back to the venue. Do your show the way you want to."

By this point, Bill Aucoin had hatched a plan. *The* plan. We were building a rabid following as a live act—we had climbed to at least occasional headlining status, especially in the heartland—but this wasn't reflected in our tepid album sales. With 120,000 sales, *Dressed to Kill* had done better than *Hotter Than Hell*'s 90,000 and *KISS*'s 60,000. But it was nothing when we considered the crowds we saw at our shows. Where was the disconnect? What was going on?

The albums didn't sound like we sounded live.

And so Bill presented his plan: a live album, a sonic souvenir of our show, which now attracted people in droves. As a model, he held up a live album by Uriah Heep that had helped that British band establish themselves. That album had worked in Britain, but the idea of career-boosting live albums by rock bands was not yet established in the United States—this was all before live albums made the careers of Peter Frampton, Cheap Trick, and Bob Seger, to name a few.

Since the only thing missing, as far as the band was concerned, was an album that truly represented us, Bill's idea struck a chord. We hired Eddie Kramer to produce the live recordings. Bill arranged to hire photographer Fin Costello, who had worked on the Uriah Heep album, and we used the title *Alive!*, from a live record by Slade. Through the summer of 1975 we recorded shows, beginning with a sold-out Cobo Hall in Detroit, where Costello shot the audience—twelve thousand people strong—for the back cover. We shot the front cover image in Detroit, too, but we went across town to the Michigan Palace, the site of some of our best early shows and our rehearsal space for a few days in the run-up to the live recording at Cobo.

People have argued whether *Alive!* is a purely live recording or somehow enhanced. The answer is: yes, we enhanced it. Not to hide anything, not to fool anyone. But who wanted to hear a mistake repeated endlessly? Who wanted to hear an out-of-tune guitar? For what? Authenticity? At a concert, you listen with your ears and eyes. A mistake that passes unnoticed in the moment lives forever when recorded. We wanted to re-create the experience of our show—whatever needed to be done, we did it. The flashpots were enhanced with recordings of cannons, because that's what they sounded like in person. The audience was jacked up to immerse the listener in the crowd. It was the only way to replicate our concert-on-steroids. We figured the people who celebrated with us at a concert wanted to hear what they remembered, what they perceived.

We also made sure the audience could be heard throughout the show—just as you would experience it live. Most live albums in those days sounded like studio recordings until the song ended, when some applause could be heard between songs. But we wanted to portray the real concert experience. And the back cover paid tribute to those fans who made all that noise and turned our shows into such powerful communal events.

We couldn't have picked a better person to do *KISS Alive!* than Eddie Kramer. His brilliance in the studio and his innovations in enhancing the recordings were not only ground-shaking, but groundbreaking. He had different audience sounds on tape loops that were sometimes twenty feet long, held taut on mic stands and going around so you would never hear a repeat of any fan response. He had all these mic stands set up in the studio with different lengths of audience participation tape running on them so we could bring in actual crowd reaction, whether it was a murmur or a roar. I certainly would never have thought of that—to create different loops of tape and have them going continuously so we could raise them and lower them and get different crowd reactions at will. It was brilliant.

One bone of contention as we put the finishing touches on the album was a long, boring drum solo. Soloing was not Peter's forte. He often sounded more like Ricky Ricardo playing the bongos than a rock and roll drummer playing a legitimate solo. Plus a solo that might be riveting at a show—when combined with effects and an audience—could be mind-numbingly dull in record form. So we edited it.

"If you don't put it back in," Peter told us, "I'm quitting the band."

Sigh.

Same old crap.

The result—basically the entire show we were doing at that point—captured the sonic magnitude of KISS live. Finally, we had something that put the listener in the audience. We had made a quantum leap forward from the first three studio albums.

The package came out great, too, with the photo of the audience, the shot of the band with basically all our effects going off at once, and the notes from each band member to the fans. We wrote the notes to personify the Starchild, the Demon, the Catman, and the Spaceman. Certainly my character has always been flamboyant, and I wrote my note without making it gender-specific. It was written to the audience at large. When I wrote "Dear lovers, nothing arouses me more than seeing you getting off on me," it could have been taken for heterosexual, homosexual, or bisexual love. I wasn't threatened by any implications of the superficial aspects of sexuality or style. I considered it a compliment to be found attractive by anyone and everyone, sought after and emulated by people regardless of gender or sexual orientation. It never felt like a threat to my sense of masculinity or identity. If I were gay, it certainly wouldn't be something I would hide or be ashamed of, but I'm not. I was just comfortable enough with my sexuality not to attach anything negative to androgyny and vulnerability. At least, not while in character. Vulnerability was not something I showed offstage. I was still too insecure.

One night on the road just after *Alive!* came out, a woman and I were lying under the sheets in a hotel bed. She turned to me, puzzled, and said, "My boyfriend told me you were gay."

"Well, I guess that didn't work," I said. "Because it didn't keep you away."

26.

After the release of *Alive!*, things felt different. It was like watching water simmer before it boils. It suddenly seemed like just a matter of time before things would explode. An electricity pulsed through the audience at shows. There was a churchlike fervor that gave our shows in late 1975 a holy-roller quality.

Up to then we had made steady progress, so I never questioned that it would happen for us eventually. And despite the grave financial problems—the extent of which I probably never grasped at the time—I never worried that our modest album sales would cause the demise of the band. But on the other hand, we were running out of bigger bands to play with, pissing off headliners with our outrageous show, and our options were dwindling.

Then, when *Alive!* came out, the doors just got blown off. The game changed overnight. Suddenly we headlined venues bigger than we had played before even as openers. I was a bit nervous in the beginning because I didn't have the experience of communicating with twenty thousand people. Once I figured it out, it was the audience whose nerves sparked, not mine. But at first I had to learn to communicate with the person in the back row. I had to send energy all the way to the back to project the atmosphere of game show/circus/religious revival we prided ourselves on creating. The bigger the crowd, the harder you have to work. Everything had to be amped twenty thousand times. And I felt anointed to do it.

Let me at them.

I want to be what they want.

I want to be the Starchild.

I want us to be KISS.

I want to show them we are exactly who they think we are.

It took me time and some trial and error, but soon enough I knew I could do it. In fact, I knew I was pretty damn good at it.

The difference between a guy who has just gotten his commercial flying license and a seasoned pilot is that the first one knows how to fly the jet while the other one knows how to deal with any and all situations. I quickly logged enough flight time that nothing fazed me.

This is your captain speaking, and you're in good hands.

When I got out there onstage, I really did get off on seeing everyone else getting off. Crowds at our shows were ecstatic, and we were all sharing in the jubilation. Our joy matched the joy our fans experienced. And they kept my insecurities and unhappiness at bay. All the problems in the world—theirs and ours—would still be there tomorrow, but we were going to have a great time tonight.

We also got to take a few heroes of mine out on tour with us. That fall of 1975 we had both Slade and Wizzard, the band fronted by Roy Wood of the Move, open shows for us. Roy Wood's band created an eccentric version of Phil Spector's wall of sound. His bass player wore roller skates. They were booed offstage. Afterwards I told Roy what a huge influence he had been on me. He was still shell-shocked from getting booed, and I was disappointed not to get much of a reaction from him. After the first show we played with Slade, we all stayed in the Chattanooga Choo Choo Hilton, a hotel with vintage railcars as rooms, all lined up on tracks behind the main building. I was a huge fan of Slade, and in fact the mirrored top hat I had seen guitar-playing frontman Noddy Holder wearing in concert years before was the inspiration for my cracked-mirror guitar. I dropped in to say hello to Noddy in his train car. He was completely delirious—so intoxicated he was incoherent and unable to stand. Your idols don't loom quite as large when they're horizontal.

We had a couple of days off and flew to New York in the midst of things exploding. When I got home to my apartment in Queens, I found shotguns in the bedroom closet.

Whoa, what the hell are these?

My girlfriend, Amanda, had started hanging around with some unsavory types she'd befriended while I was on tour. They stashed weapons at our place. *Great.* I was just a Jewish kid from Queens— the only guns I'd ever seen were the kind you used to knock over a doll at the carnival to win a prize, the kind with a cork attached to the barrel with a string. She was descending into a completely different life.

Amanda also told me that Joe Namath had given her a lift home from a club one night while I was gone. It was only after I thought about it a little that a lightbulb went off in my head and I realized Joe Namath wouldn't drive girls to their doors and just give them a peck on the cheek. I had never lied about my activities on the road since I had told her my mantra of "Don't ask me what happens on the road if you don't want to know." Somehow it had never dawned on me that the same would obviously be true of her: Don't ask me what happens *at home* if you don't want to know.

I told her things were over between us, although it was clearly halfhearted on my part, because she came along just the same when I moved into Manhattan and rented a place on East 52nd Street. We never had any pretenses of being in love anyway—we were bed buddies. But it was time to change the sheets.

The apartment was in a tall luxury building on a street that dead-ended at the East River. Construction on the building had just been completed. When I went to look at it, they offered two apartments. One on the twenty-first floor went for $510 a month; another on the twenty-sixth floor, with a beautiful view, cost $560. Despite our recent upturn, fifty bucks a month was a huge difference. I took the place on the twenty-first floor.

My new apartment was tangible proof of my ascension. I went to Macy's and bought my first real furniture—a big L-shaped green velvet couch and one of those huge ball-shaped lamps that hangs from a tall arching metal stand. I felt very cool.

Another change brought about by the immediate success of *Alive!* was an upgrade in hotels: we graduated from Holiday Inns to Sheratons. At the Sheraton, the towels had embroidered "S" logos on them. Whenever we were about to have a break and return to New York, I would stuff a set into my suitcase. Soon I had a cabinet full of monogrammed towels at my new luxury apartment.

Bill Aucoin liked to see us live an extravagant life on the road once things started to pop and he started to repay his massive personal debt. We enjoyed it, too, until we got a little wiser and saw the bills. In the dressing rooms now, people asked us what we would like to drink. It only seemed natural to ask for Champagne. *How cool—Champagne!* We ordered several bottles of bubbly, not realizing everything we ordered was charged to us. But it was fun—and, besides, who knew how long this all would last?

We certainly weren't born businessmen. Whatever the myth, we were totally green and not savvy at all about tour expenses or bottom lines. We trusted the people around us to have our best interests at heart. It took years for us to learn the ropes and to consider trying to change the way things were done.

In the meantime, I felt newly flush, whatever the reality.

One day off in New York, I went to 48th Street to pick up some things at a music store. It was a strange situation, because we had gotten quite famous more or less overnight, and yet very few people recognized us without the makeup. I could walk the streets or get a cup of coffee. I could even go to a newsstand and buy music magazines with photos of KISS in them. Of course, it was different on 48th Street. I didn't look like everybody else. I had the blue-black hair and the street versions of my seven-inch platforms, which I wore all the time. I guess there among all the music aficionados, people could put two and two together when they saw a six-foot-eight guy with mounds of blue-black curls walk in. *If that guy isn't in KISS, the circus must be in town.*

When I went to check out, carrying a couple sets of strings and a few other things, the shop owner wanted to give it all to me for free. I didn't understand. "It's on us," the guy insisted.

The irony was not lost on me.

"I can afford it," I said. "I can buy it. Give it to the next guy who comes in and really needs it."

27.

On New Year's Eve 1975, we headlined the Nassau Coliseum on Long Island, New York. Exactly two years before, we had played another New Year's Eve show, opening for Iggy and Blue Öyster Cult at the Academy of Music. This time, Blue Öyster Cult opened for us. Things were really cooking.

Backstage at that show, we received gold albums, recognizing *Alive!* for surpassing five hundred thousand copies shipped since its release in September. Everything else we had accomplished that year had been the stuff of my fantasies—whether it was moving up to headlining status, climbing the hotel chain ladder, or getting a Manhattan apartment—but receiving a gold record fulfilled a childhood dream. Elvis had gold albums. The Beatles had gold albums. Now *I* had a gold album.

The aftermath of the show was less rewarding. We had about two weeks off before starting the next leg of the tour, and I went home to 52nd Street and Amanda. Things with her had continued to go south, and this time when I got home I saw track marks on her arm. Another couple she had befriended trafficked drugs into the country—major league stuff—and I knew that even as a relationship of convenience this wasn't going to work anymore. I didn't want guns to start turning up again. I didn't want to hear phone messages about shipments arriving. And I didn't want a junkie around. "This is over and you've got to leave," I told her.

She didn't want to.

Ultimately I moved out for the final week of our tour break and stayed at an empty place Bill Aucoin had. I wasn't quite sure why he maintained a spare apartment, but I didn't care. Amanda and I had been fighting for several days when I left, and as I was going out the door of the building, the doorman called to me and said, "Mr. Stanley, she says she's going jump."

"Tell her not to land on me," I said, and left.

Soon we went back out on tour. I called Amanda's mother and told her to fly to New York and get Amanda out while I was gone.

On January 31, 1976, KISS headlined Hara Arena, in Dayton, Ohio. Before the show I could hear a deep rumbling sound. The commotion of a big crowd. Excitement.

Every night I asked the tour manager, "How're we doing tonight?" The answer had been "good" for a long run now, since *Alive!* had taken off. That night, he said, "Sold out."

The four of us were celebrating, jubilant at the knowledge that we were taking it to that next level. We were now a credible headliner, a real headliner. KISS was becoming one of *those bands*, the type we had looked up to. We had graduated.

A curtain always shrouded the stage before we went on. It wasn't the elaborate kabuki we have now, but there was always a curtain. In Dayton that night I opened it a little and peered out. The place was packed. The energy of the crowd was almost frightening. I felt a nervousness in the pit of my stomach—the same feeling you get as a rollercoaster makes the long, slow climb up the initial hill. That's what Hara Arena felt like to me.

Then the next night when I asked the tour manager how we were doing, again he said, "Sold out." And again the next night and the night after that—and all of a sudden we sold out everywhere. It was no longer an anomaly. KISS was a band selling out arenas every night. Once the floodgates opened, everything happened so fast. The pressure had been building up all this time, and then it exploded. There was no turning back.

Ads with two of my favorites—
Rush and Bob Seger, 1975–1976.

And yet, I was just a kid. I was twenty-four years old and the depth of my comprehension was fairly limited. Yes, this was tremendous. Yes, it was unbelievable. Yes, this was how I had planned it and envisioned it. But as it started to happen, the success of the band was overwhelming. It was frightening.

The rollercoaster feeling I'd had at Hara Arena became a more or less constant sensation: I was being pulled up the big hill, knowing we were going to reach the top at any moment and then plunge down the other side, falling, screaming, with no control whatsoever. I could feel the momentum, the process of being pulled up the hill. I could tell we had reached a point of no return. All I could do was hold on real tight.

The problem was, What did I have to hold on to?

Nothing. I had no emotionally meaningful connections in my life.

God knew the guys in the band weren't going to be any help.

The world we operated in now was littered with casualties of fame. Drugs were offered as a sign of friendship. Every. Single. Day. People became self-destructive. People numbed themselves. People died. Because of my insecurities and self-doubt, I was scared I would fall prey to the same temptations. My sense of self-preservation kicked in.

I'm going to need something to hold on to.

This thing was going to careen down the hill at any moment, whether I was prepared or not.

Then I thought of Dr. Jesse Hilsen.

Back in those days people sometimes dismissed therapy as a "crutch" or considered it a sign of weakness. I myself had bought into that enough to stop going to Mount Sinai once life seemed to be going more smoothly, as Wicked Lester came together. I wanted to believe I was okay.

But I wasn't. I called Mount Sinai. Dr. Hilsen had left the hospital and gone into private practice. But I tracked him down. "My band is about to become huge," I explained. "I don't know if I can handle that world. I need a lifeline."

I was determined to survive.

Perhaps therapy would be the way I kept my seven-inch heels planted on the ground.

Part III

I've been up and down,
I've been all around

28.

Early in 1976, when we were getting ready to make our next studio album, Bill Aucoin said, "You can either use *KISS Alive!* as a springboard to take you to another level, or you can be a one-hit wonder that just goes right back to doing what you were doing before."

He had a point. To go back to what we had done earlier did seem stupid. After all, it didn't work before *Alive!*, so why would it work now? The reason our first three albums didn't sell was because listeners didn't like the way they sounded—there was something intrinsically wrong with them, though I still couldn't have put my finger on exactly what it was.

Bill suggested we bring in Bob Ezrin to produce the new record. Bob was already known for the great records he'd made with Alice Cooper, and he proved to have a vast musical vocabulary. It turned out to be a brilliant move on Bill's part. Bob was a gift.

We may have had a huge album under our belts, but we still didn't know anything more than we did before *Alive!* became a hit.

Still, for a bunch of guys who thought they were hot shit, it was initially jarring to go into a studio with somebody who treated us like children. As we began work on what would become *Destroyer*, Bob made a point of letting us know he was the boss. He wore a whistle around his neck and referred to us as "campers." He told us we didn't know anything—which was true. He told us never to stop playing until he said so. Once, at the end of a take, long after a fade-out would have ended the recording, Gene stopped playing. Bob came out of the control booth and ran up to him, stuck his finger so close to Gene's nose that it made his eyes cross, and said, "Don't you ever, *ever* stop until I tell you to stop!" A trickle of sweat ran down Gene's forehead. He never stopped again.

It was humbling, particularly at a time when we thought we were God's gift to rock and roll and finally had a record to back up our claim—*Alive!* was platinum by this point. But Bob clearly knew a lot more than we did. He was trained. He was worthy of respect. And he taught us a lot.

One of the most significant things he did was challenge us not to write "fuck me suck me" songs. "No more 'I'm a rock star, suck my dick,'" he insisted. And as we worked on lyrics, he had no problem saying very plainly, "No, I don't like that."

I never would have written a lyric like "Detroit Rock City" without Bob upping our game. He pushed us far beyond our limits.

During the process of making the record, Bob lived in an apartment directly across the street from my place on 52nd Street. He had a piano, and when we weren't in the rehearsal space or studio, I spent a lot of time there. Gene and I also sometimes took amplifiers over to his place and worked. We wrote "Shout It Out Loud" at Bob's apartment.

The riff in "God of Thunder" reflected the way my limitations as a guitar player were key to what I came up with and probably helped make my songs identifiable and unique. That riff was a compromise between what I heard in my head and what I could actually play. Another example of that process was "I Want You," which ended up on the next album.

Sometimes at the rehearsal space Bob would have the four of us sit in a circle and he would say, "Who's got an idea? Anybody have an idea for a verse? Who's got a part?" Someone would play a snippet and he might say no. Then somebody else would play something and Bob would shout, "Okay, that's good. Now who has another part?" A lot of the songs came together like that—pieces of this and that stitched together with input from Bob.

Peter sat at his drums while we threw out ideas. When it came time to arrange finished songs, Bob often came up with parts. Once I saw him work with us, I understood Alice Cooper's albums much more. I could see Bob's point of view in them. Bob's fingerprints were all over things like *Billion Dollar Babies*. Suddenly I could hear his drum parts and his bass parts. I knew them from our stuff—like the bass line in "Detroit Rock City," which Bob created. That bass part is similar to the bass in Curtis Mayfield's "Freddie's Dead." Bob even came up with the guitar solo on "Detroit Rock City." He sang it to Ace and made him figure it out.

Bob was brilliant at that kind of stuff.

When it came time for the drums, we faced a real challenge. Bob spent many, many hours teaching Peter his parts. Bob came up with most of the drum parts on the album, and he would dismiss the rest of us for hours at a time to work with Peter. "Detroit Rock City" in particular had a very challenging drumbeat, and it took a lot of effort and patience for Bob to get Peter to be able to play something he couldn't have learned to play on his own if his life had depended on it.

Back then there were no click tracks, which allow a drummer to work with a sort of metronome to get a consistent tempo. But to get a track just the way he wanted it, Bob liked to be able to cut and splice from various takes we recorded, which necessitated a steady pace. That would have been difficult in our case, to say the least. So Bob created a human click track. He sat in the control room with a mic stuck into a hole in a cigar box and tapped the beat on the box and fed it to all of us, most importantly Peter.

Bob also wrote the lion's share of "Beth" using a few lines and a melody Peter brought in. Peter had a co-writer on every song he ever wrote because he couldn't really write—song structure and concepts like making your lyrics rhyme were totally lost on him. In the case of "Beth," Bob wrote most of it, even though the original idea Peter brought in had already been done with a co-writer. To get the vocal for "Beth," Bob had to record Peter singing the song probably a dozen times and cobble together a single version from the passable parts of those takes. Peter's chances of being able to sing a song off the cuff were about as good as my chances of throwing a penny and hitting the moon. It would be a challenge for him to carry a tune in a bucket. Even if we sang a note to him, he couldn't find it. But since we had always presented our Beatles-based fantasy to the world—four band members all contributing equally—at some point Peter began to believe his own press. Perception became reality to him, despite the fact that we created the perception ourselves. We made it out as if we lived like the *Help!*-era Beatles—and all made music together as equals. But that was *never* the case—and who should know that better than the people who were actually there and not contributing?

Peter and Ace's contributions were never as substantial as we made them out to be in the press. The fact of the matter was that two guys—Gene and me—were the engineers and motivators and did 80 percent of the work. Unfortunately, when we decided to create the *Help!* illusion, we never considered the possibility that Peter and Ace would start to actually believe it, and that their belief would bite us in the ass. But sure enough, their delusions started to create resentment and, eventually, fatal fissures in the band. Those fissures first started opening during *Destroyer*, as Peter struggled to record a song that was ostensibly his own, and we began to have to work around Ace, who spent much of the recording process with his priorities far from where they belonged. He sometimes played his parts with his rings and chains scraping against the fret board and pickups, and then wanted to quit for the day and take off. When I would ask him to remove the jewelry and do another take because of all the noise, he would say, "Hey, that's rock and roll."

"No, Ace, that's shit."

His alcohol abuse is well documented, but Ace also didn't hesitate to just up and leave the studio to go play cards with friends. I could not wrap my head around that at all—leaving the job to get loaded and play cards, even if it meant having another guitar player handle his parts? Making music was my dream, and skipping out on that process was something I couldn't fathom.

Sonically, Bob Ezrin didn't try to re-create the bombast of *Alive!* with its huge broken-up guitars and screaming vocals. He found power in other ways. He created an atmosphere of grandeur. He brought in elements of things I loved—liked the orchestral bells on "Do You Love Me." He gave guitar chords heft by layering them with a grand piano playing the same parts. In some ways it reminded me of what I liked about Roy Wood and Wizzard—that big, chaotic version of Phil Spector's wall of sound. Bob added things that really struck emotional chords in me.

He was also the first producer we worked with who—finally—understood the subtleties we didn't understand about using different guitars for different parts, or doubling a guitar with a different guitar, or slowing down the tape slightly and doubling the guitar over it to make the sound bigger because of the slight discrepancy in the tuning. Bob knew the essence of great production and great

Our first billboard, on the Sunset Strip in 1975. I can't tell you how many times I went to see it.

arrangements, and he brought it to bear on *Destroyer* in a way I thought was groundbreaking for the type of music we made.

Wow, this is what a real producer does.

From that point on, unless someone could tell us what was wrong with what we were doing and how to correct it—whether it was a problem with a song itself or with the sonics—I considered that person an engineer, not a producer.

With the album wrapped up, the *Alive!* tour continued. We had a few days off in L.A., and I got together with Karen, the hostess from the Rainbow. The band and I had reached a level of success that transformed my relationship with her into a physical one. I took this as a kind of validation: now I really was a rock star of a different caliber. It was gratifying, and it seemed like a normal and logical evolution. I was also now in a position to rent luxury cars for my use, so one of the days in L.A. I rented a two-seater Mercedes and picked Karen up at her apartment to go for a drive up the coast. After about forty-five minutes on the road, it started to pour. That's when the reality hit me in the face—along with the oncoming rain—that I had no idea how to raise the top. We drove back to her place in the rain with the top still down, never speaking of the obvious. We were both soaking wet when we arrived, and I finally admitted the truth. After a quick laugh together, I got right to the most pressing issue: "Do you have a hairdryer I can use?"

Near the tail end of the tour, we stopped in Hawaii. None of us had ever been there before, and now we had a gig in Honolulu and a few days off to spend there afterward. The day after the show, our pyro guy and some others—including Rick Stuart, a security guard charged with looking after me—rented a catamaran. Now, right away, you should know not to do anything risky with a pyro guy. No offense to pyro guys, but they got a hard-on making things go boom—whether that meant making a living at it or winding up in jail. The line between pyro guys and arsonists was very fine back then.

I decided not to be a wuss and went along. Sailing a boat is something better done with people who know what they're doing. Instead, I was out there with a pyro guy and Rick, whom everyone called "the Dobe"—as in Doberman—because of the studded dog collar he wore around his neck. I thought we would just parallel the shore—which was scary enough for me—but we wound up heading out to sea. As we headed out, another boat coming in yelled to us, "Be real careful! The tide's tricky and we had trouble getting back in!"

Great.

That wasn't what I wanted to hear, sitting on a cloth suspended between the two pontoons of a catamaran.

Things on shore kept getting smaller and smaller.

What the fuck am I doing?

I'd read enough *Reader's Digest* stories about people stuck on rafts for a month, eating seagulls and trying to catch turtles.

It's going to happen to me.

I panicked and jumped off the boat.

I'm going to swim to shore.

As the catamaran continued to slice its way out and away from me, I yelled at Rick, "Do something!"

The Dobe jumped in and swam toward me. Now both of us flailed against the riptide, unable to make any progress toward shore. We made our way sideways to a pair of surfers bobbing on their boards.

"We can't get in," I said. "Can you help us?"

"Fuck off," the guys said, catching a wave and leaving us out there.

After a few more minutes, I was struggling to keep my head above water, and every time I dipped down, my feet hit the spikes of sea urchins, which jabbed painfully at my soles. I looked at the shore and saw hundreds of people enjoying themselves. They weren't very far away, but they were totally unaware that we were going to die.

I don't matter.

People tossed balls around or lay on towels relaxing: the most important person in the world was dying, and the world went on.

Nobody matters.

Despite how much we fought, Mother Nature kept pushing our heads below the water. Just as I thought it was all over, that I was going to drown a few hundred feet from a beach full of people who wouldn't notice if I died, a little motorboat pulled up and people grabbed me and the Dobe and dragged us out of the water.

In the motorboat sat the owner of the catamaran we had rented. He'd been worried that we didn't know how to use the boat properly and had tracked us with binoculars as we sailed out. He saw us jump off and came out with his motorboat, realizing the tide would at the very least strand us.

I lay in the bottom of the boat. My head throbbed and my feet throbbed around the black spots where the sea urchin spikes had lodged in them like big splinters.

That was close.

Back at the hotel, I went upstairs and tried to pull out the spikes. Nothing doing. They just broke off. I called the front desk. "I stepped on sea urchins. What do I do to get the spikes out of my feet?"

"Pee in the sink and put your feet in it," the voice said.

"Very funny. But seriously, what do I do?"

"That's what you do."

As if the day hadn't been interesting enough, there I was pissing in the bathroom sink and then hoisting myself up onto the counter to soak my punctured soles in it.

Mahalo.

29.

By the time *Destroyer* was certified gold in April 1976, we were solidly in the black, after digging ourselves— and especially Bill—out of hundreds of thousands of dollars of debt incurred during the first two years of touring. But we still weren't making much money ourselves. Touring, even now that we sold out arenas, didn't fill the coffers of the band members. A manager took 20 percent of the gross from a show right off the top, and salaries and production expenses easily ate up another 50 percent, leaving the rest to be split among the four of us. That reality was still lost on us. Standard business practices meant we did the work while others took most of the money. I still lived in a rented apartment and didn't even own a car.

One night a reporter asked me, "What does it feel like to be rich and famous?"

"Well," I said, "I can tell you what it's like to be famous . . ."

That was all about to change.

Bill Aucoin always saw the bigger picture. He could tell that we connected with our fans in a way that far exceeded the norm. He grasped the extent to which people would respond to us beyond the music: he understood the potential of merchandising.

When I first saw the tour program Bill created for the later stages of the *Alive!* tour, I had never seen anything like it. He never told us he was going to do it. He just showed up one day and said, "Here's the tour program." After paging through its twenty-four pages, I thought it was terrific. Bill also thought—and was quickly proved correct—that our fans would want T-shirts and belt buckles. And that was just the tip of the iceberg. He founded an in-house merchandising company together with a guy named Ron Boutwell. Initially, the company fulfilled orders from our fan club. Bill just announced it to us, very matter-of-factly: "We're going to start marketing merchandise."

It could not have happened without Bill.

There's a myth out there that we took part in a grand plan right from the beginning. That is not the truth. We were clueless about merchandising. Nobody in the band was ever involved with the merchandising plan. Eventually, we started to have a hand in it, but that came over time. All we provided at first was the template—the music was ours, the makeup was ours, but so much of the rest was Bill's. Obviously, we were the nucleus of everything that happened, but in terms of the reach of the KISS image through merchandising, we had no more to do with that than we'd had with the fire breathing or the levitating drum set. I'm a big believer in promoting the team because you're only as good as the team. It's the team that wins the game. We weren't brilliant businessmen and there wasn't a brilliant Madison Avenue company behind us. There was just Bill, who, like us, wasn't held back by perceived limitations. He just pushed forward with an innate sense of what he could accomplish.

Bill wanted to maximize our potential on all fronts. We certainly weren't going to be marketed like Led Zeppelin. And we had more to offer than just music—we were naturals for merchandising, even if we didn't realize it ourselves at first. Back then, the breadth of KISS merchandise was often scoffed at. But I looked to the Beatles. You could get Beatles dolls and shirts after they made it big, so what was wrong with it? Obviously, nobody wanted Deep Purple dolls, but why would they? Without disrespecting their music, a lot of the bands of the day had a fairly nondescript, forgettable look. But KISS had visual appeal. That was the nature of KISS. The beauty of KISS. So I understood the desire to market us that way. And I never thought it detracted from the band.

I just wanted to be sure there was substance. In this respect, Gene and I had some differences. If someone came to us and said, "Let's make a KISS cake," Gene would say, "Let's make it ten feet high with lights all over it." I would say, "That's great but what will the cake be like? How will it taste? That other stuff is cool, but we need to have a great cake underneath. Without that we have nothing." Sizzle was great, but you needed the steak. That remained my concern as the merchandising took off. Sometimes I wondered how far would be too far—were there things we shouldn't do? But at that point the answer was no. It all seemed good. Phenomenal, even: KISS radios, KISS motorcycles, KISS lunchboxes.

As the money started to flow from Bill's merchandising concept—as well as continued sales of *Alive!*—I have to say I was impressed. It was exhilarating to hear about money going into our personal accounts. We still drew a fairly modest weekly salary and didn't take physical possession of the rest of the money, but we were told about it. Again, we didn't know much about what was going on. We didn't understand the various revenue streams, where they came from, or where they went. None of it.

In the midst of this maelstrom, Howard Marks, who was Bill's boss, approached us with an offer to manage our money. Howard had an advertising agency that had created the album cover for

Alive! and then put together the brilliant covers of our next three albums. Howard said to us, "There are a lot of sharks in the business, and you're going to need somebody to look after your finances."

It happened that Howard had a best friend who was a wealthy businessman in Cleveland named Carl Glickman. Howard volunteered to form a company with his friend to take care of our finances. His concern for our welfare made him feel all the more like family to us.

How great is this? How lucky are we?

The new financial company, Glickman-Marks, held regular meetings to update us on money matters and soon started sending someone on the road with us to serve as an accountant along the way. It never occurred to us that the road rep's taste for fine wine, expensive food, and paid companionship might be compromising nightly box office settlements. What we did notice was that the company built personal financial portfolios for us. I mean, hey, we owned an industrial park in Cincinnati at one point.

At the financial meetings we asked things like, "How much did we make?" rather than, "How much came in?" And because the figures we heard as answer to the first question sounded very impressive to kids like us, who had no experience of making real money, we never asked the second one, or its logical follow-up: "How much are *you* making?" Bill soon moved his office to an entire floor of a building at 645 Madison Avenue and ultimately rented another floor in the same building.

Bill's marketing of the band's imagery expanded our appeal beyond a rock audience. One afternoon back in New York, I went into a jeans shop on 59th Street. The register sat atop a glass display case, and on the case was a sticker Bill had distributed to promote *Destroyer* that featured the fantastical graphic novel–style album cover image of the four of us, painted by Ken Kelly. As I was poking around the shop, a mom and her little boy walked up to the

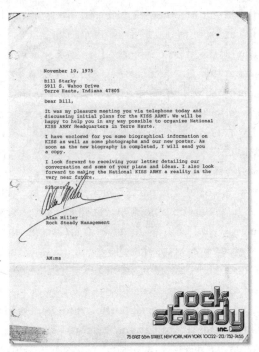

*A wonderful piece of history; the beginnings of the KISS Army,
and Bill Starkey started it all.*

counter. The boy—who couldn't have been older than four—
pointed to the image. "KISS," he said.

Cool. We're more than a band.

A band makes music, a phenomenon impacts society. And if a
kid who had no idea about music recognized KISS . . . weren't we a
phenomenon?

Not long after that, in May 1976, we jetted off to England for a
two-month European tour. To me, England represented the musical holy land. Everything I loved came from there. We even had
two nights booked at the Hammersmith Odeon, in London, where
so many of my favorite bands had played legendary gigs.

But nearly as soon as we landed, I hated it. We had become a big band in the United States. In England and the rest of Europe, we had to prove ourselves all over again. We were back at square one—nobodies. Thank God for the fans. As we had seen back home when we started out, the fans in England were also rabid in their dedication to us. On the other hand, the food was horrible and the transportation archaic. The people who ran things were very stodgy. Merchants took perverse pride in the fact that you couldn't get dry cleaning back for a week. There was no air conditioning, and, if you pleaded, they might begrudgingly put one lone ice cube in a drink for you. These things were badges of honor to the older guard of the British Empire.

But the hotel policies represented the biggest sore spot. They made it virtually impossible to take female guests to your room. You had to sign them in, and they had to leave by 10 P.M. And the staff enforced the rules.

Trouble taking girls to our rooms was a much bigger problem than the food. I could go without food, but I couldn't go without a steady diet of wild and willing women. That was absolutely essential.

Ace bought knives all along the European tour, and on the way home he taped a bunch of them to the inside of his Marshall cabinets to sneak them into the country. It pissed me off—if they were found, all our gear would be impounded. But it was par for the course for Ace. Once, on a domestic flight, our tour manager's bags had been searched, and a stolen hotel phone was found. The tour manager hadn't put it in there. Ace also stashed drugs in the bags or pockets of crew members—without their knowledge—so he wasn't on the hook if they were found. Ace was all about Ace, regardless of the cost to anyone else.

Arriving in the middle of the night back at my apartment on 52nd Street after a month in Europe, the doorman stopped me as I walked in with my suitcase. "Can I help you, sir?"

"Yeah, very funny, I live here," I said. I kept walking toward the elevator.

"Sir, if you don't stop I'm going to call the police."

I was gone *a lot*.

And I was soon gone again. As the tour continued back in States, the strain of dealing with the splintering personalities in the band meant we shuffled through more and more tour managers— all told, during the first five years of the band we probably went through twenty tour managers. Among the most colorful was "Fat" Frankie Scinlaro, an old-school manager who had worked with Joey Dee and the Starliters. His upbeat nature was contagious. He had a lot of nicknames for us—he called Peter the "Ayatollah Criscuola," Gene was "Gene the Nazarene," and I was the "He-She," because of my preening and dancing onstage. We'd begun to call Ace "Baby Elvis" because he was developing such a paunch. He ate a lot of potato salad, and in general he ate with his mouth open—he said it "aerated" the food. It was like watching a cement mixer. Fat Frankie would do anything to get us laughing, and when he did, tensions within the band faded. He could be really self-deprecating, too: he liked to say "I may have a little dick, but I can make it spin."

Some of the tour managers were fired because Bill didn't think they were doing a good job; most were ousted because of jealousies within the band—each member wanted the undivided attention of the road manager, or at least a sense of favoritism. When one of us didn't get that, that person not coincidentally began to think the road manager was no good. A lot of them quit, too. Even people who had worked with other bands couldn't deal with the growing friction in ours. It was just too trying to have four hyperactive, dysfunctional people demanding all your attention and, if they didn't get it, sabotaging you so you fell on your ass.

Through all the changes in road managers and crew, the only constant was Bill. He had a way of defusing tension and making each member of the band think he was his favorite. But Bill, too, was increasingly stretched thin. He had started trying to expand his management business and seemed to spend a lot of time now on acts like Piper, Starz, and Toby Beau. We felt somewhat spited—we made all the money, and now he spent most of his time dealing with these baby acts who never went far. Sean Delaney's attention was also diverted by these other acts. And I was annoyed by the way Bill now seemed to believe that the formula for success was simple: give a band a look and a logo and they would become as big as KISS. That was insulting—Bill and Sean's ideas had definitely helped us immeasurably, but our success wasn't so simple. There was more to us than a logo, platform boots, and makeup.

Ever since I'd haunted 48th Street as a kid, I had admired the vintage guitars that cost a fortune. Now, however, I was ready to start collecting them. I put the word out on that leg of the tour that I wanted to buy guitars. The first exotic instrument I bought was a Gibson SG double-neck, like the one Jimmy Page played. I bought it in Indiana from a guy who collected them and had a room full of double-necks. Most of them were cherry, but this one was sunburst. From then on, the promoters knew I was in the market, and often, a line of people with guitar cases would be standing at the truck entrance to the concert venues when we pulled in. It was terrific— you never knew what might turn up.

I bought my next one in Arizona from a guy who owned a store called Bob's Bizarre Guitars. That was a sunburst Les Paul— exactly what I'd always wanted—and I paid $2,200 for it. I couldn't believe I finally had one of those guitars! It had what are called white or cream humbuckers—the bobbins where the copper wire is wound were white. You don't usually see the color of the bobbin because they are encased in a chrome or nickel case on the old guitars. But if you looked under the casing, the bobbins could be black, white, or what was called zebra, meaning it had one white and one black. Most of the guitars had all black bobbins, which was considered the least desirable set-up; the most coveted ones had two white bobbins.

I was over the moon.

30

You're millionaires," our financial advisors happily told us one day in late 1976. "Beth" had become a chart hit and crossed over to AM radio. *Destroyer* had become our second platinum album. We had played our biggest show ever, to forty-two thousand fans at the California Angels baseball stadium in Anaheim, California, in late August. Our in-house merchandising business was booming.

Being told you're a millionaire definitely sounds impressive, but it didn't hit me with the same heft that getting that first gold album had. That was a true milestone that I could quite literally grasp. This? This was great, but it wasn't the same concrete accomplishment. And it was also hard to figure out what it really meant, since the money was still something abstract. I still lived in my one-bedroom apartment.

But now we had two months off in New York to let the news sink in—and to record a new album.

I bought my parents a Chrysler. It was the first time they had ever owned a new car. I also bought them a house not long after, when my dad lost his job—and his pension. Instead of possibly being on welfare and food stamps, they were in a new house, with a new car. When Ericka started school, she lived in a nice suburban school district and did extremely well. (Many years down the road, she would ultimately get accepted to an elite university, and I felt blessed to be able to cover the costs for her.) Even so, my dad called me stingy for keeping the deed to the house in my name. I was afraid he'd just sell it if it was in my parents' name.

My dad told me that my success was more luck than anything else. In my experience, people who dismissed the success of others as luck were people who had failed. It was a way to absolve themselves of accountability for failure and discount someone else's role in their own accomplishments. And the idea that success was the result of luck also made other people feel entitled, as if the "lucky" ones should share their luck without reservation. After all, it could have happened to anyone. I saw this pattern in my family.

I bought myself a Mercedes—a burgundy 450SL with saddle interior. The first time I drove out to Queens in it, to see my parents, I pulled into a parking spot a few blocks away from their place and paused, sitting in the car with the motor running.

Should I really have bought this car?

I switched on the radio. "Rock and Roll All Nite" blared from the FM rock station. I pressed AM and spun the dial. I heard "Beth."

Yes, it was okay to buy the car.

During our break in the fall of 1976, we went back into the studio to record *Rock and Roll Over*, which was released in November. It was our sixth album in less than three years' time. Our initial productivity as a band was all about keeping our heads above water. But just because we'd reached a certain level of financial security, I didn't see any reason not to remain productive. It was fun to go into the studio. I'd spent my whole life dreaming of being in the studio. The studio was also a place where I could hide out when we were off the road. I still had virtually no social life, very few friends, and the studio was a safe haven—and one where we now had carte blanche. I could go there and not have to keep an eye on the clock. Those bills would be paid without so much as a raised eyebrow.

When *Destroyer* had come out earlier that year, the album had thrown some people because it didn't sound like us live. But it did capture the essence of what we did—by creating a cinematic feel that represented the magnitude of our shows even if it didn't re-create the sound of our shows. Bob Ezrin had enhanced and broadened our sound. He had magnified the four characters. But when we asked people around us what they thought of it, they sometimes said things like, "It's different." *Different* is not a good word in that context—it's a word people use when they can't make up their minds whether they like something or not.

The truth is the change scared us, too. Maybe we didn't want to have a nanny this time around, either—someone telling us how to do everything and blowing a whistle in our faces. We figured we'd done our apprenticeship. And Peter and Ace certainly had no desire to work with Bob again. We decided to try a more meat-and-potatoes approach, go back to basics.

The first thing we did was contact Jack Douglas, who had produced Aerosmith's three most recent albums, *Get Your Wings, Toys in the Attic,* and *Rocks.* The problem was that Jack was friends with Bob, and he turned around and told Bob we had asked him. It wasn't tactful on Bill's part not to tell Bob first—the whole thing blew up, and we felt like we'd been caught hitting on a friend's girlfriend.

Then came the idea of going back to Eddie Kramer, because *Alive!* had been so good. We rented the Star Theater in Nanuet, New York, outside the city but close enough that we could all go home at night. Eddie came on board and we retreated to familiar territory as fast as we could.

Even though Eddie was from South Africa, he had the air of an English gentleman. He was part of the heritage we all loved. One thing we hoped Eddie could fix was our drum sound—after all, he'd been a part of getting that big drum sound Zeppelin had. He had Peter set up in the theater itself while we played in a studio elsewhere in the building. We linked Peter in by video camera. In theory, even a chimpanzee beating on pots and pans could sound thunderous in the right environment. But still the drums sounded tinny. Soon, however, I came to the conclusion that in Zeppelin's case, John Bonham was that sound—and Peter Criss would never be John Bonham.

Eddie didn't function as a musical director or visionary in terms of arrangements the way Bob had, and we missed that leadership. No one was there to help us write or shape songs. I was having trouble coming up with songs, so I asked Sean Delaney to come over to my apartment for writing sessions. Those informal get-togethers at my 52nd Street place yielded "Makin' Love," "Mr. Speed," and "Take Me" for *Rock and Roll Over,* as well as "All American Man," which showed up on *Alive II* the following year.

"Hard Luck Woman" was an anomaly because I never intended it for KISS. I didn't see song writing as an exercise, and normally I was good at self-editing—if I didn't think a song had a place on a KISS album, I didn't bother to finish it. But I was still fascinated by trying to figure out what made certain songs by other people tick. I had been listening to Rod Stewart's "Maggie May" and "You Wear It Well" with that in mind and decided to try my hand at something similar. The lyrical spark came from someplace completely different—a song called "Brandy," by Looking Glass, that was about a sailor's daughter who worked at a bar. Once I finished the song, I couldn't imagine KISS doing it. I planned to try to get it to Rod to see whether he wanted to record it. But with "Beth" doing so well that fall, Eddie Kramer and Gene both thought the song would make a logical follow-up for KISS. And since Peter had that type of raspy voice, like Rod's, we figured he should sing it. I had to record a vocal for Peter to follow, and again, he took many takes to provide enough material to cobble together a finished version.

The situation within the band had deteriorated even in the space of six months since we'd made *Destroyer*. Peter brought in a cassette with a disjointed sketch of a song called "Baby Driver." He always brought tapes with recordings he'd done with co-writers because he couldn't play us a song any other way since he didn't play any instruments. Peter lashed out when we worked on "his" songs. But the problem wasn't that Gene and I rewrote his songs; the problem was that the things Peter brought in weren't songs to begin with. The lyrics never rhymed, there weren't any delineations between verse and chorus. They were scraps, not songs. Yes, the band was stronger when everyone participated, but somebody had to lay down the law when something simply wasn't good enough. Bob performed that role on *Destroyer*, created "Beth" for Peter, and guided us all creatively. Now that it fell to us, it was futile to try to hold Peter to the same standard we insisted on for the rest of the material. There was leeway because, hey, we *wanted* a Peter song—that was part of the image of KISS. And now, because of "Beth," Peter expected to write the songs he sang instead of singing mine, Gene's, or Ace's. But even with the additional wiggle room as far as quality, we couldn't let his stuff undermine the integrity of a record.

Of course, for Peter's co-writer, getting a song credit on a KISS album was a gravy train, so Peter always pushed his buddies' ideas and made a stink if anyone suggested they weren't quite up to scrub. Peter spent all his emotional energy worrying about his place in the hierarchy without the ability to be honest with himself about the quality of what he brought to the table.

Ace was a shadow of his former self. He had been a bright light that looked as if it could explode—he had the talent to be as good as he thought he was. The potential was there for him to have been one of the all-time greats. But the booze and Valium and coke and whatever else now left him incapacitated almost all the time. We prayed we'd be able to get a solo out of him before he passed out. He wasn't funny anymore—in any way. When he tried to tell jokes, he had to stop and slur, "How's it go again?"

The situation sometimes made me angry. I had busted my ass for the band, and I felt that these two guys were playing fast and loose with my future based on their irrational whims and inner conflicts. And yet, because the deterioration took place in stages, I found I accepted things that I never would have initially. If you try to bend a tree down to the ground, it breaks; if you bend it incrementally, little by little, you can get it parallel to the ground without snapping it. It just took time. That was me.

There was very little band mentality anymore. The other three guys drifted off to their own social circles, and we all had our own people telling each of us how great we were. Between their sycophantic friends and all the press, Peter and Ace began to believe they were world-class virtuosos, despite mounting evidence to the contrary. When we argued with Peter over his songs, he'd say things like, "You just don't want me to do this because I wrote the biggest song" or "You don't want me to do this because I'm the best singer." And he constantly accused me of not having "paid my dues," apparently because I hadn't spent a decade before KISS playing in bands that went nowhere, like he had.

Both Peter and Ace were fucked up all the time. I'd seen plenty of functional addicts. Bob Ezrin had been doing a lot of coke and chugging Rémy Martin while we recorded *Destroyer*, but the quality of his work never flagged. Bill Aucoin, Neil Bogart, and much of the Casablanca staff were on a slippery slope, doing lots of drugs, too. Drugs and alcohol were like a Ferrari: there's a split second difference between being in control and being wrapped around a telephone pole. You're in control, and then you pass that line and don't realize it until it's too late. I hoped Bill would be able to save Peter and Ace. But that turned out to be foolish—Bill couldn't even save himself.

If Gene and I tried to defuse unpleasant situations by saying, "Come on, man, that's the drugs talking," Peter and Ace would respond by insisting they knew exactly what they were saying. Peter's insecurities got more and more crippling with the addition of drugs. The whole world was against him. One day in the studio he exploded about something and smashed my acoustic twelve-string guitar against the wall. There was a moment of deafening silence after that.

During another argument, Gene snapped at Peter: "Peter, you're an illiterate idiot who can't read or even talk correctly and never finished school."

"Yeah," said Peter, "and I'm in the *same band* as you."

To this day, that remains the smartest thing I ever heard Peter say.

Playing Tompkins Square Park in the East Village with "The Baby Boom."

Me in my bedroom at age sixteen with big plans.

I'm eighteen, living on 75th Road. That was my turquoise Ford Fairlane.

Gene, me, Peter, and Ace. In the beginning we were invincible.

Japan, 1977. The fans would make me all these dolls.

A young Starchild on the Destroyer Tour.

BARRY LEVINE

*On tour in 1977; a spur-of-the-moment decision to dress like Elvis.
Cool and all shook up.*

1977: Goodbye Uriah Heap, hello Linda

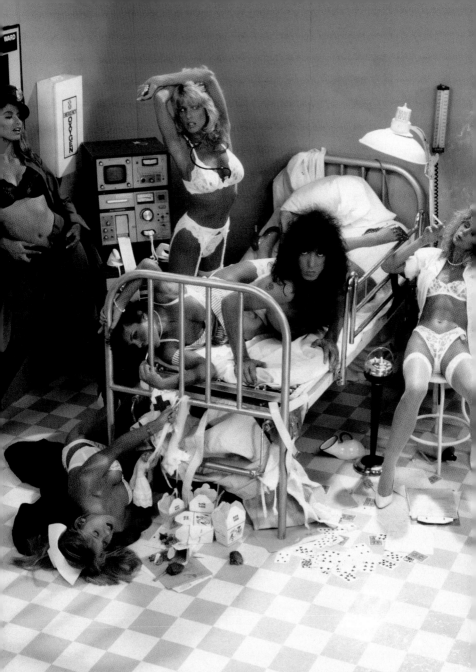

I dreamed up this insanity.

No wires. No tricks.

Preaching from the pulpit. Can I get a hallelujah?!

On our most recent tour. Mayhem in a confetti storm and it's all over.

Electric Lady Studios in 1985, recording Asylum.

Gene, Eric, me, and Tommy.

Me and Lady Gaga. She flew cross-country to come to the show and wore my boots for the entire show. She is the real deal. Holmdel, New Jersey, 2010.

November 19, 2005.

Doing one of those things I never imagined in my life. Baptizing Emily in church. Baptism for Colin, Sarah, and Emily was important to Erin so it was important to me. Evan was bar mitzvah'd and the rest will be too. There is room for it all.

Proud papa with Evan at age thirteen.

ROSS HALFIN

Phantom . . . a dream come true and I never worked harder in my life—an incredibly rewarding experience.

I painted Robert Johnson for our entry to bless the house and remind us where it all started.

With my little ones at the office.

It doesn't get better than this.

31.

One night in Texas in early 1977 a youth group attending a Bible conference gathered in the lobby of our hotel. Trying to be kind, generous, and Christian, one of them walked over to me and said, "I'm going to pray for you."

"How *dare* you," I said. "What would possibly make you think I need you to pray for me?"

Whatever judgments they had of me, it didn't stop a group of them from pressing themselves against my hotel room connecting door to listen to this messenger of Satan strip a willing local of her clothes and inhibitions.

When we pulled into arenas now, we saw people brandishing banners and placards and carrying crosses. I was astonished. These people quoted the Bible and called our music satanic.

You're talking about us?

I laughed at the protests at first. As far as I was concerned, they had their hands full monitoring their own practitioners—which turned out to be true, as scandals later engulfed Jimmy Swaggart,

Jim Bakker, and others. I found it amusing that whenever a televangelist was tempted by the devil, it was usually in a hotel with a hooker.

The person you have to watch is the one pointing the finger.

I also figured the protests were cynical ploys to get publicity. They used us as a stepping-stone to some sort of local—and later, even national—notoriety. Of course, that pointed to the fact that we had indeed become a bona fide phenomenon.

We're big enough to warrant some idiot carrying a cross in front of our show?

When you're successful, everyone wants some, I guess.

Later on I decided I wanted to counter these people. At times I thought Gene took things too far by trying to use them to fan the fire. I didn't always think that was a good thing—I disagreed that all publicity was good publicity. Antagonizing these people wasn't the answer. I didn't want to address them individually or give them the importance they were seeking, but I wanted to stop playing the game. I simply wanted to say the allegations weren't true: we were not knights in Satan's service or devil worshippers or anything else.

Yes, we had a bass player who spat blood and breathed fire and called himself "evil incarnate," but if you went to the movies, you'd also see a guy who wanted to suck your blood and another with bolts in his neck who'd been brought back to life by a mad scientist and a jolt of electricity. If they saw a guy on TV with his face painted white and his hair pulled up on top of his head and thought he was real, and that he was stating facts when he said he was evil incarnate, *they* were the ones who were crazy. Not *us.* Did these people really think we looked like this all day? Did they also think the guy who played Batman was really Batman?

The way I saw it, KISS wasn't going against anything, whether it was religion or politics. KISS wasn't even about rebellion. We didn't tell people to tear anything down or to refuse to play by the rules. We said, *Become who you want to be.* It was about self-empowerment. It was celebratory. For me, it wasn't about fighting the system, it was about picking your path and believing in yourself. The ultimate rebellion wasn't fighting the system, it was circumventing the system and living your life fully. And what the band represented for me personally, I thought it could also represent for other people—for fans. Maybe that's why our audiences were all smiles. We were singing about how good life could be and how much you could accomplish by believing in yourself. Despite what the religious protesters said, KISS was all positivity.

Hell, all anyone had to do was listen to the lyrics from our mission statement off *Destroyer,* "Shout It Out Loud":

> *Well the night's begun and you want some fun*
> *Do you think you're gonna find it?*
> *You got to treat yourself like Number One*
> *Do you need to be reminded?*
> *If you don't feel good, there's a way you could*
> *Don't sit there brokenhearted*
> *Call all your friends in the neighborhood*
> *And get the party started*

At the same time religious protesters vilified us for being a danger to America's youth, music critics killed us because in other ways we weren't dangerous *enough*—to ourselves. Apparently, Gene and I didn't live recklessly enough and were too business minded to meet the credibility criteria of some hip music magazines. The premise that some desk-bound journalist might deem me worthy of his seal of approval only if I played Russian roulette with my life had an irony to it that wasn't lost on me. Drug usage was and is sheer stupidity, and sooner or later there was always a heavy price to pay for it. I wasn't interested in being a dead legend.

Our closest contemporaries were Aerosmith. The difference

was how we were viewed. They were a rock band, and we were so much more. In some quarters there was more credibility in being a rock band, but the impact of being an all-encompassing phenomenon was more widespread and diverse. It made us more interesting to newspapers and magazines, little kids, and preachers.

The interesting thing was the way that for some people being a phenomenon didn't correlate with being a band. As if it undermined our credibility—as if the impact of the image, the logo, and all the press eclipsed what was otherwise as good as a lot of bands the critics did love. Journalists constantly dismissed us with the same basic argument—if we were any good musically, we wouldn't need any of the visual effects. What never seemed to occur to them was the possibility that we were good *and* that we *wanted* and *loved* all the rest.

Part of the perception problem had to do with Neil Bogart and Casablanca Records. The label released Donna Summer's disco anthem "Love to Love You Baby," which became a smash hit over the course of 1976. Hit singles were Neil's thing, and it altered the way he did business. He made Casablanca into a singles-oriented label and focused on acts like the Village People. He signed a rock band called Angel and positioned them as the anti-KISS, in all white outfits and ballet slippers instead of platform boots. Neil's forte once again seemed to be novelty acts not that far removed from his bubblegum days. KISS went from being the signature band on Casablanca to being part of a sideshow label—part of a menagerie. Instead of being in the company of rock bands, we shared a label with a bunch of guys dressed up like construction workers and cops and a band that wore ballet slippers. People who wanted to see us as pap or contrived had only to look at the company we were in to reinforce their suspicions. It solidified any negative impressions people had of us.

Part of the perception problem was due to simple subjective differences in how people saw things. If Bruce Springsteen slid on his knees, critics called it showmanship. If I did, they considered it some sort of scam. A circus trick. One guy was a showman and the other was a charlatan. But sometimes it had a darker side that corresponded to things we overheard—things about how we were money-hungry Jews or "kikes." As if our entrepreneurial ability weren't a positive trait, but rather a trait of deceit or manipulation—because that wasn't rock and roll, that was *what Jews did.*

The same sentiments infected the inner workings of the band, too. I think in Peter's case it had to do with his upbringing and the fact that he wasn't very bright. Ace owned a lot of Nazi memorabilia. Now, I'm sure there are people who collect that stuff who aren't Nazis or anti-Semites, but Ace was not one of them. Barely below the surface of the band's interactions was a simmering and ongoing resentment and anger directed at me and Gene. We ran the band and wrote almost all the songs and generated the ideas—not because KISS was a dictatorship, but because the other guys' contributions just didn't amount to much. Their jealousy and envy and resentment got focused on the most tangible thing they could pin it on—the fact that Gene and I both happened to be Jewish. It wasn't that different from the core of society's anti-Semitism: take Jewish immigrants out of their native soil and put them in a new country, and the next generation becomes doctors—that's hard for certain people to take. And so it was inside the band. Ace and particularly Peter felt powerless and impotent when faced with the tireless focus, drive, and ambition of me and Gene. As a result, the two of them tried to sabotage the band—which, as they saw it, was unfairly manipulated by those money-grubbing Jews.

But of course, we kept up the mythology: four guys running down the street, jumping in the air, living under one roof. Just substitute New York for Liverpool, and that was us.

Yeah, yeah, yeah!

Yeah, right.

32.

I always wanted a gold record, and I always wanted to play Madison Square Garden. I already had my gold album. On February 18, 1977, we headlined our first show at the Garden. And it was sold out.

It had been four and a half years since I pulled up in front of the Garden in my cab to drop people off for Elvis's show.

I had seen the Stones at Madison Square Garden—forged a ticket for that show, in fact. I'd seen George Harrison's concert for Bangladesh at the Garden. I'd slept outside Macy's in Queens to get tickets for that show. I'd seen Alice Cooper at the Garden. I'd seen Ringling Brothers Circus at the Garden.

Madison Square Garden was synonymous with success on a large scale. Playing there was big stuff. Really big stuff.

I was so anxious before the show that I took half a Valium. The idea that I might be sluggish? No chance. The adrenaline high was so strong on a normal night, and this was homecoming in a sold-out Madison Square Garden. I probably could have taken several whole pills and still have gotten up onstage and then run a marathon in record time. Shows like this were still new—I wasn't yet used to the idea that we were *this* big.

Standing on the diving board is usually scarier than taking the dive, and sure enough, once onstage, I felt exhilarated. That first wave of force coming from people screaming and lights coming on is very powerful. Having multitudes of people focused on you and sending you energy creates an undeniable wave of force. That might sound like some sort of New Age concept, but the feeling is staggering.

The entire show carried incredible emotional weight. But by the second song, I was home.

I knew my parents were in the audience, and I couldn't help chuckling about it: "Yep, that's my boy—the one in eight-inch heels and lipstick jerking off a guitar onstage." But I was proving something to them. They were wrong. This could be done. And I had done it.

You see? I am *special.*

And then a bottle came sailing out of the darkness and hit me in the head. I saw it at the last second and flinched just enough so it smacked into my head next to my eye instead of in my eye. The glass cut me. I bled for the rest of the show. In some ways it was cool, but I also felt hurt—not physically, but hurt that somebody would do that. And yet at the same time, I knew it wasn't done maliciously. I'd seen the impulse before. Fans wanted to touch you in any way they could, and here was someone touching me with a bottle. Our road crew, as devoted as they were, found the guy and beat the crap out of him.

Still, it was the first time I felt vulnerable onstage. There was always a dark mass of people out there while I was in the spotlight, and now I knew I really could get hurt. For the first time it occurred to me that the fourth wall could be knocked down by them instead of by me.

We had about a week in New York around that gig at the Garden, and once again I was confronted with the fact that I didn't have any real life outside the band. Most musicians I knew wanted to talk about equipment—stuff I could give a rat's ass about. I thought there was so much more to the world, even if I was still learning what that could be. I liked to talk about music, but on a historical level, an emotional level—not a technical level. I spent a lot of time dissatisfied because I didn't have friends to talk to about things that might be stimulating, educational, or enlightening.

As far as the women I hooked up with, I knew it wasn't about deep conversation. I chose them because of what I thought other people would think—and because of what I *hoped* I could convince myself: *I must be somebody worthwhile because this beautiful woman wants to be with me.* It was all about bolstering my sense of self. Being with someone to make myself feel better always meant being with a woman others wanted, a woman others envied me for having. Thankfully, I managed to meet some women who, besides being beautiful, were also smart, funny, and well-read. But even with those women I had little to offer in terms of a relationship. I wasn't open, and I wasn't going to give anything of myself. So it was more or less two people trading services.

Though it was hard for me to articulate, all of this made me feel even more isolated than I already felt.

I remember one woman coming to my apartment and starting to get itchy for cocaine after a while. She apparently had a major habit. She began to get dressed to go out and score some blow. "I'll come right back," she said.

"If you leave," I told her, "you don't come back."

You can be with somebody and still feel alone.

For me, actually being alone was worse. One evening I drove my burgundy Mercedes down to a hip restaurant and bar—one of those places that was known as a hangout. I pulled up to the curb near the entrance on Fifth Avenue and 11th Street and then sat in my car. I wanted to go in, maybe talk to some people, hang out. But I froze.

You can't go in there on your own!

I didn't know anyone. I couldn't risk being in a situation like that. I couldn't make friends. I couldn't hang out. The Starchild? Yes, of course, *he* could. And even the version of the Starchild I could muster at parties put on by promoters or radio stations or our own management. Those were controlled situations. People in that context expected the Starchild; I depended on *being* the Starchild to interact with them. I depended on presenting a likable persona and hid my real self, the one-eared kid from Queens who still didn't believe anyone could really like him and wouldn't know what to do if someone did.

Who am I? Where do I belong?

I was supposed to be a big rock star, and there I was paralyzed in my car outside a restaurant, afraid to go inside. The contrast between how I was perceived and the reality of my situation could not have been more stark.

Who would believe this?

With a last look at the entrance, I pulled away from the curb, drove around the block, and steered the car back uptown to my apartment. I didn't have the basic skills to function in a setting like that. Most people were petrified by the idea of going onstage. Not me. Whatever emptiness or insecurities I had waited at the side of the stage. I lived for those moments. I wanted the crowd to love me because I still hadn't learned to love myself enough to get over the most basic social phobias I harbored offstage.

When are we going back out on the road?

Mercifully, we headed back out soon. And by March we found ourselves touching down in Japan in a Pan Am 747 amidst a Beatles-like furor over the band. In fact, it was the Beatles' records we broke for attendance at the Budokan in Tokyo. The magnitude of our stardom in Japan was astounding.

We had arranged to pass through customs and immigration in full makeup and gear. We had it all with us on the plane and got ready when we were within a few hours of landing. But we arrived late, and the official who was supposed to be there to smooth everything along had already left. Without him, we had to remove our makeup before they'd let us in the country. After they verified we were the people in our passport photos, we did the quickest makeup job we had ever done and then walked out to find thousands of fans waiting outside. It was pandemonium. Once we got into our cars, people swarmed over them like locusts. I got nervous and claustrophobic.

"Smile," Gene said calmly, through clenched teeth.

We spent the next two weeks attending lavish parties and making regular visits to Japanese bathhouses. The bathhouses employed women who seemed to grow extra hands and limbs once your clothes were off. If I could do to myself what they did to me, I would never leave home.

While in Japan I met with executives from Hoshino Gakki, the makers of Ibanez guitars. We sat in a boardroom and I explained my views on the sonics and aesthetics of guitars, which led to my first signature model. Having my own guitars sold in music stores around the world was a milestone for me—and any musician.

After the last show, we flew back to Los Angeles. There we learned we'd been named the top band in America by the Gallup poll—over Aerosmith, Led Zeppelin, and the Eagles, among others. Soon, magazines were publishing similar results from readers' polls. In *Circus* magazine we won a head-to-head poll versus Zeppelin. Now, I had a high regard for what we were doing, but I wasn't crazy—*I* didn't see us in the same league as Zeppelin. The same publications also ran votes on readers' favorite players, and Ace and

Peter both came out on top of some "best guitarist" and "best drummer" polls, fueling the increasing gap between their self-image and their actual abilities. If only *Circus* readers realized they were barely sentient beings most of the time who didn't care and were often either too fucked up or too inept to play their parts on recordings without great effort or a nameless ringer filling in for them. I figured if we were going to disregard the critics who called us hucksters and dismissed our music, we also had to dismiss the people who called us virtuosos. Peter and Ace didn't agree. The press reinforced what they wanted to think: that they were world-class musicians. Of course, Ace could really have been one, but he was killing his talent—and his body and brain—with booze and drugs. And Peter? From *Destroyer* on, what the band wanted to do pushed the limits of his abilities or simply outstripped them.

We had a few weeks off in L.A. before we went to New York to start recording yet another album. One night I ended up going out with Lita Ford, who was then the guitar player in the Runaways. Lita and I had some fun times together. She was only nineteen, but her band had just released their second album and were about to head off for their own tour of Japan. The two of us went to a club called the Starwood for a show. The opening band, the Boyz, featured George Lynch, who went on to fame in the band Dokken. The Boyz played a cover of "Detroit Rock City." The second band was called Van Halen. I was impressed. They had another show the next night, and I made Gene go with me to see them.

Near the end of Van Halen's set that second night, Gene got up and disappeared. Little did I know, he'd gone backstage and spoken to them about taking them into a studio to record a demo. He never told me. He didn't mention it when he returned to his seat; I found out only later. It was funny, because I always thought of Gene as the one member of the band I could count on, and yet he still did secretive things like that. It was that old impulse of his—and he never felt the need to explain any of what I saw as sneaky or dishonest behavior.

During that time in California I also met and started seeing Cher's sister, Georganne LaPiere, who was then starring in the soap opera "General Hospital." Georganne was extremely smart—a member of the high-IQ society Mensa—and I loved talking with her. Georganne and I saw each other off and on for more than a year, though after a while I told her I planned to see other people as well—there was no dishonesty about it. I realized phone relationships could go on forever. You talk to somebody, have a nice conversation, and then, when you say goodnight, you go off and do whatever you're going to do.

At the end of the time in L.A., I flew to New York. The song "Love Gun" came to me in its entirety on the flight—melody, lyrics, all the instrument parts—absolutely complete. It was amazing—and rare for me. I stole the idea of a "love gun" from Albert King's version of "The Hunter," which Zeppelin also nicked from for "How Many More Times" on their first album. By the time the plane landed, I was ready to record a demo.

When I got to New York, I called a drummer I knew and went almost immediately to Electric Lady to record the song. By this point I didn't need to do demos in less lavish studios—I could do them in top-end studios, and Electric Lady was my favorite. I used the same equipment and tape that other bands cut masters on. That worked out to be as much of a curse as a blessing. Sure, the demos sounded great. But with using quality studios for demos came the risk of demo-itis. You get so locked into the version you record as a demo that you lose all flexibility when it comes time to record the track. You've worked out all the parts, and it's hard to erase them and let other people have creative input if they veer from the version you recorded on the demo. Then you're stuck recording a stiff version of the thing you already did—it robs the final recording of spontaneity. You're less open to suggestions for change because you already have a fully realized concept. Eventually, in the late 1980s, I stopped doing demos for all those reasons.

The funny thing about "Love Gun" was that even though the album version was recorded as a facsimile of the demo, when we went to cut the album version, Peter couldn't play the kickdrum pattern on the song. Once Peter cut the track, we had to bring in another drummer to play the extra kickdrum beats Peter couldn't.

We recorded the album at the Record Plant, another iconic New York studio. It was up near Times Square in what at the time wasn't a great neighborhood. When you entered the place at the ground level, the receptionist was sitting behind a glass window and had to buzz you in through a locked door. The window had shutters, and once through the locked door, you saw that the reception area was separated from the hallway by another locked door. I can't tell you how many times I left the studio to take a break and walked into the receptionist's little office. She would close the shutters and lock the door and say, "Oh, Paul!" I didn't fool myself into thinking I was the *only* one, but I was *one*. And it was terrific. Sure beat a coffee break.

During our stay in New York, Gene came up to Bill's office and played us finished demos by a band called Daddy Long Legs—it turned out that was a name he came up with to replace their original one, Van Halen. Bill and I listened intently and later spoke—without Gene—and agreed to pass on getting involved with them. Not because they weren't great. Not because they didn't have enormous potential. We passed to protect KISS, which needed our daily focus to continue building on all fronts. Gene's wandering eye was clearly a potential risk to all we had accomplished and all we were working toward.

For the *Love Gun* tour, which began in Canada in early July 1977, after the album was released, we had a private airplane for the first time. We'd flown private only one time before, when because

They showed up in drag and handed me a dress, in honor of my birthday;
left to right: *Peter, Gene, Me, Ace. Lincoln NE, 1977.*

of a scheduling conflict we had to take a tiny Learjet to get in and out of some out-of-the-way city. This was different. This was ours. It was a Convair 280, a propeller plane, filled with odd furniture— almost like a flying junk shop. The pilot and copilot were Dick and Chuck, and our flight attendant was named Judy.

Dick and Chuck fought regularly and often yelled at each other in the cockpit. "You asshole!" "Fuck you!"

It wasn't very reassuring.

Once, at the end of a flight, we landed, got to the end of the runway, turned around, and immediately took off again. They had put us down at the international airport rather than the private airport. Another day I saw flames coming out of one of the engines midflight. I told Judy to bring Dick back to see it. He came back, looked out the window, and said matter-of-factly, "Don't worry about it."

Then he returned to the cockpit. The whole operation was an accident waiting to happen.

The tour itself, however, went gangbusters. We had to add dates in a lot of markets and recorded another live album, *Alive II,* along the way. It seemed like a good idea: we'd done three studio albums and a live album, and then another three studio albums. Why not another live album? The problem was, we had to fabricate a KISS show for the album because we didn't want to repeat material from the first live album. That first one documented a standard set. The second one couldn't because a lot of those songs from the first three albums were still staples in our show. So now we had to create a KISS show that didn't really exist—with the dynamics of a real show. Even so, it didn't seem like a big deal since we had a lot of great stuff— "Detroit Rock City," "Love Gun," "God of Thunder." And once again we enhanced the ambient quality of the live recordings so they replicated the bedlam of an actual show. The onstage explosions caused compression in the microphones, so again we used recordings of cannons to make them sound right. And for the back photo, we decided to take a shot during sound check at the San Diego Sports Arena with all our effects shot off at once—just blast the entire arsenal and have us all up on the hydraulic lifts. That never actually happened all at the same time during a show, but it was an authentic documentation of the bombastic feel of the experience.

The second problem with *Alive II* flowed from the first. Using only songs from the second three studio albums, the new live album took up just three sides of a double album, not four. What were we going to do? We decided to add a side of studio tracks. I wasn't keen on the idea. We recorded the tracks at the Capitol Theatre in Passaic, New Jersey, to give them a live feel. I had "All American Man," which I'd written with Sean Delaney, but overall, the songs we came up with just weren't great. "Anyway You Want It" was a Dave Clark Five song I'd always loved, and Gene loved it, too. The original 1964 version is cataclysmic—just huge. Ours didn't come close, but we needed to fill up that final side of the record.

Ace didn't play on any of the studio tracks except the one he wrote, "Rocket Ride." Instead we had to use Bob Kulick, who had auditioned for the band during the cattle call back in 1972 and with whom I'd remained friends.

As the tour continued, we flew on with Dick and Chuck fighting in the cockpit. During the time Uriah Heep was opening for us, I constantly made eye contact with their keyboard player's great-looking girlfriend. I found out her name was Linda and the day after the band left our tour, I called our tour agent and said, "Track that girl down." The next day she was back on the tour, now traveling with me. *This* was rock and roll.

In Houston someone showed me a 1958 Flying V guitar, which was something I really wanted. It even had its original case. I asked how much he wanted for it. "Thirty-six hundred bucks," the guy said.

"Come on, that's a lot of money." He didn't budge. I bought the guitar. I had caught the guitar bug again.

In California someone told me about a guy who had a sunburst Les Paul for sale. I paid $10,000 for it. It seemed like a fortune at the time, but it ended up on the cover of the bible of sunburst guitars—*The Beauty of the 'Burst*—and is valued at as much as a million dollars now. (Best of all, that guitar is still known as the Stanley burst, even though I no longer own it.) By the end of the *Love Gun* tour, I had nine premier examples of guitars I loved—including the ones I'd already bought.

The demand for KISS concert tickets continued to rise through the year. And being onstage continued to suspend everything around me. Performing provided pure escapism and joy and elation. In my everyday life, I could never free myself of my insecurities, and the increasing rancor inside the band left me feeling more isolated than ever. One night I even decided I should try the rock star thing of breaking up a room, but as soon as I started breaking things, I stopped.

What did I do that for?

The room's messy now.

This is my *room—now I have to clean it up.*

But as I walked up the steps to play the show each night, I shed all problems at the bottom of the stairs.

I needed the crowd to love me. Nobody else did. Not even me.

It can be very lonely walking offstage when you feel like that. When so much seems to be missing from your life. By December of 1977, when we got back to New York, we had sold out three more nights at Madison Square Garden. After the first two gigs, the other guys met up with family or friends; I found myself sitting alone at Sarge's Deli on Third Avenue and 36th Street eating a bowl of matzo ball soup. On the one hand, now that I was a rock god playing a block of shows at MSG, I assumed I had succeeded in making people envy me and wish they had been nicer to me. But on the other hand, there I was having soup in a deli by myself.

That was a harsh reality to deal with.

After the final MSG show, Bill Aucoin threw a party at a swank townhouse. I flew in a girlfriend from Detroit. Santa Claus was at the party. And I had never seen so many lobsters in my life—hundreds and hundreds of them piled up on platters. They must have cleaned out the ocean for weeks. We still didn't understand that we ourselves actually paid for such things.

George Plimpton and Andy Warhol came to the party. It was always interesting to see people from other scenes like that—artists, writers, entertainers. *Oh, that's George Plimpton.* But I didn't function well except in the most socially controlled situations. I didn't want to risk getting shown up. I was too self-conscious.

I locked myself in the bathroom with a woman who worked at a radio station. When we finished, we straightened our disheveled clothes and I went back out. Andy Warhol approached me and said, "You should come down to the Factory sometime and I'll do your portrait."

I'm not cool enough to hang around people like that!

I never went. Big regret on that one.

After playing three nights in a row at the Garden, I knew one thing: what I had thought would fix me, had not.

If all these people look up to me and see me as special and a star, shouldn't I feel that way?

Maybe in theory. Maybe while I was onstage. But success and fame and the change in the way other people perceived me hadn't erased whatever was wrong behind the mask. I had reached what I was after, and it wasn't the answer. Whatever was missing was still missing. The question was, *what* was missing? *What* was wrong?

And just then, as the *Love Gun* tour wrapped up at the beginning of 1978, a funny thing happened. At what seemed like the peak of our popularity—and when being onstage provided the only respite from my emptiness and my nonexistent home life—we stopped touring. In part, it was because we simply couldn't. Ace and Peter were deeply into drugs and alcohol and alternated between hostility and incoherence. When they weren't incapacitated, they caused headaches for everyone around them. We weren't speaking to each other. We couldn't stand each other.

We wouldn't play a gig for more than a year.

What do I do now?

33

One of Bill's follies was the movie *KISS Meets the Phantom of the Park*. He thought that film was the next step for us. The Beatles had *A Hard Day's Night* and *Help!*, and we should have our film. He sold it to us as *A Hard Day's Night* meets *Star Wars*, which had come out the year before. It would have lots of cool special effects.

Nobody in the band had the slightest clue about acting. None of us read the script. We didn't care. We trusted Bill's judgment. When we started filming, it didn't take an expert in the field to know we were in deep shit and there was no getting out of it. The director asked *us* after each scene whether we thought it was good. We had no idea what we were doing. For us, a good take was one where we didn't blow our lines. If we said the right words, we moved on to the next shot.

Someone off camera fed us our lines. When we got ready to roll the camera, I yelled, "Line!" and someone said something like, "Gee, Ace, it's time we get going." Then I said, "Gee, Ace, it's time we get going."

"That's a keeper."

It was horrific—it didn't remotely resemble acting.

In one scene we levitated a box using wires. We assumed the wires would be rendered invisible by special effects people. Not so.

Meanwhile, the four of us weren't speaking unless we were delivering lines. Peter and Ace frequently left during filming. In one scene, we had to use Ace's stunt double—who happened to be black—after Ace left without notice. It was clear as day in the final version that it wasn't Ace.

We had to play a fake concert at Magic Mountain amusement park for another scene. When we were onstage, I turned around and saw some random old man in cat makeup and a wig playing the drums and chewing gum. Peter had taken off, and they threw this guy up there.

One bright spot about the production was that we had the West-mores doing makeup for us. They were the First Family of Holly-wood makeup—George, the patriarch, had set up the first makeup department for a Hollywood studio in 1917, and subsequent genera-tions became legendary for makeup and effects work. Over the years I had learned the steps and intricacies of applying the makeup to my face, and one of the Westmore sons watched as I did my own makeup one day on the set of the movie. "How'd you learn to do that?" he asked.

"I taught myself," I said. "It was just trial and error."

"Well, that's exactly the way we would do it," he said.

Cool.

When the movie was finished, we saw it at a screening at the Screen Actors Guild Theater on Sunset Boulevard. If you thought it was bad on a TV screen, you should have seen it on the big screen! People openly laughed. I slunk down in my seat. It was humiliating. The finished film was absolutely awful, and to have to stand when the lights came up while various people who had been involved with it came over to lie to me about how great it was made it that much more humiliating.

Around the time of that "concert" at Magic Mountain, Ace had first announced he wanted to leave the band. We held a band meeting on the lot where we were shooting the movie. In response, Bill and Neil had almost immediately hit on an idea to hold us together. "You don't have to leave the band," Bill said. "We'll do solo albums."

That turned out to be our next folly.

Neil said we would release them all on the same day. He envisioned shipping a million of each solo album. Bill had the idea to maintain some cohesiveness by having one artist do all four covers. And he suggested dedicating each album to the other guys in the band—to keep up the mythology.

Despite the dedications, we wished each other anything but good luck.

So after wrapping up *KISS Meets the Phantom of the Park,* we each went off to make an album with no knowledge of what the others were doing.

I had a lot of fun, actually. I didn't want to stray far from what KISS did. But it was great to be able to work with no tensions, no egos, and surrounded by talent. I started cutting demos at Electric Lady in New York, then went back out to L.A. to re-record them. After we cut a few of the songs, I realized they just didn't sound right. The demos might not have been perfect or the most fidelic, but they captured what I was looking for, so I decided to keep them and finish them. I liked the spontaneity and rawness. Then I cut another four or five new songs in L.A.—I had a band in New York and another one in Los Angeles. The only person who was in both was Bob Kulick.

As for the songs, "Hold Me, Touch Me" was about Georganne. I had flown off to see her frequently during downtime, and the song came from being away from her and hoping she was thinking of me when we weren't together. Most of the songs, however, were about Carol Kaye, a stunner in Bill Aucoin's publicity department whom I was seeing at the time and was crazy about. She was funny and smart and loved music, and the heat we generated at times could peel paint. Carol was romantically involved with someone else, too, and I had been trying my damnedest to get her to stop seeing him. I basked in the drama of that classic love triangle, but I was desperate to pull her away from him. "Tonight You Belong to Me" and "Wouldn't You Like to Know Me" are about her. "Tonight"

Me and Carol Kaye. My first solo album tells part of our story.

remained one of my favorite songs because of that tear-your-heart-out passion and pain that I knew so well.

Funny, though, because the night Carol finally said, "Okay, I'll stop seeing him," it was as if somebody had turned a hose onto the bed where we were lying. I was suddenly drenched in sweat. I had a full-on panic attack. I searched for the right words, mumbling, trying to backpedal my way out and come up with a plausible explanation for why I suddenly looked like I'd just gotten out of the shower. The truth was that so much of my life was about chasing approval, chasing acknowledgment, and chasing love, that when confronted with the chance to actually get approval, acknowledgment, and love, I was stunned. The reaction surprised me, because in my mind I really thought being with her was the answer. But it was safer to just chase things; I wasn't equipped for the real thing.

Needless to say, she didn't stop seeing her other guy after all.

I decided to mix my solo album in London at a legendary old-school studio called Trident. I wanted to fly there on the Concorde, something I'd never done. Somewhere over the Atlantic, it struck me that the plane wasn't level—it was flying at an angle. But what did I know? Then the pilot came on the PA and said in a calm voice, "This is your captain speaking. Now folks, you may have noticed we're flying at a slight angle. We've lost an engine."

We're in the middle of the fucking Atlantic with one engine!

"We're on our way back to Kennedy Airport."

If we're flying on one engine, why don't we go down to about five feet above the water instead of fifty-five thousand feet above it?

The captain came on ten minutes later: "We're using more fuel than expected because we're flying subsonic, so we're not going to make it to New York."

That's not good.

"We're going to divert to Nova Scotia."

I don't like this at all. Why are we so damn high up?

Before too long, the same calm voice came on again: "We're not going to make Nova Scotia."

Where on earth are we going to go?

"We're going to land at Gander Airport in Newfoundland—we need a long runway."

We made it to Gander and landed. They paired people up and shuttled us off to a local motel. I said there was no fucking way I was bunking with someone.

The next day, a DC-10 made an unscheduled stop and picked us up. They kept us in a sequestered compartment away from everyone else. What should have taken three and a half hours ended up taking seventeen hours. But once in London, I enjoyed it this time. A few months later, when a band called New England that had just signed with a newly formed record label asked me to produce their record, I specified that I would do it only if I could mix it in London.

When the four solo albums came out in late 1978, you could see the glass as half-full or half-empty. Selling around five hundred thousand copies each was nothing to sneeze at—2 million records if you looked at them collectively as a KISS product. But since Neil had shipped a million of each, what was he supposed to do with the other 2 million copies? It was too much hype, and because of the leftover records, a financial disaster for Casablanca.

The solo albums did quell the need for Ace and Peter to leave. But they represented nothing more than a Band-Aid on a gaping wound. They put off something that was inevitable.

34

Among the people I worked with on my solo LP were three girls and a guy called Desmond Child & Rouge, who sang background vocals on "Move On." Putting up flyers had become a big thing in New York by then, and I had seen one with a picture of these three hot girls and a guy. They had a few gigs around the city. I went to see one of their shows in a basement club that held a few hundred people—to be honest, I went because the girls looked kind of sleazy and cool in the picture on the flyer.

They sounded terrific. They had a great band, and the three girls sang their asses off, in harmony. It was sexy and vibrant. There was a Broadway element to their style, a little Brill Building, a little Drifters, and they echoed the romanticized ethnic sound of things like "Spanish Harlem." Some of the songs—as well as things Desmond wrote later, like "Livin' on a Prayer," which he did with Bon Jovi—told stories about working-class life and had real emotion. We also shared a mutual love of singer-songwriter Laura Nyro. I liked the vibe. I thought it was the best thing happening in New York. And I struck up a friendship with them.

When I first met Desmond in 1978 he was living with Maria, one of the backup singers. She was his girlfriend at that point. He had curly hair kind of like Peter Frampton. There was a sexual ambiguity about all of them that I wasn't quite able to define. I remember the four of them being at my apartment one night and thinking, *This is all kind of vague—I'm not sure where everyone in this room stands.* Desmond and two of the three girls left; one stayed behind. I now had part of the answer. I had a little crush on one of the other Rouge girls and a few months later found out in the best way possible that it was mutual. The picture became even clearer when Desmond eventually came out as gay around the time the band put out their second album, in 1979. That album was clearly about the turmoil and conflict he felt over his sexuality. I saw the band at the Bottom Line again around that time, and I could see it was over. They all seemed to be fighting for position onstage. Their manager was a travel agent by day, and I remember saying to them, "If you need a doctor, do you call a plumber?"

But it was too late. They had been mishandled, there was tension in the band, and the magic was gone.

Desmond and I started writing together soon after we met. I would take my guitar to his place, and he would sing along or play a keyboard. The first song we wrote together was "The Fight," and it ended up on their debut album in 1978. Then in early 1979 we worked on another one. It started after a night I spent at Studio 54, the famous New York nightclub. I had heard all these 126-beats-per-minute songs and listened to the lyrics and thought, *Gee, I can do that.* I went home and set a drum machine to 126 BPM and sat down and started "I Was Made for Lovin' You." It's funny that some KISS fans think the song has a sanitized connotation of disco, because it was written in a musical whorehouse.

Studio 54 was a den of iniquity; it was sordid—to a level and degree that I wasn't completely comfortable with. It was hardcore debauchery—sexual relations between everybody and anybody and drugs everywhere. It was beyond me. But I loved going there to dance. Nobody at Studio 54 wore a white suit and danced like John Travolta. I could go down there in jeans and a T-shirt and dance. Sometimes I'd go there on a Saturday night and not leave until the next morning. I'd buy the Sunday *New York Times* and read the paper in bed after one last dance with a woman I took home.

The music at Studio 54 was all about living in the moment—about having a great time. And so my song began like that, too: "*Tonight,* I'm gonna give it all to you . . ." Desmond helped with the verses of the song, and eventually, when we went back into the studio to work on another KISS album, *Dynasty,* the producer of that album, Vini Poncia, helped with the chorus.

Bill Aucoin brought in Vini—who had produced Peter's solo album—to appease Peter. By this point we were stuck in an ongoing yo-yoing process with Ace and Peter. *Are they in or out? Can we keep this going?* Bill and Sean Delaney's relationship was fraying at the same time. Sean was sent off to work on a few of Bill's other bands, and then he just disappeared. We basically never saw him again once he and Bill split up. So Bill needed Vini to be the peacekeeper.

We found out later that anyone hired to work with us at this time got briefed by Bill about what you could and couldn't say to each guy. He made sure we were insulated in this artificial world where nobody ruffled our feathers. People were told what we each liked, what offended each of us, what we each needed to hear. People were paid to tell us what we wanted to hear, and it was hard to make a distinction between motive and heartfelt opinion. We were in an Elvis bubble. People literally held open doors for us. Someone opened the door at the studio, and there was always a catered meal. Bill knew us inside and out. He knew how to placate each one of us and keep us happy. That is a manager's job, particularly when confronted with four people as volatile and combustible as we were at the time. But those people were enablers, too; nobody wanted the gravy train to stop.

To Vini's credit, though, he didn't want Peter to play on *Dynasty* despite their relationship. For Peter, Vini was a buddy. But for Vini, this was a job, and Peter was no longer capable of playing what was asked for and needed. So Vini brought in Anton Fig to play the drums. Anton had been in an Aucoin-managed band called Spider and had played on Ace's solo LP. He later went on to play in David Letterman's house band. We worked out a deal: Anton was paid well, but we weren't paying for secrecy. Rumors did swirl that Peter wasn't on the album, but we never felt the need to address them. We never thought about actually kicking Peter out—at least not yet. For now, it would remain the four of us, as always.

With Vini at the helm, the album wasn't really a rock album. But then again, we weren't really a rock band anymore. We were a bunch of rich guys who lacked a primal spirit. Of course, we also never felt we had to play by anybody else's rules—what was musically acceptable to us broadened over time. For some people, it was fine that we did things our way—until we didn't do things *their* way. That constituted a betrayal.

When I heard "I Was Made for Lovin' You" being played back in the studio, I was blown away. Yeah, it wasn't "Detroit Rock City" or "Love Gun," but it was undeniable. Another band came into the studio while it was playing, and they loved it, too. It was universal, something that grabbed you the first time you heard it.

Was it calculated? Yeah. Was it calculated to succeed? Yes, ultimately it was. But was that a bad thing? It started as a challenge to myself to see whether I could write in that style instead of meat-and-potatoes rock and roll. It was no different from the challenge I gave myself with "Hard Luck Woman." The only difference was the style. No apologies for a hit that people worldwide still want to hear and sing along to.

The show we mounted to support the release of *Dynasty* was no longer a rock show. It was more like "H.R. Pufnstuf on Ice." It was something that perhaps in some ways we consciously maneuvered toward. Over time, the band had evolved to include a broader demographic than in the beginning, but the change in our live presentation was just one of many missteps made at the time. We wore ridiculous outfits for the *Dynasty* tour—like Vegas or Disney characters jumping around in our colorful outfits. I don't consider what we normally wear to be costumes, but the clothes we wore on that tour certainly were. I had a layered lavender top—I guess the thought was that the black-and-silver look we'd always had was too hard-edged, so now we were going to add an individual color for each guy based on the halo color on each of our solo albums. It was horrible.

I had designed the stage—hexagonal with elevators that brought us up to stage level. We paid a fortune for a laser curtain to ring the whole stage. This was the early days of lasers, though, so they were very dangerous, and water-cooled, and big. It never worked properly. We spent years in court trying to get our money back for that laser curtain. We also had two complete stages built in anticipation of the need to leapfrog to alternating cities. We could add dates in one city while another crew erected the second stage at our next destination, allowing us to satisfy ticket demand in one place and then play the next place without an off-day to tear down and rebuild the stage.

Without Sean around, Bill brought in a choreographer named Kenny Ortega to try to tinker with the show. Kenny went on to work on stage shows for Michael Jackson and Cher; movies like *Dirty Dancing*, *Ferris Bueller's Day Off*, and *High School Musical*; and the music video that some blame for killing Billy Squier's career, "Rock Me Tonite." Bill also brought in a guy named Joe Gannon to work as a stage manager and direct our show like a Broadway musical.

Perhaps not surprisingly, the tour was in trouble from the start. It wasn't a good omen when our first show was canceled. We figured we would be doing multiple nights in most markets, but for the most part, that didn't happen. We had already had a few two- and three-night stands on our last tour, in 1977, so what was next? More nights, obviously. Nope. Fewer. The bottom got pulled right out from under us. It was shocking and scary to see that instead of getting bigger, we were getting smaller, as it seemed people were having second thoughts about coming to see us.

Why aren't they coming?

We had sanitized ourselves and were well on our way to extinguishing the fire that had propelled us so far. We stayed at a hotel opposite the Forum in L.A. when we played there, and I looked out the window and broke out into a cold sweat because I saw so many kids and families standing in line—which at that time could only backfire on us. The line could just as easily have been for the circus. There was an upside, though—I saw a lot of apparently single moms with their kids in tow. I could tell somebody, "Blond mom in row three," have her and junior come backstage after the show, and then send junior off for a tour of the stage. But it was all wrong.

Peter was completely unmanageable. Whatever we did was never right. If we let him sleep late on a day off, he would get angry and say he wanted to travel on the off-day. If we traveled on an off-day, he would say he wanted to sleep. If he said it was too hot backstage, we turned up the air conditioning; then he complained it was too cold. One time he punched a mirror and got a serious deep cut on his hand that needed microsurgery and stitches.

It wasn't unusual for Peter to throw his drumsticks at me or Gene or Ace if we stepped in front of his drum riser. Never mind that he was up on a drum riser—meaning we didn't block the audience's view of Peter even if we did pass in front of his kit.

If he wants to be at the front of the stage, he should learn to play the damn guitar.

But then one night near the end of the tour, in December 1979, Peter had been bingeing on drugs and playing particularly erratically. When I turned around during one song and let him know his tempo was too frantic, his reaction was to start slowing songs down and then speeding them up again, apparently out of spite. That crossed a line. It's one thing to sabotage things offstage—and god knows he'd done plenty of that. But this was different. This was in front of fans, people who had paid to see us.

Immediately after the show, Gene, Ace, and I spoke about it. We were all stunned by the betrayal. The unspoken rule had always been that you left your shit in the dressing room; no matter what was going on, when we went onstage, we were a band. The stage was sacred. Peter's purposeful sabotaging of the show was the ultimate treachery.

We decided we wanted Peter gone.

Ace can say whatever he wants now, but he voted to fire Peter without any prodding or strong arming. It's a tribute to Ace that he did. As far as my own vote, I didn't think it was cold or calculated to dump Peter. It was just survival. Was I going to let his problems drag down the entire band—and me with it? No way. Gene felt the same way.

We called Bill and told him we had to get rid of Peter. We said we wanted to cancel the rest of the shows and go home. How could we go on? Bill smoothed things over enough to get us to delay taking action and continue the tour rather than fire Peter immediately. We had just a few dates left. Peter didn't see the train that was about to hit him—but that was par for the course.

Immediately after the end of the tour, in mid-December 1979,

Peter married his second wife, Debra Jensen, a *Playboy* Playmate. The situation was weird. I couldn't help but wonder: would she marry him if she realized she was marrying the *former* drummer of KISS?

Early in 1980, Bill had to break the news to Peter that he was out. But instead, Bill persuaded the other three of us that we should

give Peter a second chance. So we didn't finalize a decision, and after a few months—a period when we were off the road anyway, recording *Unmasked*, with Anton Fig on drums again and Vini producing—we agreed to have Peter come back and try playing with us. In the interim Bill had arranged for Peter to take drum lessons from Jim Chapin, a famous jazz drummer. The day of the audition or rehearsal

Peter, Debbie, and me: Black tie in New York.

or whatever you wanted to call it, Peter walked in carrying a music stand and sheet music. The first thing he said was, "I'll have to have all your songs on sheet music because I read music now."

I whispered to Gene, "Are we on 'Candid Camera'?"

Peter sat down, put his sheet music on the stand, and studied it for a while. Mind you, this rehearsal was of *old material*, not the new stuff we had written and recorded for *Unmasked*. We wanted to see whether he could even play the songs he already knew. The rehearsal did not go well. It was over.

My philosophy had always been that if somebody was drowning, you tried to save the person. But when they started to pull you under, you cut them loose. That's what was happening. All the talking and advice and trying to get him help got us nowhere.

We shot a video for the song "Shandi" after the decision to let

Peter go had been confirmed. He came to the video shoot knowing it was the last time he would appear with KISS. At the end of the day, he took his makeup case with him and left. It wasn't tearful, but it was a big moment. Peter was leaving. We had fired him, and this was the last time we were going to see him in the band.

Oddly enough, Peter didn't seem to care. He was likely in his own drug haze and saw this as his big opportunity. In his mind, he wrote the biggest song we ever had, and now he was free to go out and become the big star he should be.

Wow, Peter's gone.

It's the end of . . . something. But the end of what?

It was difficult to envision the band not being the four of us. Dysfunctional or not, we were the four musketeers. It was a scenario we had never contemplated. What if somebody no longer wanted to be there? What if somebody was no longer doing his job? Whatever tension there was inside the band, we had always remained a band. Then all of a sudden one person was no longer part of the band. It shook all of us to the core. What do we do? Do we break up the band?

The rules had changed. KISS clearly wasn't going to continue as it had.

35.

As the drama with Peter was unfolding during the first half of 1980, we were also involved in a drama with our record label. Casablanca was absorbed by PolyGram, and for some reason the lawyers of the new company hadn't checked Casablanca's contracts with a fine-tooth comb. PolyGram assumed they were buying KISS and Donna Summer along with the label, but we had a "key man" clause, meaning that in our case, the deal was predicated on the presence of Neil Bogart. And from what we heard, the same was true of Donna.

Now, we may have been in some decline after *Dynasty* if you gauged things by the tour—when we'd had to cancel some shows and witnessed the changing demographics of the audience. But the way PolyGram saw it, *Dynasty* had been a huge hit, and in addition to making the charts at home, "I Was Made for Lovin' You" had been our most successful single outside the United States by far, hitting the top ten all across Europe and topping the charts in Australia and New Zealand. The label risked looking like idiots if they let us walk away—which we were entitled to do once they canned Neil. The situation could not have worked out better for us. Poly-

Gram ended up giving us a new and very lucrative deal as a face-saving move. Negotiating a new contract under these disastrous circumstances for them proved extremely advantageous for us.

The truth was that up to that point, we hadn't made much money—particularly if you compared what came in with what came to us. We found out later that KISS brought in about $100 million in merchandise sales in the three years between 1977 and 1979. Of that, the band members together took home less than $3 million. The overheads of Bill's operation were eating our lunch. But again, at that point we still didn't know enough about business to realize it.

We had credit cards, but we'd never seen actual money. Still, the idea of having a gold credit card was a big deal. My parents had never had credit cards. And since the bills went to Glickman-Marks, who took care of paying them, the cards lent a sense of unreality to the act of buying things. I had a little magical piece of plastic that allowed me to take things out of stores.

Now that we suddenly had a chunk of money from the new record deal, I decided I wanted to buy an apartment instead of continuing to rent. You didn't get anything out of renting—you didn't build equity, so in a case like mine it was pointless.

At first I wanted to look at places overlooking Central Park along Fifth Avenue. When I explained this to a real estate agent, she said to me, "I can take you to the places you want to see, or I can take you to the places that will let you in."

"What do you mean?" I asked.

She started talking about "nouveau riche" and being an entertainer. She paused. Then she said the buildings along the park were owned by "blue bloods and old money." She might as well have said, "You're a Jew," which I would learn was indeed unspoken grounds for being rejected by many of the prime buildings I was interested in. My agent had been through this before and knew the situation all too well.

"You mean, I can't live where I want?"

She explained the system of co-op boards. In New York City, most buildings were jointly owned by all the inhabitants, and a board created by the joint owners had to approve any new buyer. It was different from condos, where you just bought the unit from the previous owner. Co-op boards could—and did—block applications to buy from people they didn't want in the building. Jews and blacks were often those people.

Eventually I settled on a place on 80th Street and Madison Avenue, one block away from Central Park and the Metropolitan Museum of Art. I finally owned my own shelter, my home, my sanctuary, my refuge. It felt very different from renting.

The apartment was a duplex with three terraces. I had a music room, and on one wall I had tall glass-front built-in cabinets installed where I suspended and backlit all my collectors' guitars—like a cross between the Bat Cave and a museum installation.

The bathroom had a tub as big and deep as a small pool. One day I was paging through *Penthouse* magazine and liked the look of the woman on the cover. I called Bill Aucoin's secretary and said, "Find her." A few days later she was in that massive tub with me. Cliché or not, there we were with a bottle of Dom Pérignon. Not long after, my mom asked me whether I was seeing anyone special. I smiled and told her to pick up the most recent *Penthouse*. Needless to say, she was speechless at some of the very revealing shots. I have to say I loved her bewilderment at the debauched road I had taken. Over time, my mom grew accustomed to the shocks of my lifestyle and began to view it all with a resigned sense of humor.

My bedroom was amazing, too. When you walked in you saw a black lacquered chest of drawers, and stretching from that all the way to the ceiling was plate glass etched with branches and birds, lit from below—it was a room divider. My bed was on the other side of the glass. And above my bed was a huge mirror that kind of flowed out of the etched glass. I spent a lot of time looking up at that ceiling mirror and remarking on how great life was. When I saw myself lying next to a beautiful woman, I thought, *Hey, that's me! That's me in bed with that gorgeous woman!*

One night I was lying in bed with the woman from *Penthouse*, watching a documentary on TV about the 1970 Kent State shootings during a campus demonstration against the Vietnam War. She started getting kind of frisky and I pushed her away. "Hang on," I said.

"What?" she said.

"This is important," I said.

"That really happened?" she said.

Since I was choosing the women I spent time with based on a single criterion—their looks—I had to expect them to act within the boundaries of who they were. And the fleeting sense of fulfillment I felt looking up at the ceiling did make it easier to be at home rather than on the road. For a time, at least.

I started seeing a lot of women around town. At one point I was seeing two different chorus girls from the show *Sugar Babies*, a Broadway musical starring Mickey Rooney. I took my father to the show one time, and we went backstage to meet one of the girls. She was nearly six feet tall, exotic and ravishing. As we walked out I said to my dad, "She's really hot, isn't she?"

"She seems like a nice girl," he said.

"She's not a nice girl," I said. "She's just hot."

For him, sex appeal and sexuality had to be tempered, sanitized, and neutered. I had found a different point of view and wanted him to know that I reveled in the raw honesty. I had come to grips with the fact that sometimes there *was* nothing more to it. This woman wasn't nice. She was just very hot. And that was plenty.

One morning a woman called me, and after we had talked for a few minutes I said, "That was a really great time last night."

And she said, "Yeah . . . who do you think this is?"

Oops.

Another time I went to pick up a former *Playboy* Playmate at a new apartment she'd moved into. When I rang the doorbell, a different woman I'd been seeing answered the door. They had moved in together and decided not to tell me. They thought it was hilarious. Believe me, if you saw these two, I was lucky to be the brunt of the joke.

I was seeing quite a few women at the same time, and went through a period of sending women flowers when I was screwing someone else. If I spent the night with one woman, I'd send flowers to another. It wasn't insincere exactly, because I wasn't making any pretense of being exclusive with any of them, but I wanted them all.

I was living a triple life. There was the Starchild. There was me without the makeup—the perceived me, that is. And then there was the real me, who, despite fame and adulation, still felt insecure. There was a reason I spent most of my time in my apartment, sometimes with women, often alone. Some people took me for snobby or aloof, but the truth was, I was still shy and insecure. It wasn't that I didn't *want* to talk to people and make friends; it was that I *couldn't.*

I still had just one ear and was deaf on one side. I still shrank back in social situations. I didn't know what was going to happen with my band, which was the only support structure I knew.

Now what?

The neighborhood around my new apartment had quite a few shops and galleries specializing in art nouveau antiques. I had liked colorful Tiffany glass lamps since I was a kid. My parents used to buy old furniture at junk shops and refinish it. Some of it they kept, some of it they sold. And over our dining room table at home hung a glass lamp. It was just an ice cream parlor lamp, but people called any colored glass lamps Tiffany lamps back then. When I moved up near the Metropolitan I spent time enjoying the museum's collection of real Tiffany glass.

One day as I walked past the Macklowe Gallery in my neighborhood, a Tiffany lamp in the window made me stop in my tracks. I still didn't have any furniture in my place beyond the bed and my vintage guitars hanging in the glass-fronted cases lining the wall of the music room. But I went into the gallery to see the lamp up close. The price tag said $70,000. I bought it on the spot and carried it the two blocks home. When I got home, I put it down in the middle of the empty living room, on the wall-to-wall carpeting, and plugged it in. I lay down on the floor and stared at it for hours as the sun set and the stained glass glowed brighter in the gathering darkness. Here I was in my own place with this beautiful lamp.

Life is grand.

I became intoxicated by the idea that I could buy whatever I wanted.

Maybe buying fancy things can make me happy.

I would stroll Madison Avenue, see a pair of shoes in a shop window, and ask, "How many colors do they come in? Just give me all of them." I was draping the scared little boy inside me in another image—projecting a big persona with a shell of fine clothes.

Once, I wanted to go in a jewelry store that had Rolex watches displayed in the window. At first, they wouldn't buzz me in the locked door. Then, after they finally did, they were rude and condescending. After looking around for a little while, I pointed to a watch and asked, "How much is this one?"

"Twenty thousand dollars," said the salesman, looking down his nose at me.

I pulled out my wallet—by this time we had that kind of cash in our personal accounts—and counted out that much in front of him. Then I said, "Guess, what? I'm not buying it. You shouldn't treat people like that."

36

Unmasked tanked in the States and we spent most of 1980 inactive. We didn't have a drummer anyway. The single "Shandi" was a hit abroad, however, and we booked a tour of Europe and Australia for the fall. But before we could play live, we needed a drummer. Auditioning people was very strange.

We didn't want big-name drummers. We wanted somebody to come out of nowhere. It wouldn't have made sense to have Anton Fig or some other known commodity dress up as a black-and-silver giraffe or whatever.

Bill placed a cryptic ad in some music magazines, and we also spread the word. Bill started to get tapes and photos and bios and lots of phone calls. He went through the materials, and we periodically invited groups of potential replacements he had filtered to audition with us. We decided we didn't want a drummer who played like Peter. The ones who made the best impression on us played what you might call "English." They played on the backbeat, and whether they were playing double bass drums or not, they revered the same bands we did. Peter had enough trouble keeping time on a single bass drum and snare, so the idea of him playing two bass drums was out of the question. It wouldn't have made sense in the context of what we were doing anyway. Using a double bass drum in rock came about as a way to emulate what John Bonham of Led Zeppelin managed to do with one bass drum. His foot was so fast that it took most drummers two kick drums and both feet to mimic it. We didn't set out to find someone with a double kit, but we also didn't want to impose boundaries or limitations on a new member. As long as we were getting somebody new, we figured we should be willing to move forward.

One guy who auditioned was a little stove repairman from Brooklyn named Paul Caravello. He was tiny, with a huge head of hair and no airs or attitude. The first thing he did was ask for our autographs. At first, I wasn't blown away by his playing, but everybody else in the room, including Vini Poncia and Bill Aucoin, thought he was great. We brought the guy back for a second time, and he turned out to have a good voice, with the same raspy quality Peter had. He was also a quick learner.

We had found our guy.

Paul wanted to change his name, and we wanted him to change it, too—we didn't need three Pauls in the band, since Ace also shared that name. His first suggestion was Rusty Blades, which we vetoed quickly. Thankfully, the name game was short-lived when his second suggestion was Eric Carr, a name that sidestepped any obvious cartoon rock star moniker.

He seemed like a good soul. Some of the other people who auditioned had acted like rock stars, thinking they would gain points for that. Eric was sweet. He eventually proved to be tortured in his own way, but he certainly was a much-needed breath of fresh air in the wake of Peter's departure.

He had told us stories about repairing stoves—going to an

apartment and opening up stoves to find all kinds of bugs and beasts crawling around inside—and we wanted him to know he wouldn't be a second-class citizen in KISS. So once we told him he was in the band, we did two things to welcome him. First, we bought him a silver Porsche 924. I somehow became the guy who was supposed to watch over him and groom him, teach him. He approached me after he got the car. "Can I have it painted camouflage?"

"Absolutely not," I said. I didn't think he should take a sleek imported sports car and turn it into a circus mobile.

Then I took him shopping at a place called the French Jean Store. They sold—surprise—French jeans. I helped him pick out a new wardrobe—he'd need it since we were leaving for a European tour soon.

It took some time to figure out a character for Eric. Heaven forbid we put him in a character people already knew. That seemed too obvious to us, and maybe sacrilegious. Originally, he was going to be the Hawk. We had a costume built with a protruding chest and feathers all over it. He painted a beak on his nose. But he looked like the mascot for a high school football team—all that was missing were the big foam chicken feet. It was horrible. Fortunately, he came up with the idea of the Fox. He wore the same size boots as Peter, so we used existing boots and had the platforms built up even more. The boots ended up being like stilts, and he still looked tiny next to us.

Eric got thrown in at the deep end of the pool. We had become comfortable dealing with the world we operated in—basic stuff, like handling women's sexual advances and the media, or acting properly in a restaurant. Eric had to learn on the fly.

The second night of the tour, on August 31, 1980, in Genoa, Italy, we heard a commotion outside the locker room that was serving as our dressing room at the sports arena where we were playing. Then we started to hear people chanting, "KISS Fascista! KISS

Fascista!" Security started screaming, "Lock the doors!" Baseball bats started pounding on the door and smashing things outside. They wanted to kill us. It was bad enough that we were going to get killed for playing music, but worse still that I was apparently going to die in platform boots and makeup.

We consciously avoided espousing any political views, and yet to them we represented all the evils of American capitalism. That was the first tour where people asked us about politics—Europeans' way of thinking seemed more tied into politics and world events. Gene took any opportunity to be seen or heard; his Achilles heel is his need for attention, regardless of the source of the attention. I had no intention of making political statements. At the end of the day "Love Gun" wasn't about guns—I was just singing about my dick.

We had fun messing with Eric on that tour. It was like having a little brother around. One nickname we came up with for him was Bud Carr Rooney—because we joked that he looked like the love child of Buddy Hackett and Mickey Rooney.

The first night we were in Paris, Eric wore a brand-new white suit to dinner. His first. Not ten minutes into the night, he spilled a huge glass of red wine all over it. At times like that he would close his eyes and mutter, "What a schmuck." He sent that suit to the cleaners so many times—hoping against hope the stain would come out—that when it finally came back white, the sleeves fell off when he put the jacket on.

He was impressed that we could get by on a little pidgin version of the local language on that first tour across Europe. In Paris, he decided he wanted to try. "How do you ask for butter in French?"

"Well," I said, "*s'il vous plait* is 'please,' and what you want is *fapouge*." The French word for butter is *beurre*. I made up the word *fapouge*.

The waitress came to our table, and Eric said, "*Fapouge s'il vous plait.*"

She looked at him and said, "*Fapouge?*" He did this thing we used to call "the Ronald Reagan," where his head would start to shake from side to side when he got nervous. He did that now. "*Fapouge,*" he repeated, with his head shaking.

Me and Ace in Australia, 1980 . . .
I like remembering the great times.

Another night he really liked the food we'd had, which had come on a sizzling hotplate. Eric was still like Oliver Twist in those days: "Please, sir, may I have some more?" The waiter brought another searing hotplate, carrying it with tongs, and Eric reached up and grabbed it with his bare hands. You could hear the *sssssss* sound as it singed his fingers. He just closed his eyes and said, "What a schmuck."

Another night in France a guy at a nightclub started hitting on Eric, making him uncomfortable. He went over to Ace and said, "That guy over there is trying to come on to me." Ace, in his inimitable logic, said, "Let's make out so he thinks we're together. Then he'll leave you alone."

And the kissing began.

Armed military personnel guarded the airports in some parts of Europe back then. One time, at an airport where security had AK-47s, Eric got pulled aside. He was wearing a camouflage jumpsuit and bullet belts. They took him through a door and out of our sight. But he was back surprisingly quickly. "What happened?" we asked.

"I told them I'm a musician," he said. "So they took me to another room and had me play a piano." Once he played a little piano, they let him go.

Though Eric was two years older than me, he seemed like a kid.

His life experience had been limited, and he was naive and gullible. One night in England he took a female journalist to his room from the hotel bar where we were all hanging out. The next day we asked him what happened. "Well, we talked and then she wanted to take some pictures of me without my clothes on," he said.

"What!?" I said.

"She said she wouldn't print them."

"Are you crazy?"

"Oh, shit, did I do something wrong?"

"You let her take pictures!"

"But she said they were just for herself . . ."

Sure enough, when the next week's issue of the journalist's magazine came out, there was Eric looking like an idiot, naked in the bathtub with his huge head of hair and a glass of Champagne.

He closed his eyes. "What a schmuck."

37

The atmosphere in the band was much better without Peter's constant negativity to contend with. It was eye-opening what a difference it made—we had alleviated such a huge problem and so much uncertainty, strife, and hostility. It was as if the sun had suddenly come out—and that was only Peter. Ace was still in a downward spiral, but at least now we had half as much turmoil.

Ace had lost an ally, but he hadn't lost a buddy. Whatever relationship he'd had with Peter was strictly mercenary. Ace was smart, and he manipulated Peter to help him vote for things he wanted. If he missed Peter at all, it was on that level, not as a friend. Now it was me and Gene and this other guy who didn't have the same seniority or power as a full member. Ace was the odd man out as far as the decision-making process. I knew it bothered him, but it wasn't an immediate issue while we were on tour.

When we arrived in Australia for the first time, in November 1980, it quickly became clear that things were going to be crazy.

Melbourne, Australia, in 1980, with 50,000 of my closest friends.

We'd been told KISS was massive there, but you never know what to expect. You can only comprehend things you've already experienced; Australia was like nothing we'd ever experienced. Huge here meant not being able to leave the hotel. It meant taking a helicopter from the hotel to the stadium we were playing.

The phenomenon we witnessed became known there as "KISS-teria."

We had an entire floor of the hotel, with one suite devoted to our own Australian public relations staff. And no wonder, since we were on the front page of the newspapers every day accompanied by headlines like, "KISS in Midnight Cruise on Sydney Harbor." We had to keep the curtains drawn in our rooms. The place was crawling with bodyguards, and there was a constant drone of screaming outside. "You're not going anywhere," we were told.

Thankfully, Australia had its own *Penthouse* magazine, and a number of *Penthouse* Pets came over to the hotel to keep us company. Paparazzi camped in front of the hotel, and whenever we went anywhere, we had to hide on the floors of vans. Every single night, the promoters threw parties, which were packed with models and actresses. Some parties were women-only. We would show up at a club or ballroom that had been taken over, and the place would be filled with beautiful women. Australia was one giant Chicken Coop.

Eric, however, would often leave the parties and go out and befriend some waif he met on the street. He identified with the fans. Maybe he felt more like them than like one of us at that point. He sometimes brought girls to his room who had been camping outside trying to catch a glimpse of the band. For his comfort, he chose women like that over models and *Penthouse* Pets. Issues shape personalities.

The first hints of Eric's troubles started to come out, too. One day he rented a car and driver to spend a day in the countryside with a girl he'd met. He was so nervous, he told us, that he got awful gas and had to stop the car every ten minutes to go to the bathroom. He was depressed afterwards about what an idiot he felt like. He also went on about how he was losing his hair. His hair was so big that when he moved forward, it moved backwards—it was always moving in the opposite direction from the rest of him. And yet he constantly wanted me to look at his head. "Look, is it thinning here?"

Left to right: *Me, Bill Aucoin, and Elton John, out to dinner in Australia, 1980.*

And strangest of all, Eric struggled with the idea that he wasn't the original drummer of the band. I didn't understand it. I mean, of course he wasn't the original drummer. He was the second drummer. So what? There was no talking him out of his funk when he started obsessing over the fact that he would never be the first drummer.

In Australia I began to seriously question Bill Aucoin. His cocaine use had become more extreme, and since splitting up with Sean Delaney, his general behavior had become reckless, too. One morning I went to his room and found a boy in his early teens eating a bowl of cereal in Bill's bed. Another morning I found a different boy there.

Bill was out of control.

When we got back to the States, a boy who had won a contest had been flown in to meet us, along with a photographer from the magazine that had sponsored the contest. Bill was clearly hitting on the kid. The next day I said, "Bill, tell me you didn't."

"Yes I did. And the photographer."

Bill had crossed a line into an area I saw as criminal and immoral. I was no longer laughing.

Back home, the band had more time off. Even though we hadn't toured in the States for a full year, we figured we'd make another record first. We decided to work with Bob Ezrin again, the producer who had served as our captain and Svengali for *Destroyer*.

That was it! We would make another *Destroyer*.

The problem was that the stuff we were writing was no better than the songs on *Unmasked*. In fact, it was probably worse. We'd lost the plot. My songs were nothing to write home about; Gene's were no better. But then Bob entered the picture, and he floated the idea of a concept album—which really came out of left field. Gene quickly bought into it and came up with a generic, vague, typical concept: it was about a kid who was the chosen one. Bill got behind the idea, too. It would be our attempt to woo the critics.

"Let's put out an album that makes a statement," he told us. "One that shows everybody how talented you are." Trying to show people how talented and bright you are is the best way to make an idiot of yourself, and we ended up doing that with flying colors.

Looking back, we wanted peer acceptance and critical approval and lost sight of the fact that none of that had mattered to us in the beginning. The people who so vehemently disliked us were more

KISSTeria in full swing, on a private yacht with the Penthouse Pet of the Year. Australia, 1980.

tied up in their own issues than in what kind of music we were making. The fact that the dislike and distaste was so pronounced, almost obsessive, throughout our career should have been a clue that it had little to do with us. If people wanted to waste their time wringing their hands over how much they hated my band, that was pathetic; what may have been more pathetic was that we tried to overcome it by pandering to those people. But we were clueless and decided to try to elevate ourselves, to separate ourselves from where we had started. We assured ourselves that we would impress a lot of people. Finally, we would make an album that garnered critical acclaim—our *masterpiece*.

Gene, Eric, and I moved to Toronto in March 1981 to work on the album—Bob wanted to do it on his home turf. We didn't know at first, but his drug habit was now dictating his choice of location.

Ace didn't even travel to Toronto. It's all well and good for him to say in retrospect that he didn't like the musical direction the band was taking, but the fact is that even if we had been doing exactly what he wanted to do musically, he was too wasted to play. He didn't need an excuse to drink; he was a drunk. He was bombed all the time.

As work trudged on, Bob's substance problems became so acute he didn't show up, either. I had always been aware that Bob had a drug problem, but he had managed it in the past. Now his 24/7 cocaine use had taken on epic proportions. The captain abandoned ship. He was supposed to serve as the visionary behind the concept, and all we were getting were notes sent to the studio by messenger after Bob listened to cassettes we sent to his home.

Eventually we got so far behind in the production that Gene and I started working simultaneously in two separate studios, both of us sending tapes to Bob and getting back notes, doing the whole thing piecemeal. We had virtually no idea what the other guy was doing, and we couldn't reach Bob on the phone. His wife relayed messages because Bob was too fucked up to get to the phone.

Poor Eric—this wonderful guy who thought he had joined a hard rock band—was suddenly playing gibberish with a fox costume in his closet. He was completely thrown by this band that had lost its way and was stumbling along a ridiculous path. He wasn't comfortable making explicit objections at that point, but he did express bewilderment and discomfort. "You know, this isn't what I was expecting," he said. But he was never in a position to draw a line in the sand. He must have had serious doubts, though. He kept playing us a new band called Metallica—he was into stuff like speed metal and thrash way before we were.

The songs we recorded had no teeth. We were gumming the music at that point. We had forsaken everything we loved and embraced. We were intoxicated with fame and success. We were no longer the band everyone loved—and clearly we didn't love that band anymore either. How else to explain the way we veered away from what we did? For a band like ours to be doing something like *Music from "The Elder"* truly reeked of the little Stonehenge coming down on the stage during *This Is Spinal Tap*. If only we had realized.

For the cover, we intended to use my hand instead of a model's hand. But the day before the photo shoot, I slammed my finger in a window and had a purple nail that had to be retouched. This should have been an omen.

When we were finally finished in September, we went back to New York. If I played the tape for anyone at my apartment, I insisted on silence—as if I was exposing them to brilliance—and they had to sit through the entire thing straight through. We also had a listening party for the record company, with the same insistence that they listen to it in a manner befitting its artistic merit. The reaction at the end of the listening session was like the audience when they heard "Springtime for Hitler" from *The Producers*. Mouths wide open. I already knew somehow that it wasn't because the sheer greatness of the album had taken their breath away.

The record label hated the album. It was originally sequenced in a way that vaguely told a story. But that meant you didn't get to anything that resembled a rock song for quite a while. So they made us change the order. As if it wasn't already bad enough, they basically did the equivalent of tearing all the pages out of a book, throwing them up in the air, and then binding them together again.

In preparation for the launch, we also changed our image to accommodate how we now chose to look offstage. We didn't want to have long hair anymore. I had razor-cut hair, a bandana around my head—I still needed to hide my ear—and a necklace that looked like I got it from Chiquita Banana. Gene had a little braided ponytail hanging over his shoulder. Ace was still in the photos even though he had in essence left the band. We were delusional. We had drunk the poisoned Kool-Aid, so to speak.

I went into a record store down on 8th Street in the Village the day the album came out in November 1981 and saw a poster for it. I had a panic attack. I looked at the poster and it hit me like a sledgehammer.

What the hell have we done?

38.

For the first time in the history of the band, we didn't do a tour following the release of the album. In fact, two full years would pass between the end of the 1980 Australian tour and the next time we played live, in late December 1982.

I grew a beard.

I spent the bulk of my time one-on-one with a number of women, either ones I knew around New York or ones I flew in from elsewhere. I didn't attend big social events; I just laid low in a series of relationships with multiple women.

A swimsuit model I was seeing at the time said to me, "You'll never be happy because you're so tough on people and so judgmental."

She was right—at the time I didn't realize just how right. That was how I functioned, how I controlled the world around me. Everything had its place. I controlled my environment, but I didn't really live in it. Now, I'm not crying in my beer, because hanging around with beautiful women was like spending my days and nights at Disneyland, no matter what my motivation was. And it certainly beat the alternative way people dealt with similar feelings of emptiness—like filling it with drugs, surrounding themselves with people who constantly told them how great they were, or winding up blue on the bathroom floor.

The allure of buying fancy things was wearing off. I realized while the band was idle that it wasn't about what I could buy with

the money. It was about what I didn't have to do—simply put, money gives you the ability to stop worrying about money. It provides a level of freedom, but it doesn't change you. At the end of the day you're still the same good guy or the same prick you've always been. Or in my case, the same scared little kid.

With my dad at the Record Plant studio in 1980. With a long time off from touring, I decided to go incognito.

One afternoon I asked Kenny Ortega, the choreographer we had used on the *Dynasty* tour, to drop by. I handed him a suitcase and told him, "Take whatever you want."

I sold my collection of vintage guitars—the entire batch—to a dealer for $50,000. They no longer meant anything to me. Luckily, my life turned out alright, and the decision doesn't haunt me— because that collection is worth about $2.5 million today.

The racks of clothing and other possessions had become oppressive. Whatever I thought they were satiating, they were not. Ultimately, the stuff became not just clutter, but a looming reminder of my inability to make things right.

But I needed to try something else to address the fundamental unease inside me. Then, during a visit to my therapist, Dr. Hilsen, he said, "I found a guy for you."

"What do you mean?"

"I found somebody who I think can do reconstructive surgery on your ear."

He had read an article about a Dr. Frederic Rueckert and then tracked him down. The surgeon worked at a hospital in Hanover, New Hampshire, home of Dartmouth University.

I was excited. I wanted two ears.

I flew up to Hanover to meet the doctor. Fred Rueckert was a warm, grandfatherly figure who exuded confidence and security, reinforced by all his experience. We hit it off immediately. He explained that the first part of the process would be to remove pieces of cartilage from my rib cage and carve them into the framework of an ear. Then the frame would be implanted and covered with a series of skin grafts. All in all, it would involve about five surgical procedures, taking skin and additional cartilage from my good left ear.

Nobody my age had ever had the surgery. They typically used this new technique on kids. But given the fact that I had such a tangible symbol and cause of so much pain, why wouldn't I try to change it? Suddenly, I had hope. I hoped having two ears and erasing that constant reminder of my childhood would help me feel more complete on the inside. I wanted to move on.

The first thing they needed to do was cut out the sections of my rib. Before the surgery Dr. Rueckert warned me, "You're going to be a little sore."

You sometimes hear people talk about being aware of things even in a state of anesthesia. I guess it can be a terrifying experience. I was aware of everything during my first surgery—as they cut my chest open, I could hear what they were saying even though I couldn't open my eyes. I heard the doctor take out the piece of cartilage, heard him carving it, and then heard him say, "That looks good." A nurse agreed with him.

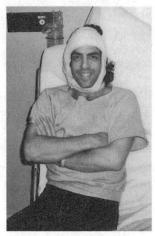

First ear surgery in 1982 at Hitchcock Clinic in Hanover, New Hampshire.

The next day I had searing pain if I tried to move even slightly. "A little sore"? It felt as if somebody had put a sword through me.

The healing process after the skin grafts didn't go so well. Circulation didn't develop in certain areas, and I had to stay in the hospital for a few weeks as they monitored and worked to correct the problems to avoid the skin dying from lack of blood supply. My parents and niece were there with me in New Hampshire. Gene came, too. He was going through a period of being very afraid to fly, so I gave him a lot of credit for visiting and really appreciated it.

After the first procedure, although it wasn't standard, I opted for a local anesthetic for the rest of the surgeries. So after each subsequent revision surgery, I could walk from the hospital to the Hanover Inn—a cozy old hotel right on the green in the middle of town. I took painkillers and watched TV and slept. It was all part of something very personal, so being alone felt good to me. I enjoyed doing it on my own—and anyway, I didn't know any other way to do it. There was nobody I would have felt comfortable asking, "Will you go with me?"

By the time I left Hanover and went back to New York, I was still in bandages and dressings that needed to be changed daily. Normally, a doctor would handle that, but I ended up doing it myself—and I actually enjoyed it because it gave me a sense of participating in the process. It was hard to look at, but it connected me that much more to my own development and—I hoped—improvement. I also was sleeping with protective plastic over my ear that was held in place by a thick leather head-and-chin strap. I had to wear it for months after each surgery.

I always tried to express to Dr. Rueckert the life-changing role he was playing for me. It seemed to catch him off-guard when I brought it up. He told me that for the most part, he heard from patients only when things didn't go well. He was a humble man who helped countless children avoid the experience and turmoil and endlessly compounded problems I faced as a kid. He helped give me a new lease on life; I gave him a Rolex watch when he retired. I could never figure out a way to truly show him how much he meant to me.

Finally healed, I cut my hair short and started hanging out at an Upper West Side watering hole called Café Central. I decided to take a break from spending time in music circles. Café Central was more of an actors' hangout, a bar with tables, and people spent entire nights table-hopping. Regulars included Christopher Reeves, Peter Weller, Raul Julia, and Al Pacino, and Bruce Willis was a bartender for a time.

If musicians bored me with talk of gear and guitars, I soon found out that most of the actors I met wanted to talk about only themselves. They seemed to endure listening to their peers only so they would get a turn to talk—about themselves. Still, I welcomed the change of scenery for a while. I started going to the theater almost every week. I had a ticket broker and I'd call and say, "What have you got for tonight?"

I found it interesting that so many people in New York—myself included—talked about the culture of the city but never actually experienced it. Here was an opportunity to do it. I went to see whatever was playing—from the big-production British musicals like *Miss Saigon*, *Cats*, and *Les Miserables*, to more serious plays like *American Buffalo*, *Waiting for Godot*, and *Death of a Salesman*.

I took some acting classes, too. I sat in on Lee Strasberg's classes once or twice. At one class, a woman got up to do a scene in front of him and broke down crying before she started the scene.

This is nuts.

I thought you acted from joy, not torment.

Strasberg's wife Anna took a liking to me, and I went to a few parties at their house. I came away with the impression that none of these people wanted to be happy because they feared it might compromise their acting ability. They had to be brooding and miserable, and hence everyone in the room seemed to be under his or her own personal dark cloud. I felt as if I should have taken an umbrella.

This is not for me.

One night when I was out at a restaurant having dinner, the actress Donna Dixon and a model friend of hers walked in. Donna was staggeringly attractive—so much so that it was intimidating. So much so that I went for the woman who turned out to be her roommate. Donna was just too beautiful. But after I had seen her friend a few times, I admitted to myself and to her that I was actually interested in Donna. And somehow it worked—I started seeing Donna. I loved having such a gorgeous girlfriend. As superficial as it may have been, she was beautiful in a way that made me happy.

With hindsight, I can see that dating her was clearly another example of my trying to eradicate my own imperfections by being with someone seemingly perfect. Anyone who could date a woman who looked like that *must* be special. But at the time, I was very taken with her. When she entered a room, the room came to a halt. And I was with her!

Donna had landed her first big role, starring opposite Tom Hanks in the TV show *Bosom Buddies*. She shuttled back and forth to L.A. for that, and we continued to see each other.

During this time, Ace announced he wanted to quit the band. I drove up to his house in Westchester and spent the day with him.

We went to the mall, drove around, talked. "Don't leave," I told him. "Stay in the band."

"I need to go," he said.

I found out years later that he didn't remember I had been there. Many pages of Ace's past are now blank. That's how blasted he was. He was living in a constant state of blackout.

Bill worked out a deal to let Ace leave but have him make promotional appearances for the next album, which we planned to make in Los Angeles. In some ways I was glad Ace finally left—we couldn't go anywhere with him the way he was. Everybody around the band seemed to be suffering from the same disease. It's one thing to be useless; it's another to be a detriment.

Bill had gone from sharing office space with Howard Marks Advertising to first having one floor and then two floors of a building on Madison Avenue plus a Los Angeles office. He had people developing film projects and dozens more people on the payroll—I had no idea what they all did. He had a huge luxury apartment near St. Patrick's Cathedral that he'd spent a fortune decorating but that he rented rather than owned.

He was now making such bad decisions that I often followed up on meetings he had on our behalf. "What did he agree to?" I'd ask. Then I'd have to nullify things.

It was clearly the drugs. Eventually his drug habit became so all-encompassing that he could no longer go to the office. He was home freebasing, holed up with a pipe.

When things change incrementally, sometimes you don't realize how far you've gotten from where you started. That's basically what happened with Bill. When I looked at him, he still appeared to be the person I knew; when he was lucid, he still sounded like the person I knew. But he wasn't that person anymore, even if it took me a long time to recognize that fact. Bill had gone from being our visionary mentor, our manager, a father figure, a fifth member of the band, to being a delusional, drugged-out whack job. It was so bad that heart-to-heart talks I had with him went nowhere except to confirm the worst.

"What are you doing?" I'd ask him. "You're spending all your money."

"I don't care," he'd reply. "I made it once and I can make it again."

It was a reckless attitude. And it mirrored Ace and Peter—they all took things for granted.

Watching all these guys go down the tubes with drugs or booze, seeing their demise, I realized that it's all a question of what people do with the freedom that success affords. There were times when Gene wanted to have company in his stance of "*We* don't drink or take drugs." But that wasn't my stance. I had nothing against drinking, and I had smoked pot when I was younger. But when I saw what the Casablanca office turned into, what Bill turned into, or what Ace and Peter turned into, I didn't think that transformation was just the luck of the draw. They made their own destinies.

Finally, after Gene, Eric Carr, and I convened in L.A. to start work on the next album, *Creatures of the Night*, Gene and I discussed parting ways with Bill. It was sad and scary to contemplate letting go of someone who had been so instrumental in our careers. It would be a monumental change. Not something to take lightly. We had worked with him for almost a decade.

Despite what was going wrong, all the good stuff during the formative years wouldn't have happened without Bill. He was instrumental in our development, and he was the glue that kept everybody together. He knew how to press the buttons in each member to keep all of us happy. Each of us felt like his favorite.

But we realized we had reached a point where rebuilding KISS was going to mean getting rid of everything we had known. We were already rid of two members, and we had experienced such waste and coddling that it had taken away our autonomy and independence—which is in essence what it's designed to do. Bill's system had catered to our needs but cut us off from reality. It was life in a bubble, and it was killing us.

I even suggested we take our makeup off, to make a complete break with the past. In the end, Gene didn't want to take off the makeup, but we did decide that Bill had to go.

We called him from L.A. "Bill, we're going to fly to New York to meet you."

I always believed you owed it to yourself and the other person to look that person in the eye at the end of a relationship, whether it was a business relationship or a romantic relationship.

When we arrived at his office, Bill said, "I know why you're here."

"It's time," we said.

He smiled wistfully. We shook hands, hugged, and walked out on a big chapter of our lives.

39.

As we prepared to make our next album, *Creatures of the Night*, not a lot of A-list producers were knocking at our door. In fact, people weren't even returning our phone calls.

Finally, in the summer of 1982, I scheduled a lunch in L.A., where we planned to record the album, with a guy named Michael James Jackson. We met at a restaurant called the Melting Pot, on the corner of La Cienega Boulevard and Melrose. Michael, it turned out, had no real experience with rock and roll bands, though he had just worked with Jesse Colin Young, the founder of the band the Youngbloods, who had some hits in the 1960s. When we started chatting, Michael said, "What you guys need to do is write some hit songs."

Gee, why didn't I think of that? Fucking brilliant.

But I liked him despite being momentarily thrown by that "insight." He was very introspective and intellectual, and we began to hit it off. Also, even though I wasn't sure what he had to offer musically, we needed *someone*. I knew that Gene and I weren't at a point where we could be productive together because neither of us wanted to compromise our respective musical ideas. We needed an intermediary in the studio, somebody to be the swing vote.

Gene and I never wrote songs together anymore. Michael brought up the idea of bringing in outside songwriters to work on the record with us. I suggested Bryan Adams, who had written a minor hit called "Let Me Take You Dancing" together with Jim Vallance. Even though his voice was sped up and sounded like a girl's on that track, I thought there was something there. When we flew him to L.A., though, Bryan ended up writing with Gene, and they came up with "War Machine."

With Ace gone, we put the word out that we were looking for a new guitar slinger. Among others, we auditioned Steve Farris of Mr. Mister, Robben Ford, who was a great blues player, and Steve Hunter. Richie Sambora, who was in a newly formed band called Bon Jovi, flew in from New Jersey to audition. He wasn't yet the consummate player he would become, and he didn't get the gig. It's funny, but years later I heard him say he hadn't really wanted the job because he wanted to be in something more blues-based. First of all, it's hard to imagine that he flew to California to audition for KISS just because he liked airplane food; also, Bon Jovi's done a lot of great things, but they don't sit next to Howlin' Wolf in my record collection.

Another person I spoke to was a really sweet young kid named Saul Hudson. He told me his mom had been a seamstress for David Bowie and that his friends called him "Slash." He was very well spoken and engaging, but he seemed really young. Finally I asked him how old he was. "I'll be seventeen next month," he said.

I had turned thirty earlier that year, and Gene was twice this kid's age. "You know," I said, "you sound like a great guy, but I think you're too young for this." I wished him well and always remembered him because he was so nice and unaffected.

In the end, a lot of different people played solos on *Creatures of the Night*. It was a way to try people out and to see who might fit the feel of a given track. Eddie Van Halen came to the studio one day knowing we were looking for a guitar player. He listened to some of the stuff we had, including a solo on the title track by Steve Farris. "Wow, why don't you get *that* guy?" asked Eddie. He was blown away. The fact was, we had rehearsed with Farris, but the fit hadn't been right.

Eddie was really unhappy at the time and called me at home a few times. He was pretty out of it, and he wanted to talk about the KISS solo albums. "Why did you do it?" he asked. "Why did you go off and do solo albums?" It was clear that this had something to do with his own band, which was in turmoil at the time, but he didn't say exactly what was happening. He seemed to be looking to me for answers, but I was never sure what the question was.

I wrote the songs "Creatures of the Night" and "Danger" with a guy named Adam Mitchell who had been in a Canadian band called the Paupers. Adam had also written with a guitar player named Vincent Cusano, and even though Adam didn't have a lot of nice things to say about Vinnie as a person, he said he was a very talented singer-songwriter and that his guitar playing might fit KISS. It was a scene that would play out often—people always talked about Vinnie's talent and ability, but they never had good things to say about him as a person. *Hmmm.*

The first time Vinnie came to the studio, he started doing a solo and got down on his knees. I thought it was one of the goofiest things I'd ever seen. You just didn't do that at an audition. He seemed wrong somehow—he was odd looking and shifty—but we were between a rock and a hard place, and Vinnie ended up playing on a lot of tracks for the album.

For us, *Creatures* was done with the shock and realization of how completely lost we had gotten. The album was a declaration of intent to get back on track. Eric was relieved, as this was what he had expected all along. He was definitely happier all through the recording process.

One afternoon a carload of little kids and what I presumed was one of their dads showed up at the studio, and Gene ushered them into the room where we recorded. They gathered around a microphone. They were there to sing background vocals on a song.

What the hell?

Gene, it turned out, had made a deal with a Hollywood producer—if the guy could send his kids and their friends to sing background vocals on a KISS song, Gene would get some brownie points for some acting work out of the guy.

Are you fucking kidding me?

I was furious. And not just because Gene hadn't asked in advance for my okay. He was whoring us out and compromising our album for his own benefit. It offended me that he tried to get acting roles in that way. I had been studying acting long before he had the idea to get into movies—in fact, he had told me he had no interest in acting. To me, the path was obvious—you studied acting and then auditioned for parts. That was the "right" way to go about it. Gene didn't see it that way. He just went out and brown-nosed his way in.

If you walk behind an elephant, you end up cleaning up the shit.

I spent my free time in L.A. with Donna Dixon. Part of the reason I invested so much in Donna was because she still managed to keep me at arm's length—no matter the closeness we had developed. That ignited my old compulsion to see the relationship as a challenge to overcome. Even though we were together, there was still something lacking—and I kept trying to get whatever that was. I was awed by her beauty and placed her on a pedestal, which quickly must become one of the most boring and unsexy places for a woman to be. My dad, though, would no doubt have approved.

Donna Dixon tells how her fear of bizarre rock star finally turned to love

BOSOM BUDDIES star Donna Dixon has overcome her fear of bizarre rock guitarist Paul Stanley of KISS — and now, she admits, she's crazy about him.

"He's a perfect person to be with, a gentleman, very handsome and very bright," the 24-year-old blonde says.

"He's the straightest person I've ever met, he's very, very dear — and yes I'm crazy about him!"

Donna's new love is famous as a weirdly painted face cavorting with equally weird musicians in KISS.

"Because of the makeup he wears on stage," she says, "people have all these wild fantasies about the way he really looks and how old he is.

"But I can tell you he's 30 years old, he doesn't smoke, he doesn't drink and he doesn't take any drugs.

"He's very handsome and, most important of all, he's very bright."

Donna, who won a talent contest over 20,000 women to get a co-starring part in the series, admits she was more than a little perturbed about Stanley at first.

"I've known Paul for almost three years," she says, "ever since I was modeling in New York. But when I first met him I have to admit I was more than a little afraid of him. I said to myself:

"'Oh no, this is a rock star, and he's probably crazy.'"

But Donna — who has been romantically linked with Fall Guy star Lee Majors and Happy Days' Scott Baio — says she soon found out that Stanley was not what he appeared to be.

"Paul is a real sweetheart — probably the sweetest man in the world," she says. "When I first got to see him perform, I couldn't believe it.

"I could see why people have all these wild fantasies about him. But they shouldn't judge him by the way he looks on stage.

"He is the perfect gentleman — he stands up when a lady walks into the room."

But Donna's heavy work schedule means she doesn't get to see Stanley as often.

"I only see him when he comes out to Los Angeles or I'm in New York," she says.

As well as spending long days on the set of Bosom Buddies, Donna has to give up her Tuesday and Thursday nights in acting classes, her Monday and Wednesday nights in dancing classes as well as her Saturdays in singing lessons.

She had no acting experience when she was picked for the role of Sonny.

She told the ABC series' producers, "I'll take acting lessons. I'll study night and day." And that's exactly what she has been doing.

"My life is so busy that at night all I can do is crawl into bed and memorize the next day's script," she laments.

Donna has made a TV movie, Margin For Murder and she is anxious to do more. "That's why I'm so serious about my acting studies," she says.

"When my chance in the movies comes, I don't want to blow it. But I want to be accepted because of my talent and not because of the way I look."

Donna Dixon and KISS rocker Paul Stanley without makeup. Donna says of Stanley, famous for his weirdly-painted face: "He's the straightest person I've ever met."

1982—life in the tabloids. You can keep it.

Once we finished recording *Creatures,* I spent much of the rest of the year going back and forth between L.A. and New York to see Donna. She came to New York a lot, too, and lived out of my apartment. After her TV show *Bosom Buddies* got canceled, she auditioned for a movie called *Doctor Detroit.* She told me after the audition that she thought Dan Ackroyd, the star of the film, was a genius. I thought that assessment was a stretch.

Donna was looking for a new financial advisor, so I introduced her to Howard Marks. Howard had a potbelly and always wore his pants below his stomach, using suspenders to hold up his trousers. Not uncharacteristically, the day we went to see him, he'd probably had a few stiff drinks beforehand. He was eating his lunch at his desk when we arrived. He gave Donna a big talk about saving for the future and how important financial planning was and, after this long dissertation, he stood up and started to walk over to a side table in the corner of his office with the remains of his lunch and his dirty napkins on a lunch tray. As he got up—it was as if it was happening in slow motion—I could see his suspenders dangling down. He must have taken them off his shoulders while sitting at his desk.

As he started to cross the room, his pants began to shimmy downward until they dropped to the floor.

Howard looked down, threw his tray in the air, reached for his pants, and screeched, "Oh, my God!"

"Is this normal?" Donna asked me.

She landed the role in *Doctor Detroit,* and I visited her on the set in Chicago—and gave her a diamond ring. I didn't call it an engagement ring. The relationship was stagnating somewhat; something was lacking for both of us. But I didn't want to lose her, and I didn't want to be left.

Sometimes, Donna would drop out of sight, and I wouldn't hear from her for a few days. She was living out of my place when she was in New York, and just before Christmas I found a new fur coat in the closet. She said she'd taken it from the wardrobe department of something she was working on. It wasn't too long before she blindsided me by suddenly talking about having never been on her own and needing space. I told her that I didn't want to be just another guy dating her and didn't want to share her. Although there were more unanswered questions now and more distance between us, we dropped the subject and didn't bring it up again for a while.

Then I saw among her things a little T-shirt with "Martha's Vineyard" on the front of it. Martha's Vineyard? When had she gone to Martha's Vineyard? She would explain her disappearances away—kind of. I didn't ask too many questions, either, because I wasn't sure I wanted to know the truth. And anyway, when someone was inconsiderate or dishonest, it reinforced what I thought of myself.

This is what I deserve.

If only I can get her to like me . . .

40.

KISS shot a video for "I Love It Loud" with Ace. Then he went with us to Europe for some lip-synced promotional appearances at the time of the release of *Creatures of the Night*. He was very fragile, and in Europe he said to me, "I'm on the verge of a nervous breakdown. I can't do this anymore."

When we flew back to the States, that was it. Ace was gone for good.

Ace, Peter, Bill Aucoin—all gone. People were dropping like flies all around us. Neil Bogart had died of cancer while we were making *Creatures;* even though he wasn't involved with the record company anymore, his death severed another tie to our past. Richard Monier, a recent tour manager and one of my closest friends, was the first person I knew to die of AIDS—that same year. And Wally Meyrowitz, one of our booking agents in New York—another buddy and confidant—died from a combination of booze and barbiturates.

Where did everybody go?

Gene seemed fixated on Hollywood and spent as little time as possible on things related to the band. In his inimitable dismissive self-serving style, Gene liked to say, "Well, Paul only wants to be a rock star. I want so much more in life."

I didn't understand why everybody was jumping ship. We were still KISS. And I still looked at the band as my life raft.

WHERE DID EVERYBODY GO?

We had a tour scheduled to start on December 27, 1982, and we didn't have a permanent replacement for Ace yet. I'd felt from the get-go that Vinnie wouldn't work in the band. And in the interim, some nasty rumors had spread about him stealing equipment from the rehearsal studio. But nobody else was on the horizon. When the decision was made to bring him in, I said to Gene, "I just want to go on record saying that this is a bad move."

With the *Creatures* tour coming on the heels of several financial disasters, we'd had to tighten our belts, so Vinnie didn't get a Porsche.

Vinnie wanted to change his name to Mick Fury when he got the gig. Why did everybody come up with cartoon names? I just looked at him like, *Are you serious?* We settled on Vinnie Vincent. After playing around with ideas for his makeup, I designed the Egyptian ankh image.

As far as his knowledge of and understanding of the guitar, Vinnie was terrific. I'd written with him and heard him play and sing, and knew his talent. The problem was that he had no sense of what to play or when, and he had no ability to self-edit. His playing was like puking—it just came splattering out. He wanted to show how fast he could play, how many notes he could play—he didn't think things out. This became more problematic when the tour started.

Onstage, Vinnie was hell-bent on using every solo as an opportunity to showcase himself. But it doesn't work like that. It's all about context. Vinnie never seemed to grasp that. He was intensely jealous of guys like Randy Rhoads and Jake E. Lee because he thought he was as good as them. He wanted his "just due," and his solo spot in the middle of the show became ungodly long. We used to call it the high point of the show—because everybody in the audience left to go get high.

Not that many people saw his wannabe guitar heroics—the *Creatures* tour did horrendously in most markets. Before we went onstage, we'd hear "You wanted the best, you got the best, the hottest band in the land . . ." and we'd walk out to find nobody was there. Sometimes there would be only a thousand people in an arena that could hold eighteen thousand.

We had packed the same venues a few years before, but now, if I threw my guitar pick too far, it sailed over people's heads and landed on the floor. We'd pull into arenas that looked as if somebody had forgotten to turn off the parking lot lights after an event was long over. And then we'd get inside and hear the echo from the main hall and know for sure it was empty.

We left blood, as they say in the business. It was a death march for us and for the concert promoters.

At first, the instinct was to blame other people. *Oh, it's the promoter's fault.* But if people want to see you, it doesn't take an incentive to get them to a show. And if they don't want to see you, the promoter can't make them buy a ticket at knifepoint. We had to face the fact that people didn't come because they didn't want to.

Obviously, we had to pay penance for *Unmasked* and *The Elder.* We got back on track with *Creatures,* but fans were not that forgiving. It was going to take years to win back our fans and make new fans. We had betrayed them. We had betrayed ourselves, too, and we weren't going to be easily forgiven.

It's shocking in hindsight what we had done. And we spent years making up for it. The people who turned off to us weren't going to come back just because we said we were sorry. We had to prove it, and that took a lot of time. *Creatures* alone was not enough.

But nothing can prepare you for the shock of vast empty spaces. It was unfathomable that from one tour to the next, the audience just disappeared. The bottom had fallen out.

I loved the position that I had—I loved the stature of the band and how I was perceived. And losing that was horrible. *Horrible.*

I dealt with the depression by sleeping. It was my way of checking out. I was so depressed that I couldn't keep my eyes open anywhere. It got so bad that I fell asleep in the dressing room before shows. Sometimes, I dozed off before I did my makeup; sometimes I dozed off in my makeup. The crew had a hard time waking me up.

I still looked to Donna for a sense of calm and security. I could spend hours talking to her on the phone every day. She was gearing up for the release of *Doctor Detroit*. She told me once again that she needed space. I told her I still wasn't prepared to be one of several people she was dating, and that if she really wanted to break up, she had to face me in person. I bought her an airline ticket to our next tour stop. She flew in. And it was over.

My depression deepened.

I don't know whether the tour situation or the overall band crisis affected Gene—he wasn't fully vested in the band at that point. After all, he had brought in a carload of kiddies to sing on the album and was clearly looking elsewhere. He's never been one to verbalize his feelings, so it wasn't something we talked about, even though we were both certainly aware of what was happening.

Eric, for his part, didn't understand the financial side—he wasn't aware of how the disastrous turnouts related to our budgeting. He just loved being in the band and loved playing the material from the new album.

A few months after my all-or-nothing ultimatum to Donna, I decided it was just too hard—nothing and no one had filled the void. Anything I got from her was better than nothing. I took a deep breath and called her. She seemed stunned. I told her how I felt, and we started speaking frequently on the phone again. Talk of missing each other wasn't uncommon. We even got together when KISS played a show in L.A.

One morning just before we left for South America for the last leg of the tour, I glanced at a copy of the newspaper and a small article caught my eye. *The actress Donna Dixon has married her Doctor Detroit co-star Dan Ackroyd, newly discovered paperwork shows. The marriage license came to light in Martha's Vineyard.*

What? Martha's Vineyard?

It turned out they had already been married for three months. I was stunned to realize that during the time that we had been talking again, she had been on the verge of getting married, and then in fact had gotten married.

Suddenly I felt like I was underwater. I could barely move.

I called her. "You were married when we were talking?"

She said something about how she hoped I would find what she had found. No explanation, no apology.

I hung up.

From then on, it was a struggle to do anything. Depression held me like a vise. I had to push myself every day: *Get your ass out of bed.*

Everything around me was caving in.

Just keep moving. Otherwise, you drown.

The press seemed to take delight in seeing KISS implode. After I struggled out of bed one day to get to an interview, the reporter asked me, "How does it feel to be on the *Titanic?*" Writers looked at us as a commodity and forgot that we were people. Another interviewer asked, "How does it feel to be dying?" They were so hateful. Their coldness and perverse joy was not lost on me. Still, I realized something when fielding mean-spirited questions like that, day after day.

Nobody is going to tell me when this is over.

Sure, everything around me had gone wrong. But what about me? What about my survival? That was up to me.

How does it feel to be dying?

Those pricks on the phone were not going to decide whether I got the thumbs up or thumbs down in the arena.

KISS was *everything* to me.

And right then I swore I would do whatever it took to keep my life raft afloat.

KISS will never die.

Part IV

Under the gun

41.

In June 1983 we flew to Brazil and played to 180,000 screaming fans in Maracanã Stadium in Rio. It was the biggest audience we had ever performed in front of. Taking the stage in the soccer stadiums of South America, I realized the stadiums we think of as big in the States were miniscule by comparison. Tiny. When you walk into a stadium like Maracanã, you feel like you're in the bottom of an oil drum.

Another difference is the security. During the afternoon, when we were checking things out, armed militia milled around with dogs.

There's no way to describe the amount of energy that a crowd that big puts out. And all the energy was directed at us up on the stage. You might say the air was electric or that there was a sense of anticipation, hysteria—call it what you will. But when it's all directed at you, it's like a huge wave that can consume you. The amount of power pushing at you is incredible. It can almost take you off your feet.

And yet, as exhilarating as it was to play those venues, the writing was on the wall. It was only a matter of how the dominoes were going to fall, not whether they would fall. We could still play the biggest stadiums in South America, but we were in a very shaky position in North America. We knew we had to build KISS from the ground up, all over again.

Back in the States, I once again urged Gene to agree to do the most radical thing we could do: take off our makeup. Some people saw this as a bold move; I saw it as our *only* move. Our U.S. audience hadn't dwindled by chance. It had dwindled because what we were doing no longer rang true. People were tired of what KISS had become.

With the new characters, we were one step removed from Teenage Mutant Ninja Turtles. I mean, what the hell was Vinnie's ankh about? Rather than keeping the original personas and images alive, we had become a ridiculous menagerie. What was next? Turtle Boy?

As we began to record *Lick It Up,* we thought about getting a manager to replace Bill. Up to this point, Howard Marks had taken over the business aspects of Bill's job, and we were basically managing ourselves. So we went to see a famous manager in L.A. and told him that we had decided to take the makeup off. "Why don't you keep it on half your face?" he said.

On half *of my face?*

That was when we realized how out of touch and out of sync most people were with KISS. After all, *Creatures* was a good album. The problem was that people were listening with their eyes instead of their ears. If people didn't like what they saw, it was unlikely they were going to like what they heard.

Agreeing to take off the makeup was—understandably—much harder for Gene. It was easier for me to do than for the guy with a ponytail on top of his head spitting blood all over the stage. But when *Creatures* failed, common sense led us to the conclusion that we simply had no choice. Taking off the makeup gave us the best chance to continue.

Even so, Gene didn't agree to jump until we were at the edge of the cliff. It was a leap of faith that was necessary for our own survival. We were going to have to find out whether we were a good enough band to exist without the makeup. If what people always said about us was true—that we were a gimmick—then I felt it was time to call it a day because we didn't deserve to continue.

Was I nervous? Not really. I knew that what I did was from the heart, whether or not my face was white. It had become innate. I was going to continue to be exactly the same character.

When people gave us kudos or told us we had guts for doing it, I was the first to say that we didn't do it for anything other than our own survival—there was no alternative. I don't mind taking credit for things done in the spirit of risk-taking, but this wasn't one of those moments. It wasn't a brave or noble move because it wasn't done from a place of strength. We were backed into a corner.

I was also still reeling from finding out about Donna's marriage. I felt dazed and numb. I was seeing a psychiatrist at the time, and in the middle of a conversation one day he said, "The best thing to help you forget a woman is another woman." That was one of the most eye-opening things I ever heard during a therapy session. I was like, "What? That's not deep. Really?" I was looking for some Zen piece of advice, and this caught me totally off guard.

Well, okay, I guess I can go with that.

After that session I thought to myself that maybe one way to feel better was to write a song about feeling better. The best way to move forward might be to sing a song about moving forward. I read somewhere that when Beethoven wrote his second symphony in 1802, a piece that as a kid I'd found extremely uplifting, he was suicidal. Maybe I could write myself out of a funk, too.

Vinnie and I wrote the song "Lick It Up" in my place on 80th Street in the music room—with its now-empty lighted guitar cases. Before we wrote, we tried to figure out what sort of thing we were going to try to do, and the therapist's words rang in my ear. We quickly came up with the title "Lick It Up," which sounded great.

Life's a treat and it ain't a crime to be good to yourself.

It was a universal sentiment, and something that I still certainly believed, whether or not I was living it every minute. It sure felt better than singing a song about being sad. Plus, the act of writing a great song—regardless of its sentiment—made me feel good. That was part of seeing the light at the end of the tunnel. That was part of working my way out of the darkness.

Creating was a way I was able to reestablish my footing.

Other songs on *Lick It Up*—like "A Million to One"—hewed more closely to how I was feeling. I think we all like to believe we're irreplaceable in a relationship and that nobody will ever give the person we love what we did, and "A Million to One" came out of that sentiment. Of course, it was a bit unrealistic and self-serving, in addition to not being true.

Even though there was an excitement about taking off the makeup, it didn't mean our music had to change. We had been happy with the production on *Creatures* and felt confident working with Michael James Jackson again, continuing to build on our return to rock and roll.

As the album neared completion, I felt excited when I saw the proofs of the cover. There we were. It was a declaration of sorts, and for all we were leaving behind, it was really saying something. I thought we were making a statement about the band and about the validity and credibility of it in our own eyes—taking off the makeup said something about how much we valued the band. We could have just thrown in the towel and gone home. Instead, we were willing to shed our armor.

I also realized that as soon as the record came out, I would no longer have that separation to cushion the impact—positive and negative—of success. The person who was famous would be the same one as the guy walking down the street. But that could be fun, too.

I was going to be much more recognizable and visible, so in that sense it couldn't be bad—especially when it came to getting women. And anyway, I'd had years of adapting to fame, and all those years in makeup had provided a transition. So it wasn't going to be like diving into a pool of ice water.

Up to that point, MTV had always ignored us. We had filmed one of those "I want my MTV" promos, and they never aired it. The video we had shot for *Creatures*—"I Love It Loud"—didn't get played. They chose not to give us any exposure, even though we desperately needed it in the wake of *The Elder* debacle to show that we had recommitted ourselves to doing what KISS did best. We were considered uncool at a network whose taste was led by a bunch of college interns.

Suddenly, when we unmasked ourselves, all that changed.

MTV finally embraced us at some level. We came up with a made-for-MTV unmasking. If you think about it, it was really just the unmasking of me and Gene. The other two guys were pretty much unknown commodities—that's not meant to disparage Eric or Vinnie, but having played on an album that barely registered in the pop consciousness, they weren't much of a draw as far as unmasking went. To most people, KISS was still the Catman, the Spaceman, the Starchild, and the Demon. But the cat was already out of the bag, so to speak. As was the Spaceman. So in this case, to a certain extent, we sold a lot of sizzle without a very big steak.

Still, "KISS unmasking" made a great sound bite, and people bought into it. We managed to turn that into something of an event and get press out of it.

And it worked. I was convinced that *Lick It Up* wasn't as good as *Creatures of the Night,* but the album sold way, way better—probably four or five times as many albums sold in just the first few weeks after its release in September 1983. It wasn't the music the people hadn't liked. It was how the band had looked.

Once we took off the makeup, we no longer wore the platform boots onstage, and we adopted a more generic style: tight, colorful clothes, sexual and flamboyant. We slid into what was pretty much the common look at the time. I mean, Robert Plant had cut his hair and was wearing parachute pants for God's sake. Nobody was impervious to what was going on—even the Who and the Stones were affected by what was considered the fashion of the time. We just kind of morphed into what became known as a hair band.

We looked like dozens of other bands. There was no place anymore to be different. We had gotten rid of our calling card. We had taken off what made us different, so pretty much all we could look like was a run-of-the-mill rock and roll band. MTV had opened up the opportunity for a band from Idaho to look like a band from L.A., which could look like a band from London. There was a more homogenized look, because every band suddenly realized they could go buy hairspray and tease their hair up high and wear their mom's makeup and roll around on the floor with their guitars, just like they saw in somebody's video. It was the current state of bands: big hair, spandex, jewelry, femme makeup.

A lot of bands with that look made a lot of awful music. It's mind-boggling how bad some of that stuff was. It had no soul, no roots. I know it was aping a lot of British blues-based bands, but as far as I was concerned, you couldn't play that type of music credibly unless you were at least aware of the likes of Hubert Sumlin, Howlin' Wolf, and Robert Johnson. Jimi Hendrix didn't start off playing "Purple Haze." If you wanted to learn guitar, you had to go back.

Most of the hair bands were horrible, with noodling guitar players, tapping away without really being able to play. But we had to fit in with what was going on. So we did. And, for better or worse, it got us through a couple of decades.

Since MTV had covered our unmasking, we figured that this time around they would probably play a music video if we made one. We weren't going to get a world premiere slot or anything, but we were hopeful it would get played. The video for "Lick It Up" was a bigger production than "I Love It Loud," but we managed to keep the costs fairly low. Some artists were spending hundreds of thousands of dollars on videos at the time, and that seemed crazy to us, especially in light of MTV's track record of not playing us in the past. We wanted to make "Lick It Up" for a reasonable amount of money.

The video opened with an image of skulls, and if you watch very closely, you'll see one of them wobble a little—they were made out of latex. We shot the video in a burned-out area of the Bronx. Aside from a few props, like the skulls, that was all real—we didn't do anything but show up. It looked like Dresden in 1945, a postapocalyptic wasteland. But it wasn't a stage set. I'd never seen anything like that before; I hadn't spent much time in the South Bronx. The crazy thing was that it wasn't just one small area. It was huge, like an entire bombed-out city or a massive movie set— broken down and decaying buildings as far as you could see, piles of bricks and rocks and garbage everywhere. It was the weirdest, most surreal thing I'd ever seen.

When I saw the complete edited video, I thought it was cool. It was an "MTV video"—it had girls, it had fire, it had weird hairdos. It had all the things MTV videos had.

Eric hated it because he had these little drumstick legs, so he's walking and you see these little feet with high pointed shoes and these thick legs. And people seeing Vinnie asked, "Is that a girl?" When we shot the cover for *Lick It Up*, Vinnie wore a wig, and it looked great. Afterwards he gave us a hard time and insisted on not wearing it again. But then his hair kind of looked like the Gerber baby. He was very odd-looking anyway, and in that video he looked extra odd as he tried to look sexy for the camera.

Lick It Up went on to be certified double platinum. That blew *Creatures of the Night* away and reaffirmed for me that my suspicions had been correct. It wasn't that people didn't want KISS. They wanted KISS to drop something that no longer seemed genuine. Losing the makeup forced people to focus on the band. And they embraced the music.

Lick It Up felt like a rebound in other ways, too, because shedding the makeup meant, in a sense, shedding an era, shedding a persona, and finally being out there, at least on the surface, as *me*. The person who was offstage was the same person in the videos.

I felt we had taken one very big step forward, and it meant that we could soldier on and continue to try to rebuild this thing I loved, KISS.

The next test would be playing live without makeup. Were we just a bunch of knuckleheads in spandex and grease paint who blew shit up? Or were we a *band*, able to go toe to toe with anybody else?

We were about to find out.

42.

The show—in Portugal in October 1983—started with our normal introduction: *The hottest band in the land* . . . And then, suddenly, there we were onstage without any makeup on. And we were in rock clothes instead of platform boots and batwings and the usual armored accessories. For the first time ever.

I looked over at Gene.

He looks just like he did during sound check—and there's an audience out there!

The crowd didn't understand what was going on. The show had been promoted as a makeup show. Posters all over town showed the old characters. It took a few minutes for people to catch on.

Did it have the same visual impact? No. I could feel the difference from the stage. But we had to leave all that behind to find out who we were.

I wasn't sick of the makeup—I was sick of what it had become. We had to give it up to save what we loved most—the band. This was *exciting*. And liberating, too.

I relished the chance to prove ourselves all over again. And not just to critics and the audience, but also to myself. On that tour, I realized that the most difficult part of taking off the makeup wasn't performing without the star. It was adjusting to getting my picture taken. Since we had originally determined not to be photographed without makeup in order to enhance our stage personas, I had a neurotic sixth sense that allowed me to feel cameras anywhere, even if it was in my peripheral vision or far off in the distance. When we took off the makeup, I still reflexively covered my face whenever I detected a camera.

Vinnie continued to baffle me. He still refused to sign his contract. He kept promising to sign it, but he never did. And there was no way to make him. We were stuck with no choice but to continue.

We played in Oulu, in northern Finland, at the end of November 1983. It was the closest I'd ever been to the Soviet Union—maybe a hundred miles from the border. We traveled all day to get there, and when we arrived at the arena, it was bitter cold. I had to wear gloves and several layers of clothing in the backstage area. We were also starving after traveling all day and were very happy when a huge bowl of hearty beef soup was served. We sat around the family-style cauldron and ladled the soup into our bowls. It was so good—vegetables and beef in a flavorful broth, nice and warming. Vinnie ate part of his bowl and then, saying he was finished, dumped the leftovers back into the cauldron in the middle of the table. We all looked at him in disbelief.

"Where did you grow up? What are you doing? You just ruined our food!"

Things with Vinnie were getting worse and worse. He kept pushing his solos to more and more ridiculously epic lengths, stalling the show. The final straw came at a concert back in the States, in Long Beach, California, in January, 1984. That night he went on for so long that Gene and I just walked back onstage as he was still playing. I went to the mic and said, "Vinnie Vincent, lead guitar!" Solo over.

When the lights went down after the next song, Vinnie came over to me in the dark and said, "You bastard, you humiliated me!"

I swear, if he raises his arm, I'm going to knock him out right here.

It was a tense moment. I thought for sure the lights were going to come up and that prick would be lying on his back on the stage.

He was done.

When we were ready to record our next album, *Animalize*, we started searching for another guitar player. Although to say "we" is a bit of an exaggeration. Gene had basically disappeared by that point, too. While *Creatures* had been a band effort, and Gene had participated in *Lick It Up*, I felt abandoned when it came time to make *Animalize*.

After informing me without any warning or discussion that he wouldn't be around for the album, Gene went into a studio and crapped out some demos as fast as he could. Then he was off to do a movie. He left me with a pile of mostly unusable junk. Great.

A guitar maker named Grover Jackson had put me in touch with a goofy oversized guy named Mark Norton. Mark wasn't the sharpest pencil in the pack, but he played in the style that had then become popular. Eddie Van Halen had completely changed the game by this point, and everybody wanted to be fast and flashy, tapping, playing with two hands and their nose if you let them. Mark, who called himself Mark St. John—everybody was saint-something-or-other in the eighties—proved somewhat difficult to work with, too, though for different reasons than Vinnie.

One afternoon I told him, "Come in tomorrow with a solo for this song." He came in and played it the next day. It was pretty good. "Cool," I said. "Now play it again." He played a completely different thing.

"What?" he said. "I can't play the same thing twice."

"That's how this is done," I said.

Another time I said to him, "You know, sometimes it's not about what you play—it's about what you *don't* play. Listen to Jimmy Page, listen to Paul Kossoff, listen to Eric Clapton."

"I can play faster than *those* guys," scoffed Mark.

Houston, we have a problem.

In the end, I managed to get *Animalize* done basically on my own. I fixed Gene's songs, fixed the band situation, pulled solos out of Mark, and saw through the making of the album. I also named the album, designed the album art, and arranged the cover photo shoot. On top of it all, I spent big chunks of time in our office personally promoting the album, glad-handing radio people, cajoling MTV into playing the videos, and doing all the things a manager would normally do. But despite his minimal involvement, Gene still wanted his name on the album as a co-producer. And naturally, he still expected a share of the money equal to mine. I didn't think it was fair. I wasn't getting half of whatever he was getting paid for his extracurricular indulgences.

Gene still felt an entitlement to nearly half the songs on the album—and subsequent albums—but there was no quality control. Most of those songs are forgotten today, and not by coincidence. He simply wasn't putting enough time and effort into the band. I didn't care who wrote the hits, but if he wasn't even trying, there was no way we should pretend it was a partnership. I started to get pissed off about all the time he spent on other things, whether it was movies, working with other bands, or cutting ribbons at shopping centers.

I felt very strongly that we needed to commit to the band for it to survive. It was a crucial time. Whether or not he liked it, he was still *Gene Simmons from KISS,* and I didn't want him to destroy what he was standing on as he reached for other fruit. He was taking the band for granted—or worse, he was abusing what we had built together. And for what? A lot of the things he was doing would prove a waste of time. I didn't understand his need to bask in whatever questionable spotlight he could find; I saw one of his movies and thought it was embarrassing.

At the same time, Gene spent 24/7 putting himself in the spotlight and also chose to distort the public image of the band by increasing his perceived importance within KISS even as he was withdrawing from active involvement in it. Resentment started to simmer in me.

After we'd shot the cover photos—showcasing Mark—he came down with a rare arthritic condition. It often affects people's knees, but in Mark's case, it struck his hand. If you're going to have one part of your body swell, it shouldn't be your hand. Mark couldn't move his fingers. "My doctor says it will go away in two weeks," he told us.

I called him every day. "Any better?"

"No."

Finally, we had to go out and tour. *Animalize* came out in September 1984 and kept the momentum going, selling even better than *Lick It Up*. I called Bruce Kulick, whom I had met through his brother, Bob, and who had played a solo on one of the tracks of *Animalize*. I asked him whether he could tour with us for a few weeks as a stand-in for Mark. He agreed.

We traveled for quite a while with Bruce playing onstage each night and Mark hanging out backstage. We kept thinking he would wake up the next day and be able to play again. Tomorrow. Tomorrow. Tomorrow. Mark never played a single show on that tour, and finally we let him go and Bruce became the permanent guitar player.

Bruce was a real mensch, and very funny. If you asked him how he was, he would give you a ten-minute dissertation about how his fuzz box wasn't working quite right, or describe his upset stomach in details better left unspoken, or complain about how he had gas the day before. But he was a terrific guitar player and a great team player.

Bruce became our fourth guitar player, and at some point I

couldn't help thinking, *What the fuck?* I didn't want KISS to become a backup band for me and Gene—or just for me, for that matter. We weren't Ozzy or Bowie, shuffling through musicians; or at least, I didn't want to be. This was supposed to be a *band*. I tended to frown on groups that went through numerous lineups.

But even so, the chemistry we looked for had nothing to do with what happened offstage or outside the studio. That ship had sailed. We looked for functionality. We hadn't socialized as a band for a very long time, and while we didn't dislike being around each other, each member of the band was there just to play a role. We weren't riding around in a station wagon telling jokes anymore.

We spent October and November of 1984 touring Europe again, this time with Bon Jovi as our support act throughout. We had an impressive track record of picking winners: Bob Seger, John Mellencamp, Tom Petty, AC/DC, Judas Priest, Rush, and Iron Maiden were all among the acts we'd chosen to open tours. Bon Jovi had a minor radio hit at that point called "Runaway." Jon Bon Jovi was a smart guy and always sat with us at the hotel bar and asked questions about how various production expenses broke down. He was intent on getting as much information as possible, and he asked business questions. Now that we were basically managing ourselves, we had the answers.

Near the end of the tour, Bon Jovi's manager, Doc McGhee, approached me. "Would you be willing to write with Jon for their next album?"

"If you want to write with someone great," I said, "call Desmond Child." I gave Doc Desmond's number. Maybe a year later, Desmond came over to my apartment and played *Slippery When Wet* for me, the album he ended up writing with Jon and Richie.

I was impressed and called Jon afterwards. "I think this could be a big album for you," I said.

An understatement, to say the least.

43

We now had back-to-back platinum albums. People were starting to trust us again. We filled—and even sold out—venues again, bringing in ten thousand people, which if not quite up to the old days, certainly put us in very credible company. The needle was moving in the right direction.

Most importantly, I was making money doing what I loved: playing guitar, jumping around onstage, and screaming and preening a lot.

And yet, despite selling 2 million copies each of *Lick It Up* and *Animalize,* we certainly weren't top dogs anymore. Some bands— Van Halen, Def Leppard, and soon Bon Jovi—were selling 10 million copies of their albums.

Despite the fact that we were making money, our record label could not have cared less about KISS. I think the label was dominated by kids barely out of college who were busy going after bands like Dan Reed Network. And no wonder—thirty years later they're still a household name, right?

Electric Lady Studios in 1985, recording Asylum *with* (left to right) *Bruce, Eric, Me, and Gene.*

When we played concerts in New York, nobody from our own record company would bother to come. They would all be in some downtown club watching a band fresh out of a fraternity house basement. Nothing against Dan Reed or his Network, but it was annoying and even hurtful to be taken for granted like that.

The non-makeup albums became successful because the fan base gave us a second chance. The record company did fuck-all for us.

As we set to work on a follow-up album, *Asylum*, the problem for me was that my ostensible partner had the same attitude as the record company. Gene just didn't care. He would show up in the studio after being up all night with some third-rate band he was producing, exhausted, with some half-assed song he wanted to put on our album that he may or may not have actually written. Again, he felt he should get a quota of songs on the record, and again, he wasn't delivering the goods. He didn't devote the time to it.

If I suggested he was spreading himself too thin, he said, "No, no, I'm giving 100 percent."

My feeling that there was a traitor in the midst grew daily every time Gene denied his subpar and often nonexistent contributions to the band. Somebody wasn't playing for the team; somebody was thinking only about himself. KISS was a distant second on his agenda.

You are the one person I thought I could always count on.

When I voiced my sense of betrayal, Gene said, "Well, you can go do things, too."

That was evasive bullshit. If I did, there wouldn't have been a band or any albums. I wasn't about to see the band disintegrate, and he knew it.

Not only that, the license he offered to me to go "do things" was predicated on his own decision to do things. I wasn't looking for an excuse to do other things; he was. It wasn't like he conferred with me about what or when he was going to do things. He was just looking out for number one, with little regard for me.

He also developed a new habit of using the KISS logo and his KISS makeup for personal projects—without my approval, knowing full well it was needed. When I raised objections, he would offer a weak, insincere "sorry," only to be repeated again next time as though we'd never spoken about it. He was clearly going to do whatever he wanted to, regardless of any objections from me or even his legal obligations under our partnership. For Gene, "sorry" was a meaningless hall pass to placate me until he would of course do the same thing again when he thought it would benefit him. In actuality it never meant "sorry for what I did"; it was purely "sorry that it bothers you." In addition to being offensive and insulting, his total disregard hurt my feelings.

Apparently I just had to play by his rules. I had the choice of walking away or of doing the work of two people. The catch was that I had to share the credit, even if I did double the work.

The animosity continued to build.

I also started to see more and more interviews where Gene took credit for things he was only partially responsible for or in some cases had nothing to do with at all. And he never refuted or corrected misinformed or inaccurate assumptions from interviewers about his outsized role. When I would call Gene on it, and show him quotes from countless interviews, he would emphatically tell me, "I didn't say that!"

Now, I wasn't new to doing Q&A features or taking part in a taped interview that was going to be transcribed and published later. The number of times I read something attributed to me that was untrue could have been counted on one hand with fingers to spare. If James Brown was the Hardest Working Man in Show Business, then Gene Simmons was—at least according to his account—the Most Misquoted Man in Show Business. I didn't buy it.

Being lied to and having my role and the role of others diminished and even negated was not only selfish, it was unkind. It hurt. One thing Gene and I had always agreed on was that we were each other's brother. What we obviously did not agree on was how you treat your brother.

One of the results of Gene's diminished involvement was that, at least in the context of the band, I shared the spotlight less. It became my spotlight. It wasn't by chance that my songs became the popular songs. Nobody else was putting in the time to write decent songs. If Gene wanted to *be* more than the bass player, he had to *do* something more. Anybody can write a song in five minutes. The difference is that since we had a record deal, Gene got to put his songs on an album, whether or not they were any good.

When I wrote songs like "Heaven's On Fire" or "Tears Are Falling," it was because I had to. I was the one doing the work, and I enjoyed getting the credit I deserved. During the height of MTV's popularity, I became a sort of eighties pretty boy—though it was certainly a different time, and with feathered earrings, rouge, and pink gloves (courtesy of Van Halen's stylist, whom we hired), I looked as much like a drag queen as anything else. Let's just say the criteria for what was considered attractive was a little different during the hair band era.

I had a few girlfriends during those years, but for the most part, relationships were still just about companionship and sex. I didn't want exclusivity and didn't expect it from women. I just wanted to have a good time.

I had things sorted out so that even when we were off the road, I was never alone. I split my time between New York and L.A., renting apartments out there or living at hotels like the Sunset Marquis. L.A. was the place I went to indulge in what always started as carefree excess with women; when those relationships inevitably got too complicated, I would go back to New York.

Despite the newfound attention through KISS music videos, I wasn't comfortable being a public figure all the time. With his movie career in mind, Gene sought to surround himself with the most famous people possible; I came in a distant second in that department. It was fun to read about who I was involved with in the gossip magazines—but it wasn't so much fun to read about a breakup. Once, I peered over the shoulder of a woman who was reading an article in the *Star* in which the actress Lisa Hartman explained why she would never marry singer Paul Stanley. I could have done without that stuff.

The kind of people who lived in the tabloids considered themselves only as important as the amount of press they got. That was how they defined themselves. When I was around people like that, in addition to dealing with my own shit, I had to deal with somebody else's shit—like how hurt they were that their segment on *Access Hollywood* wasn't longer.

One woman I dated in L.A. worried that her house was too far east—on the eastern edge of Beverly Hills rather than smack-dab in the middle. Another one apologized that she lived in the Valley rather than on the Hollywood side of the hills. I spent time in those superficial circles, but I knew that I didn't want to live in them.

None of the relationships was leading anywhere, but they did stave off the loneliness. One night late in the year we played a show in New Jersey before heading home to New York. A *Penthouse* Pet I knew came backstage after the show and said, "I have a Christmas present for you."

I said, "I'll give you a ride back to the city in my limo."

Once on the highway she undid my jeans and gave me my present. Then she lifted her head and said, "Merry Christmas."

Hey, what about Hanukkah?

As far as my sexual exploits, during the seventies I had paddled around the pool, so to speak; during the eighties I was doing backflips in it. I went to a party one night at the Playboy Mansion, and as soon as I walked in the door I found myself standing in front of a Playmate of the Year whom I had seen in the magazine and thought was incredibly hot. We spoke for a few minutes, and then she said, "Do you want to leave?"

"Sure," I said, half-wondering what would happen if she were to reply, "Then why don't you get the fuck out of here?"

Instead, she said, "Let's go."

We continued the festivities at her place.

My class at the High School of Music & Art set up a fifteenth reunion that year, too—the class of 1970. I had missed my tenth reunion because of the tour in Australia just after Eric Carr joined the band, so I wasn't going to miss the fifteenth. More than seeing how everyone's lives had turned out, I knew I wanted to rub my success in their faces.

The woman I was seeing in New York at the time was—surprise!—a *Playboy* centerfold. I thought about taking her to the reunion, but then I thought about that date I'd had back then—with the coolest girl in school, Victoria. The date where I ended up talking to Victoria's dad as she went off to bed. The date that resulted in the hottest chick in class snickering at me for the rest of high school. I decided I would go to the reunion by myself. I told my bunny I'd give her a call once I got the lay of the land at the reunion. What I didn't tell her was that I sort of hoped I could finally bang my failed conquest.

I had a suntan earned at the Sunset Marquis, and I wore a sharp, tailored blue silk suit. I couldn't wait to see all these people who had considered me the least likely to accomplish anything.

The event was held at the school, and when I walked in, all I could think was that everybody was too big for the furniture. The atmosphere was surprisingly somber, and most of the people had not aged well. I still pictured them all as young people, full of vitality and dreams and aspirations, and here they were looking like they were at a Halloween party dressed as old people. They looked old and broken.

Fifteen years later, Victoria had short mousy hair and was wearing clunky orthopedic-style shoes and a frumpy skirt—she wasn't so hot anymore. At first I felt a brief jolt of vindication at seeing her like that, thinking of the way she had never let me live down the folly of our one date. But then I wished she could have looked as good as she had fifteen years before. This was just depressing.

Another guy there had been a real Adonis in high school—handsome, with long curly hair, and a great voice. He could howl like Robert Plant and carried himself that way. Now he was pasty and bald as a billiard ball. The best-looking guy in school didn't necessarily remain the best looking, and me, the guy nobody thought would ever win a race, turned out to be a marathoner.

The whole thing was uncomfortable and disappointing. I left quickly and picked up my waiting girlfriend and went out for a nice dinner.

I had found no joy in rubbing my success in people's faces. And I never wanted to go to another reunion.

44.

*A*sylum sold nearly as well as *Animalize*, but the band started to peter out again after the album was released, and by early 1986 we were off the road again for about a year.

Howard Marks, our business manager, called me one afternoon and said he'd gotten a call from Tom Zutaut, an A&R man famous for signing Mötley Crüe. "Tom just signed this band," Howard said, "and wanted to know if you want to go check them out. They're looking for a producer."

Well, Gene was off making another movie. We weren't going to work on the next record until the following year. Why not?

Howard came with me to meet the band—a bunch of young guys called Guns N' Roses. We had arranged to meet them at an apartment their manager had rented for them near the corner of La Cienega and Fountain. I introduced bald, pot-bellied Howard as my bodyguard, as a joke; but after looking around for a few minutes, I could see why they didn't get it.

Izzy was unconscious, with drool coming out of the side of his mouth. It wasn't clear whether he was sleeping or dead—that's how rough he looked. Duff and Steven were very nice, and Steven was just glowing about what a big KISS fan he was. I didn't realize that the half-comatose, curly-headed lead guitar player who called himself Slash was what had become of the sweet kid I'd spoken to during the interviews before the recording of *Creatures* a few years earlier. Then Axl chatted with me and played a few songs on a crappy cassette player they had lying around.

When he played "Nightrain" I thought it was really good, but I told him that maybe the chorus could be used as a pre-chorus instead, and there could be another chorus added afterwards. That was the last time he ever spoke to me. Ever.

Slash roused himself, and he and I started talking about the Stones. I showed him Keith's five-string open-G tuning, which was the set-up Keith used to write all his stuff. I took a string off and retuned a guitar, and he thought it was very cool. I also offered to help Slash get in touch with people who could hook him up with some free guitars—we were sponsored by all sorts of instrument companies, and I figured a young guy like him could use some help getting equipment to record with.

That night, I went to see their gig at Raji's, a little dive in Hollywood. I thought the songs they had played for me were good, but they didn't prepare me for seeing the band live. Guns N' Roses were stupendous. I was *shocked*, given the collection of wastoids I'd seen earlier that afternoon, and I immediately realized I was witnessing true greatness.

I went to see them perform again at another club, called Gazzarri's—it later became the Key Club. They weren't happy with the guy mixing their sound, and Slash asked me out of the blue to help out. Decades later, Slash's recollections of the night would be faulty at best. He liked to pretend I had *dared* to meddle with their sound. God forbid this guy from KISS would have anything to do with

Guns—I mean, what could be worse than a guy from KISS, of all things? He also recalled that I had a blond trophy wife with me. But I wasn't married and was in fact there with a short brunette named Holly Knight, who was a songwriter famous for "Love Is a Battlefield," among other hits. There is obviously a reason why defense attorneys never want to put alcoholics or drug addicts on the witness stand.

That was years later, of course. Immediately after my interactions with the band, I started to hear lots of stories Slash was saying behind my back—he called me gay, made fun of my clothes, all sorts of things designed to give himself some sort of rock credibility at my expense. This was years before his top hat, sunglasses, and dangling cigarette became a cartoon costume that he would continue to milk with the best of us for decades.

I didn't wind up being involved with G'n'R's album. No surprise there. The surprise came a few months later when Slash called me and wanted to follow up on my offer to help him get some free guitars.

"You want me to help you get guitars after you went around saying all that shit about me behind my back?"

Slash got real quiet.

"You know, one thing you're going to have to learn is not to air your dirty laundry in public. Nice knowing you. Go fuck yourself."

45

Five-string open-G tuning wasn't the only thing I learned from Keith Richards. When I ran into him in person, he told me he'd been offered the chance to buy anything he wanted from our storage space in New York—part of a warehouse where we kept old stage sets and equipment, all the makeup-era outfits, lots of instruments, all sorts of things.

"Yeah, mate," he laughed. "Could've bought the lot of it."

At first, I simply didn't understand. Was this the legendary English sense of humor? Was it some misremembered anecdote he'd somehow mangled? But the more I thought about it, the more worried I got. Now that he mentioned it, I had noticed things disappearing. Several times I'd gone to the warehouse to grab guitars I wanted to use, only to come up empty. Once, it was a guitar that I had stashed there only a week before. I *knew* it had to be there.

The solution to the mystery was depressing: Bill Aucoin, who somehow still had keys to the warehouse, was secretly selling our stuff out the back door. By then, he had spiraled so far down that he was couch surfing from one friend's place to another. His last client, Billy Idol, had left him. When Billy Idol abandoned you for your drug use in the 1980s, let's just say it must have been bad. So we relocated. We had a few things torched or cut down for scrap—like the stage set from the *Animalize* tour—but we moved most of it first to New Jersey and later to L.A.

Bill's activities soon turned out to be the least of our worries, however. I still lived in a one-bedroom apartment and had only one car, but Howard Marks started saying I needed to tighten my belt. He told me I had to cut back on the money I was giving my parents. That raised the hairs on the back of my neck.

It wasn't that I expected tour money when we weren't on tour. But what about all the money that had been invested on our behalf? Where was that?

I'm not living ostentatiously. I'm not living some ridiculous lifestyle. Something tells me HE's making too much money.

Eventually, I said it straight out: "If anybody's going to get less money, it should be you." That didn't go over so well.

The music industry has never been kind to artists. In the case of our business managers, I didn't want to believe they had acted in bad faith. But certainly, some decisions had been made that smelled pretty bad once I started sniffing around.

The big wakeup call came from an odd source: my therapist, Dr. Jesse Hilsen. I started talking about my misgivings and all the things being said about my finances, and he started asking questions—about my earnings, about retirement accounts—none of which, embarrassingly, I could answer. I wasn't supposed to show our financial statements to anyone—which, again, should have been a red flag—but Dr. Hilsen agreed to have a look at some of them.

And what he asked after examining some statements was a shock: "Do you know that you owe the IRS millions of dollars?"

"What!?"

"Yeah, and it's overdue and they've given notice that they're going to come after you."

"How is this possible?"

Howard had been like a family member. I had always trusted him. Our long relationship represented an increasingly rare instance of stability with the band. Now I had uncovered many examples of highly questionable judgment. I didn't want to nitpick over legality—the point was that a lot of decisions had been made that clearly weren't in my or the band's best interests—decisions that wouldn't have been made the same way if our business managers had been making them about their own money. There were investments with people who just happened to be associated with them and our attorneys. There were tax shelters that had gone awry and never been addressed. There were reckless decisions. A lot of it smacked of the same sort of cronyism I'd seen elsewhere inside the music business, and I had always thought we were immune to it because of Howard. Now I wanted to spit at him. It was a huge betrayal.

I called Gene. "Listen," I said, "we're in financial trouble."

"Nonsense," said Gene.

"Things are not as they appear, I'm telling you."

I met up with him and tried to explain. He scoffed and acted dismissive and irritated. So I had him meet Dr. Hilsen, who showed Gene what was what in the statements. Gene was very defensive, even antagonistic. But the problems were all there in black and white.

Within a day or so, I told Gene that I was leaving Howard. He wanted to stay. "You can stay if you want," I said, "but I'm out of here. You do whatever you want."

He was stunned that I was jumping ship with or without him. It wasn't going to matter. As it sunk in that I was dead serious, he began to waver. Eventually he said "I'll go with you."

I wouldn't take Howard's calls and never spoke to him again.

It was not a happy day parting company like that with yet another member of the team who had let us down. Howard was the last vestige of the original team to fall by the wayside, but there was no way to explain all that was there in black and white, filling countless files and documents. We got outside legal advisors and started trying to untangle the mess, which they agreed wasn't as it should be.

From that day forward, we never let anyone else sign a single check in our names. I've used a lot of ink signing my own name since then, whether it's for my monthly phone bill or the construction of a massive stage set. No matter how small or large, Gene and I kept everything close to the vest from then on.

Maybe we had finally learned our lesson—by taking our lumps.

But it certainly wasn't a case of being brilliant. It was a case of being *resilient* and seizing an opportunity to rectify the situation once we recognized something was wrong. Interestingly, even though it was me who got us out of a situation that was a ticking time bomb and would have decimated us, Gene continued to be lauded as a savvy businessman. I guess people just look for simplistic distinctions—as in, "Gene's the business guy and Paul's the creative guy." But it wasn't Gene who realized the ship was sinking, and it wasn't Gene who changed course.

As far as I was concerned, Gene's most successful venture in business was promoting the perception that he was a savvy businessman. That has been an undeniable success.

But then again, given that he seemed to spend 24/7 promoting that perception, perhaps it was no surprise. I didn't fault him—that was something he saw as a life accomplishment. For me to compete in that arena would have taken away from other pursuits and challenges in my life. Gene was about nonstop self-promotion; I was about ongoing self-discovery. I wanted to figure out how to be happy, and that was far more important to me than building a myth that wouldn't change the reality of who I really was.

After all, just because you can get other people to believe something doesn't mean that *you* believe it. Didn't I know it.

Transitory external factors seemed to make Gene happy, and he wasn't interested in looking inside. That may even be soft-peddling it—Gene resolutely resisted looking inside. For him, perception was reality. The surface was the all. That distinction summed up the stark difference between us.

And maybe that is also why any sense of unity created by our decision to break away from Howard was short-lived. That episode brought us together to fight what we both perceived as injustice, but as soon as we started to work on our next album, *Crazy Nights,* I found myself right back at square one.

Gene would stagger into the studio after not sleeping all night—he was too busy once again making movies or working with other bands, including one called Black 'N Blue who had opened for us on the last tour. Gene ended up writing some songs with the band's guitar player, Tommy Thayer. Or he spent the whole time on the phone, working this or that angle.

The few songs Gene brought in seemed to have been written by other people, with Gene pasting his name on after the fact. Needless to say, once again the songs were not impressive.

His lack of involvement had become a running joke in the studio, but it wasn't funny anymore. If anything, the confrontation with Howard only increased the sense I had that Gene was screwing me. In his own way, he had betrayed me as much as Ace and Peter had. At this point he was riding my coattails. If Gene wanted an equal share, he should have to do some of the work of keeping the band going.

I was seriously pissed off.

I can't live like this anymore.

Outside the studio one afternoon, I asked Gene to get in my car. I took a deep breath. Whatever the consequences of what I was about to say, I knew it had to be done. I couldn't go on like this, feeling like I was in a pressure cooker, dealing with everything to do with KISS on my own and still obligated to treat someone who was AWOL as an equal partner.

"This isn't okay anymore," I told him.

It wasn't as uncomfortable as I'd expected. In part because it felt good to finally let off the steam. "I'm done with this. You can't expect to be my partner if you're not going to hold up your end."

That was the beginning of a heart-to-heart conversation that began there in the car and then continued over the phone for several more days. As I vented, I never raised my voice. I've always believed that the person who yells loses.

Quitting the band was never an option for me. I also did not relish the idea of taking over the band on my own. But if Gene's reduced involvement was going to continue, I wanted to be paid and recognized for my ever-increasing responsibilities. I wasn't sure what to expect, but apparently the talk resonated with Gene, because a few days later he approached me and handed me a Jaguar brochure. He said he wanted me to pick one out for myself. He wanted to buy me a Jag to show his appreciation for all I'd done to keep the band going.

It was a nice move on his part. But I had my eye on a Porsche.

When we shot the video for the second single from *Crazy Nights*, "Reason to Live," the storyline involved a beautiful woman blowing up a car. It was a black Porsche 928.

And I drove it home from the video shoot, compliments of Gene.

46.

The song "Crazy Crazy Nights" became a hit in Britain, and we played a European tour in the fall of 1988. At the end of the tour I stayed behind in London to hang out with the English singer and pinup girl Samantha Fox, whom I had started to see.

She and I went to the box office smash musical *Phantom of the Opera* that I'd heard so much about. I loved the big-production shows I'd seen in the States earlier in the decade, and *Phantom* promised more of the same. As I watched it, though, I could feel it affecting me in a way nothing else ever had.

In one climactic scene, Christine, the beautiful singer at the opera house, was alone with the Phantom, a dashing but mysterious musical genius who wore a tuxedo and a white mask over his face. It was a dramatic scene—and when she suddenly ripped off his mask and revealed his hideously disfigured face, I gasped. The drama touched a psychological nerve. The parallels to my own life should have been obvious—the tormented guy who covered himself in a

*Me, Mike Tyson, Samantha Fox, and rocker Billy Squier in 1988.
Mike's arm on my shoulder made it impossible for me to move.*

cool disguise but was a shell underneath. But I didn't connect the dots in the moment. A thought did occur to me, however, that showed I understood the parallels at least at a subliminal level: *I know I could play that role.*

Nothing in my background suggested I could do musical theater. But I *knew* it somehow. And I never forgot it.

I could play that role.

After the show, Samantha and I went back to my hotel. We hadn't slept together yet, but that night she said, "Would you like to take a bubble bath with me?"

"Yes. Yes, I would."

Back in the States, all was not well inside KISS. Eric had stopped talking to me during the *Crazy Nights* tour. He sometimes got into ruts and shut down. He seemed mad at me about something, so finally, after months—months!—I had to sit him down and read him the riot act. "You just can't pull this kind of shit for this amount of time."

It might have sounded dictatorial, but the fact was he was there to play drums and be a member of the team. The silence and tension had become unbearable. "This noncommunicative bullshit stops today," I told him.

And it did. It seemed he needed help to force his way out of a self-imposed prison.

Things with Eric were definitely getting increasingly weird. But they had always tended to be odd. Whenever we were both in L.A., I would invite him to come over and hang out with me. "Is anyone else there?" he would ask.

If I had people over, I told him, "Eric, they're nice people, we're hanging out. Come on over, it'll be fun." But if anyone else was there, he refused to come.

On the *Crazy Nights* tour he had started to obsess over not being the original drummer again. The whole thing was so irrational. What could I say? It was true, he *still* wasn't the original drummer. He would *never* be the original drummer.

And then there was Gene. Despite the Porsche he bought me as an apology, Gene still hadn't contributed anything of quality to *Crazy Nights*. More troubling than that was the fact that he didn't seem *interested* in contributing. And when it came time to cut a few new songs to put on a greatest hits compilation—*Smashes, Thrashes & Hits*—I was once again left on my own.

At that point I thought, *Fuck this.* Grudgingly, I decided to take center stage. The way things were functioning, KISS had devolved into my band. I had never wanted it that way, but there we were. It was the reality of the situation. KISS records were in essence solo albums for me—again, a situation I definitely did not want. But I had no choice. On the cover of *Smashes, Thrashes,* I was front and center.

Fuck it.

And in the videos for the new songs, "Let's Put the X in Sex" and "(You Make Me) Rock Hard," I didn't even hold a guitar. It was unambiguous. I was the frontman. KISS was my band now. Whether I liked it or not.

Aaaaahhhh, the videos. What can you say about those?

To begin with, the songs were horrible. "Rock Hard" was written by me, Desmond Child, and Diane Warren—a case of three great minds gone terribly wrong. "X in Sex" wasn't much better. We brought in an extremely talented woman named Rebecca Blake to make the videos. She had been involved with a couple of Prince videos and also put out an interesting book of highly stylized fashion-fantasy photographs. We felt we needed a new look, and Rebecca had a vision.

She picked the women for the videos and dressed them and everything. When I showed up for the shoot, I said, "These women all look like they need a sandwich. They look like underfed pelicans." They had no tits and no ass. And they strutted around as if they were in a Robert Palmer video—hands on hips, icily turning—like runway models, not eighties hair metal video girls.

Then there were my outfits. I wore a chainmail tank top and white tights while swinging on a trapeze. I danced around in a corset and licked my fingers while a bunch of emaciated women goose-stepped in the background. In the course of those two shoots, I wrote the textbook on what *not* to do in a music video. I mean, I didn't walk around on the street in tights with bicycle reflectors sewn on them or Body Glove tank tops cut off just below my nipples. This was a whole new level of bad taste and judgment. Definitely not my finest moment.

With the *Crazy Nights* tour in the rearview mirror and *Smashes, Thrashes* set to take up the slack for a year or so, I had something else in mind: a solo tour. I was fed up with the situation in KISS and needed to flex my muscles a little on my own—and cut the cord between me and Gene.

A certain complacency had developed in KISS, especially once we had a stable lineup again for a few years. We played everything a million miles an hour—Gene equated that with excitement, but it caused a loss of groove. On the *Crazy Nights* tour we'd even had people on the side of the stage playing keyboard sound pads—to enhance the rhythm guitar so I could slack off and jump around more, and to fortify the background vocals for that big eighties "gang" vocal sound. Looking back, I can see there was no mystery about why the audience dwindled.

My inclination was to put together a band of people I had never played with—just for the sake of doing something different—even though I planned to play a lot of the same songs. After all, KISS songs were my songs, something I felt even more strongly over the course of the non-makeup albums. Those albums may have said KISS, but the parts of them people remembered were me. Why shouldn't I play the stuff I wrote? I also figured playing on my own would probably bring something good back to the band—it was a chance to get out from under my frustrations, a chance to play with other people and think about things differently.

The only times I'd ever played live with anyone outside of KISS was when I'd recently played in a fun little cover band for a few gigs at the China Club, a New York bar popular with musicians. The combo was put together more or less spontaneously just before the gigs we did, and there was a rotating cast of characters; the only constants were me and a bass player friend of mine named Bob Held. We basically cranked out Zeppelin and AC/DC tunes.

For my solo tour, I had no illusions of playing arenas—I just wanted a little creative space and the chance to play with different musicians. So I booked a string of club gigs and put together a band. Bob Kulick was my guitar player of choice—our studio work together over the years gave us some familiarity, and gave me full confidence that he could pull it off. Bob brought in the bass player, Dennis St. James, and I turned to a keyboard player named

Gary Corbett—he sang, which was important, because I needed another voice for harmonies. As for drummers, two names came up as I searched. One was Greg Bisonette, who had played with David Lee Roth, and the other was Eric Singer. Dennis suggested Eric, and I also heard good things about him from other people. So I called him.

Eric Singer was recording in New York at the time in a band called Badlands with Jake E. Lee, who had just left Ozzy's band. The studio they were working in was right around the corner from the office we'd set up to self-manage KISS. Eric came to the office and gave me some CDs of work he had done in Black Sabbath. He had also done all the demos for the Cult's *Sonic Temple,* and had toured the year before with Gary Moore, the legendary Irish blues guitar player.

Eric seemed promising, so I asked him to come to a rehearsal studio and jam with the rest of the band members. It was hard for me to assess him, because with drummers it's about more than just keeping the beat—they need to play in front of the beat, on it, or behind it in a way that's sympathetic to everyone else's playing, in this case mine. But even in that first session, he sounded terrific.

The band was assembled, and off we went, playing dates on both coasts.

I don't think Gene cared about my solo tour at all. If anything, my decision to go out on my own probably made him feel better about what he was doing and not doing. Eric Carr, on the other hand, was forlorn about my doing something outside of KISS. He also seemed hurt that he couldn't be in my solo band even after I had explained to him that the whole point, for me, was to do something different, on my own. "You're the drummer in KISS," I told him. "You can't be my backup drummer."

It was exciting—and liberating—to go onstage as myself. One night we played a very crowded gig in Brooklyn at a famous club called L'Amour, and a guy ran up onstage and tried to hug me. All of a sudden there was a huge ball of hair on the stage—the stage invader had ripped out some of my hair extensions. Everybody had hair extensions back then, and when one of mine got pulled out, it looked like a dead rat on the stage.

When the tour stopped in Manhattan for two gigs at the Ritz, Eric Carr came to one of the shows and sat in the balcony with his head resting on the railing through the entire show. Afterwards he came backstage and, out of left field, turned to Eric Singer and said, "You're going to replace me."

"What are you talking about?" I said.

"He's going to replace me in KISS," said Eric Carr, nodding at Eric Singer.

"Listen, Eric, you're the drummer in KISS, and he's the drummer in my solo band."

Eric Carr was not a happy camper by the late eighties. He had started to drink more and may have been doing drugs as well, though I wasn't sure. People tended to conceal drug use from me since they knew I was adamantly opposed to it. I don't know whether Eric's increased drinking exacerbated whatever he was going through, or whether the drinking was a result of his unhappiness. But he started to get erratic.

By the time KISS reconvened and began to tour our next album, *Hot in the Shade*, in late 1989, Eric Carr stopped talking to me entirely.

Hot in the Shade hatched a hit single, "Forever," that allowed us to go out on a major tour again. The video got into heavy rotation on MTV, and we put together a package tour, rotating in some young MTV-friendly bands like Faster Pussycat, Danger Danger, and Winger. One of the bands, Slaughter, had basically started as Vinnie Vincent's backup band after we kicked him out of KISS. But they too had tired of Vinnie, left him, ditched the name Vinnie Vincent Invasion, and, lo and behold, became really successful once they were no longer with him. Their record label kept them and let Vinnie go.

Funny thing about "Forever": because it was somewhat uncharacteristic for KISS, people pegged it as "a Michael Bolton song," since he was co-credited as songwriter. Surely *I* couldn't have written it. In fact, after an all too brief initial writing session at the Sunset Marquis, Michael had so little to do with it that once it became a hit he asked the KISS office to fax him over a copy of the lyrics. Only then did he start performing the song in concert—and introducing it as a song he wrote for KISS.

When our record label first heard "Forever," it was the first time in a decade that an A&R man at our label actually weighed in with an opinion on one of our songs. He sat me down in his office and said I needed to re-edit it so it faded out on the chorus. That was song-arranging 101, and even though it could be effective in some cases, it wasn't right for that song—the ending was one of the qualities that made "Forever" unique.

This desk expert pushed his opinion relentlessly, and with a tone that made it seem like more of a directive than a suggestion. I'd had enough. "I was doing this when you were in grade school," I told him. "I was at this label before you were here, and I'll be here after you're gone. So thanks, but no thanks."

That was the end of the meeting. "Forever" reached number eight on the Billboard singles chart, giving us our first top ten single in more than a decade. Not long after, that record company expert was replaced with the next one.

Also at the time of *Hot in the Shade*, we brought in my therapist, Dr. Jesse Hilsen, to run the KISS office and oversee the organization. I signed a formal release saying he was no longer my therapist and would not act further in that capacity. From then on, we rarely spoke about anything but business.

Outside of the band, eyebrows were raised about the wisdom

and even ethics of my former psychiatrist working for me, given that earlier relationship. I understand that point of view, but when did KISS ever play by the rules? Our very success was built on ignoring the rules, writing our own rules, and sometimes throwing *those* out, too. Hilsen sought out unconventional people to align ourselves with in a business often plagued by inside deals and favors done at the artists' expense. He brought in Bill Randolph, a Wall Street corporate attorney with no experience in entertainment law. For accounting,

Jesse Hilsen, M.D.
1449 Lexington Avenue
New York, New York 10128

March 14, 1988

Mr. Paul Stanley
429 E. 52nd Street
Apt. 21H
New York, NY 10021

Dear Paul,

As you have requested, I am writing to resign as your physician and psychiatrist, so that you and I may discuss business relationships that you have asked me to consider engaging in with you and certain of your business associates.

In my professional opinion, you need no further psychotherapy, and you have advised me that you desire none at this time. However, if you should desire any therapeutic intervention at any time in the future, I would be happy to make several referrals.

Sincerely,

Jesse Hilsen, M.D.

he again avoided the big specialized New York firms and instead found Aaron Van Duyne, a savvy certified public accountant with an office in New Jersey. Van Duyne had the knowledge and software to calculate the royalties due to songwriters and recording artists, but his lone music clients were Eddie Brigati and Felix Cavaliere of the Rascals. Both Bill and Aaron remain cornerstones of our team to this day, and their maverick approach and fierce dedication have built each of them a well-deserved broad roster of clients.

Unfortunately, the same can't be said of Hilsen. He left his wife and children around the time he joined the KISS office, and I began to hear talk of his avoiding settlements and child-support payments—accusations he vehemently denied to me. Eventually, the claims became more public, and a case was built against him. I watched as someone who had earlier in my life been a source of stability became increasingly secretive, evasive, and paranoid. It was hard to see this person whom I had known through so many of my personal changes vanish, first figuratively and then literally. Hilsen became a fugitive in 1994, and I never saw him again.

On July 3, 1990, we did a show in Springfield, Massachusetts, followed by a day off. Since Springfield is fairly close to New York, I decided to go home after the show and spend the off-day at my apartment. I hired a car to drive me there. On the highway, not far from New York, the driver tried to change lanes, and the limo got hit on the passenger side and went into a spin.

I wrapped my arms around the seat in front of me and pressed my head into it—we were spinning totally out of control, knocking over lampposts along the side of the road. Then the car slammed head-on into an embankment, and I flew over the front seat and under the dashboard. The car folded around me.

Somehow, the driver and I managed to wriggle out through the smashed windshield. When a state trooper arrived on the scene, he looked at the car, which was totaled, turned to me and said, "You were *in* that car?"

It was the middle of the night. I went home to bed.

The next morning I could barely move. I went to the hospital, where they x-rayed my body from head to foot. I was severely banged up, but I refused to stay there for observation and was helped home.

We had to cancel the next few shows. Yet nobody from the band called me.

When I returned to the tour, I woke up every day unable to turn my head or bend down. I still had such bad back spasms that I had to have a physical therapist loosen me up before each show. Even so, nobody from the band ever asked what had happened. Nobody ever asked how I was feeling.

Nobody ever mentioned it at all.

I was in a car crash, for god's sake! You're my bandmates!

I couldn't understand it.

At the end of the tour I went straight into a studio in New York to fool around with some demos. Studios are like fortresses or casinos, with no windows and no clocks. Real life is shut out. Whatever studio I worked in always became my asylum; it kept me cloistered away from the world. One night, alone in the studio, it hit me.

It's not that you need to be here. It's that you have no place to go.

I had no meaningful relationships, no real connections to the world. Not even within the band that had long served as my de facto family. I had the luxury of being able to go into a studio whenever I wanted. I also had the luxury of going into a studio as an alternative to having nothing else to do.

When I got a call about the possibility of producing a band on the West Coast, I quickly booked a flight. When I boarded the plane, I sat down, feeling fine, just like any other time I had ever flown. But all of a sudden my hands started shaking uncontrollably and my lips went numb.

I started gasping for air. I couldn't breathe.

Am I having a heart attack?

I was terrified and had no idea what was happening to me. I jumped up, grabbed my things, and ran off the plane.

What just happened?

Once I calmed down, with the help of a Valium, I went straight to a doctor's office. The doctor told me not to worry: it was just a panic attack.

47

I always find it interesting when people watching talk shows think the guests on the show are telling the truth. They believe the host and the guest are having an actual conversation—like they would in their own home or at a coffee shop.

They're performing!

Talk-show guests always have an agenda and know how they want to come across and what they are selling. That's the case whenever you're in front of the media, whether you're faced with a camera lens or a microphone. When I was in bed with a dozen women being interviewed for the documentary *The Decline of Western Civilization Part II: The Metal Years,* it was no different.

Once KISS took off the makeup, I got to be the same guy I was onstage even without the greasepaint. I enjoyed having that line erased. And yet, even though the line had been erased, it wasn't actually me. It may have been a little confusing—truth be told, I think some women were disappointed that I wasn't like that guy onstage when I was behind closed doors with them. I could perform like that; I could act like that; I could be like that in bed—but it wasn't real. Women were often thrown that they weren't getting what they expected. In some ways, I was much more boring and uptight than they had hoped.

The scenario in *The Decline of Western Civilization* wasn't totally unrealistic. It was having all the women there *at one time* that was unrealistic. Having that many wasn't—it's just they would be with me over the course of a week. But I wanted to take it to an absurd limit. I created that character, yes, but I also had a sense of humor about it.

I'm sure some people thought, "What an asshole." But I thought it was funny. I was chuckling along with the viewers.

Look at him!

I was playing Superman. Still, as I approached my fortieth birthday, I began to think I needed to find someone, settle down, and have a family.

Playing Superman was well and good, but it seemed like my career, or how I was perceived, was a detriment to finding that person. Sometimes that led to situations where I felt I had to give a disclaimer—as if the life I lived necessitated an apology. I tried to tell some of the women I dated, *Hey, I'm not really like that.* Or, *I'm really a nice guy.* Or, *I'm really down to earth.* Those things would either prove themselves to be so, or not, but I felt the need to explain myself. That was a bad precedent for a relationship. People either got it or they didn't.

I thought back to the early eighties and a club I used to go to in New York called Trax. There was always an older guy hanging around there, with a telltale hairline. Back then I thought to myself, *I never want to be that guy.* Now, a decade later, I felt I was in danger of becoming that very same guy. I didn't want to be the guy with the comb-over still hitting on young chicks. It was ugly, awkward, and embarrassing. I also didn't want to be alone.

How was I going to fix this situation?

I know! I'll get married!

I wasn't shy about telling people about my new goal. I had finally relocated permanently to L.A., and I figured the best way to meet someone was to let everybody know what I was looking for. I put the word out.

Soon a guy I knew told me about a woman he knew—as a matter of fact, he had dated her. He said if she gave him the okay, he would pass along her number. She said no, because she had just ended a relationship. That piqued my interest. If something was unavailable, I wanted it. I kept insisting until finally she agreed to let him give me her number. She was an actress named Pam Bowen, who had made one-off appearances on shows like *MacGyver, Moonlighting,* and *Cheers* and was the spokeswoman character for a big computer company.

On our first date, she was late. When we finally got to spend a bit of time together, she told me that she hadn't wanted to meet me because she was having a hard time getting over her European boyfriend, Claude, who had gone back to Europe to marry his other girlfriend. The other girlfriend was pregnant by him, and he felt it was his duty. I would later see firsthand that even duty had its limitations.

For our second date, I arranged to take her to opening night at the Los Angeles Opera, together with Bob Ezrin and his wife, Fran. My assistant told me confidentially that Pam said she didn't have anything appropriate to wear. "No problem," I said. I arranged a fitting for a rented gown, the way celebrities often do for award shows.

For some reason, she wanted to meet me at my house rather than have us pick her up. Twenty minutes before the curtain was to go up, Bob, Fran, and I were looking at each other in my driveway, wondering where Pam was and whether we could possibly make the show. Still no Pam. Fran turned to me and said, "Is she always like this?" I shrugged. Finally Pam pulled up in her car. "I followed a car up the wrong road," she said through sobs and tears.

Huh?

We all climbed into the limo, and the driver managed the impossible, getting us downtown in record time, just as the theater lights were going down.

As Pam and I began to socialize more together, we spent our time with her friends because I had so few of my own. But I didn't think much of her friends. One was Marla Maples, whose claim to fame was breaking up Donald Trump's marriage. Not exactly a pillar of society. But Pam had a very charitable attitude when she spoke of a number of other people I found questionable. "They have a good heart," she would say.

"For what—a transplant?" I answered.

It's not about how good your heart is, it's about what you do with it during your life. These people were bad based on their actions and life experiences. To me, you can't discount that by saying somebody has a good heart. Even so, I told myself I was in a realistic, normal relationship that could lead to marriage.

There was also a lot of drama in the relationship. Right from the start we constantly sent cards and letters back and forth about being alternatively disappointed or sorry and trying to explain things. The problems definitely went both ways. But I always thought I could fix whatever was wrong—with me and with her.

I want a relationship. I want marriage. I want a family.

I want a life out of a Norman Rockwell painting.

Then one afternoon in early 1991 Eric Carr called me at home. He had just gotten home from the doctor's office. "What's wrong?" I said.

"I spat up some blood, so I thought I'd go get checked out," said Eric.

"Everything cool?"

"I don't know," he said. "But I'm really worried. They gave me some kind of scan and found a finger-shaped growth going in and out of my heart."

"Did they say anything?"

"They said it could be cancer."

"Nah, don't worry about it," I said. "Everything always seems worse than it really is. There's no reason to think the worst-case scenario is the one that will happen. The chances that it's serious are so small. And even if it's cancer, you'll get it taken care of."

Unfortunately, a few days later he called me again. "It really *is* cancer," Eric told me.

Worse still, it was an extremely rare form of cancer. The number of cases of heart cancer every year is in the single digits. But I still thought everything would be okay.

He left L.A. for a hospital in New York City, and Gene and I flew out to be with him during his open-heart surgery. As far as I understood it, they took part of his heart out and then reconstructed it with what was left.

Not long afterwards, we were asked to record "God Gave Rock 'n' Roll to You" for the movie *Bill & Ted's Bogus Journey*—with Bob Ezrin producing, trying to capture some *Destroyer*-era magic and erase the memory of *The Elder*. Eric desperately wanted to work on the song, but he was still very frail. "You have to pay attention to your health now," I told him, "whether that means recuperating on a tropical island or just resting and focusing on yourself."

If I knew then what I know now—I never thought this might be his last chance to perform—I would have let him play, but at the time I was sure he would beat the odds. So Eric Singer played that session, though Eric Carr came to L.A. and sat behind the drums for the video shoot. He had lost all his hair from the cancer treatment and had to wear a massive wig to replicate his natural puffball. He played like a man possessed during the video shoot, duplicating Eric Singer's parts in take after exhausting take.

"God Gave Rock 'n' Roll to You" came out really well, and we decided to try to make another album with Bob Ezrin. When Bob is in top form, he's hard to beat, and I think he wanted to prove something—he, too, was embarrassed about *The Elder*—and he wanted to buckle down and create a hard-edged, quality album. *Hot in the Shade* had been a hodgepodge; it was obvious the band was fragmented. If Gene was going to reengage and we could get back to doing what we did well, I was all for it.

We told Eric Carr that we were going to record an album without him. We assured him we would pay all of his bills and keep his insurance going. I reiterated that in the grand scheme of things, the band mattered little. He had to focus on doing whatever he could to get well, without compromise.

Bob brought in a bunch of drummers to rehearse with us as we started working on *Revenge*. We played with Aynsley Dunbar for a while, who'd done stints in Journey, Whitesnake, and the Jeff Beck Group, among many others. He was a great classic English drummer, but he just didn't fit. At some point, we brought Eric Singer back. Whether you work in a band or at a factory or in any other kind of job, you have to work together with other people, and that connection affects the overall quality of the work as well as the atmosphere. As fate would have it, Eric Singer fit perfectly. He really was replacing Eric Carr in KISS—at least for a few months in the recording studio.

Throughout it all, I never considered the possibility that Eric Carr might die. I figured he'd be weak for a long time—that the status quo would go on and on. That was how I insulated myself and protected myself against the worst-case scenario.

I was wrong.

That fall of 1991, as we worked in L.A., I got a call from my friend Bob Held in New York. What he was trying to tell me was confusing. Eric Carr had suffered a stroke. The cancer had spread to his brain. He'd been found in his apartment after calling 9-1-1. When the emergency responders showed up, Eric was already unconscious, so they paged through his address book and randomly chose someone to call—which turned out to be Bob.

But from that moment on, we couldn't get any information. His parents wouldn't talk to me. I called daily, to no avail. I didn't understand why nobody would talk to me—or to Gene, for that matter.

A few weeks later, on November 24, 1991, my assistant called me and said, "Eric is dead."

I called Gene and told him the news.

It was shocking—partly because we hadn't been able to get any information about his situation.

Gene and I flew to New York for Eric's funeral. It was an open casket funeral, which was ghastly. The body in the casket, which was holding a set of drumsticks, didn't look like Eric. It didn't look like a human being. It looked like a mannequin. Eric's girlfriend, a *Playboy* Playmate he'd been with for several years, briefly took the drumsticks out of the casket for some reason, and Eric's fingers moved as she did.

The scent of flowers was overwhelming. You could barely breathe. But I could also smell hostility all around us—people bristling at our presence. Peter and Ace were there. Peter, who everyone knew resented and disliked Eric, tried to tell me that Eric had been calling him all the time. Nothing seemed to make sense. Eric's girlfriend was also filled with anger at me and Gene. It turned out that Eric had painted us as the bad guys—he said we'd booted him out of the band and didn't support him, which simply wasn't true. Everyone there seemed to have the impression that Eric had been cut off. But he hadn't been cut off. Once we told him we were going to record *Revenge,* he cut himself off from us. I didn't feel like the bad guy, and it was strange to be treated that way.

During the service, it was as if a switch had been thrown inside me, and I started sobbing uncontrollably—just bawling my eyes out.

In the wake of Eric Carr's death, I continued to spend a lot of time wondering whether I had handled things correctly. Though I thought I had made the best choices at the time, I began to realize I'd been wrong. We *had* cut Eric off in perhaps the worst way, by denying him what mattered to him most—his place in KISS. That had been lost on me while we continued to do everything we thought was important, everything we thought we could and should do.

It was wrong to keep Eric from the thing he loved most, what for him was a lifeline. KISS. And I should have *seen* that, since the band functioned the same way for me, and I wasn't even sick.

I should have *known*.

48.

A few months later, in January 1992, Pam threw a surprise fortieth birthday party for me at the Hollywood Athletic Club. I was caught totally off-guard and was thrilled to see a large turnout that included my parents, whom Pam had secretly flown out to L.A. She also hired a KISS tribute band called Cold Gin to play the party. Cold Gin had started to pack the Troubadour club doing classic KISS songs in makeup—at a time when tribute bands were not yet a big thing.

The guy playing Ace in the band was guitarist Tommy Thayer. I knew Tommy a little by then and had tried writing with him, too. He played the parts faithfully and knew every lick. I was impressed. He had clearly worked at learning those parts and put pride and persistence into it. It was also really fun for me to see a band doing what I no longer did.

Tommy told me that he had shifted his professional focus. Aside from the tribute band, he was mostly concentrating on producing and managing bands now. He didn't want to be the oldest guy in a band still trying to make it, living with a stripper on Franklin Avenue. He didn't want to be the oldest guy in the club, a sentiment I totally understood and that impressed me.

Listening to Cold Gin was also an interesting reminder that KISS had started out as a classic rock band. That early material sounded more like Humble Pie or the Who than the hair bands. It felt good to have *Revenge* in the bag, since it was a credible album on which we got back to doing what we did well. Music would always go through changes. We had thought that we weren't current, but that had been a misjudgment. We didn't need to chase trends; we needed to do what we did, and do it well.

Soon, we had to get ready to tour *Revenge*. Even though Eric Singer played on the album, we had never made any promises about his touring with us or, after Eric Carr's death, joining the band. Now we had to decide what to do.

Gene and Bruce didn't know Eric Singer as a person at all. They had crossed paths with him only for a few hours here or there in the recording studio. But I could vouch for Eric's work ethic and his sense of responsibility as a result of working with him on my solo tour. Eric Singer had been a team guy when it mattered—during the long hours spent together on the road.

The next dilemma sounds silly in retrospect. Eric Singer had dyed blond hair back then, and Bruce, Gene, and I actually had a meeting to discuss whether we could deal with that. Everybody in the history of the band had had dark hair. Could we have a guy in KISS with blond hair?

Fuck it, we weren't going to make a decision at this point in our lives based on the color of someone's hair.

So Eric Singer—as Eric Carr had eerily predicted—became the new drummer in KISS. We rehearsed and played a few club gigs in April to break him in. One thing we quickly learned about Eric was that he also had an amazing voice. Even though he had toured with my solo band, I had no idea. As soon as we started rehearsing the classic material, Eric said, "Okay, which vocal parts do you want me to sing?"

I thought he was joking. Gene sang him a part. "Can you sing that?" It was too low. So Gene took that part and Eric tried a higher part. Eric was phenomenal at the high harmonies, and soon we shifted duties around so he was basically singing all of the high parts, which in KISS usually carried the main melody. I shifted down to one of the other parts. It was great, because it was tough to have to do it all—talk between the songs, sing the lead, and sing the main melodies of the harmonies, all night long. Having such a great background vocalist join the band was a godsend.

As we got ready to go to Europe for the first leg of the *Revenge* tour, I was planning to ask Pam to marry me. And when she became pregnant, I knew this was the time to ask. I bought a beautiful engagement ring. I picked the stone myself and had it set in a band designed to look like a vintage ring she loved. I was very excited when I got it, very excited when I asked her to marry me, and very excited when I went home in June and we prepared for our July wedding.

With Pam pregnant and our wedding day fast approaching, we finally went to a meeting with separate counsel to discuss a prenuptial agreement. I had insisted on the meeting because of the vast discrepancy between what we were coming into the marriage with—both monetarily and materially. By this time, I was happily paying virtually all of Pam's bills. But I still wanted to try to come to an agreement at a time when goodwill prevailed. Not five minutes into the meeting, she ran from the room hysterical. I ran after her.

When I caught up to her, she told me that we could have the baby without getting married. She said she wanted nothing from me if things didn't work out down the road. "Where I'm from," she said, "your word is your bond."

Overtaken by the fear of losing her completely, I told her I still wanted to get married—without any agreement.

A few days before the wedding, Pam miscarried. We were both devastated, but we went ahead as planned. Everybody at the wedding knew what had happened, and the air of gloom was undeniable. The silence in the face of sadness was all too familiar to me.

When KISS headed out on a full arena tour in October, Pam never seemed to know where I was or whether I had a show that day or a day off. I would call her, and she literally had no clue about where I was and what I was doing. I began to waver back and forth, sometimes wondering what I had gotten myself into and other times thinking I had to do whatever it took to make it work.

I can make anything work.

The European guy Pam had just broken up with when I first met her never stopped calling her, and she never stopped talking to him. Early on, Claude called her several times a week from Europe. I asked her why. I mean, I could understand his showing no respect for me or our marriage, but I didn't understand why Pam didn't seem to, either. Especially after I told her that the calls bothered me a lot and asked her to stop. She didn't want to hear it. Making any concessions or adjustments wasn't part of her concept of marriage. She saw anything like that as a loss of her freedom, as limiting her ability to be whomever she wanted, whenever and wherever she wanted.

Although it wouldn't cure the core problem, I came up with what I thought was a sobering threat: "Why don't I call Claude's wife to see whether she knows you guys talk constantly, and see how *she* feels about it?" Pam looked at me with daggers. I was stifling her freedom, she said.

The contact didn't stop, I would later learn—it just happened when I wasn't around. I seemed to be back in a disappointingly familiar place—seeking approval or acceptance, and not getting it.

Pam and I pushed each other's buttons in a way that didn't leave either of us happy. "You don't let me be who I am," she would say. "So you'll never get to see the real me."

We talked about issues like that until we were blue in the face. But I had chosen to be in the relationship. I had seen the signals from the beginning and chose to ignore them or dismiss them. I had no grounds for surprise now.

She went to Mexico at some stage to shoot a short-lived TV series called *Land's End*, and I flew down during a break in the tour. When I got there, I found a message from Claude on her hotel phone.

Come on!

The calls persisted, and my continued requests that Pam stop talking to him were met with more angry refusals. I felt like neither me nor our marriage meant much to her. Actions speak louder than words, and in this case the actions were speaking loudly.

Still, I wouldn't quit.

We seemed to be at odds over just about everything, and I almost innately understood that our marriage was doomed. But I didn't want to admit failure.

There must be a way to get this right.

49

Once the *Revenge* tour ended at the end of 1992, KISS was in for an extended quiet period. The music industry landscape was changing dramatically, both because of grunge and because of a general downturn in the economy.

On the professional front, we spent the next two years on a couple of homegrown projects. Gene came up with the idea of a photo-heavy coffee-table book on the band, called *KISStory*, which Jesse Hilsen brilliantly suggested we create, print, and market ourselves. Gene also had the idea for a series of KISS conventions. For both projects, we turned to Tommy Thayer.

Tommy was from Portland, Oregon. His family owned office supply stores, and his father was a retired brigadier general. Tommy was bright and diligent, and despite tasting a little success with his first band, Black 'N Blue, he had moved on, cut his hair, and started working on the sidelines of the business. Tommy also *loved* KISS.

When work began on *KISStory*, Tommy started the months-long process of going through boxes and boxes of photos and clips in our archives. Not surprisingly, he bore down on the material. He had an encyclopedic knowledge of KISS, and in a pre-Internet era when every bit of minutia wasn't readily available, his brain was a unique and genuine resource for a project like we had in mind.

Eventually, when the photo editing was done, Tommy moved to Gene's guesthouse, where a computer had been set up to produce the book. Jesse figured out how to market the book through an 800 number. He figured selling directly would work better than using a traditional publishing company. And his hunch was correct. Once we finished the book and had it printed in Korea, we hired a tele-marketing company to take phone orders and ship the books, and it was a huge success.

The conventions would be a traveling KISS museum of sorts, where memorabilia collectors and fans would congregate to cele-brate the band. Concert promoters had no interest in acts perceived as hair bands, but we figured that, as with the book, we could do it by ourselves—rent ballrooms at hotels and put on the events with-out a promoter. Again, we needed someone to handle the logistics, and again, we turned to Tommy, who had proved so knowledge-able and hardworking during the making of *KISStory*.

The conventions were really Gene's baby, and I had very little to do with them. I did help Tommy get custom mannequins from a shop in Burbank and then apply the makeup on their faces. Our original plan was to use normal store mannequins, but they didn't look right. I remember being struck by how different the faces looked after the face paint was applied to them—even though they were all identical mannequin heads. The makeup seemed to change the whole structure of the faces.

We also had the four wax heads from the Hollywood Wax Museum. When I looked at mine, I didn't think it looked like me. So I got out some sculpting tools and altered the face.

Gene, Tommy, and I started going through boxes at our storage space. We went through crate after crate and catalogued what was in each one with the help of a photographer. It was fun to pull out the old outfits and have a look at them again. Day after day we went through the stuff and slowly decided what to display and how to display it. Tommy and I drove down to a place in Buena Park, near Disneyland, to a workshop where they built custom-made Plexiglas enclosures. We designed a set of collapsible display cases and ordered them.

All along, we paid close attention to the budget, since we were paying for everything out of pocket and doing it all on our own, with no advances. It was a real education.

While the book and conventions were still in the planning phase, we also began to discuss a new album. Bob Ezrin wasn't available, but it didn't matter, because Gene had a bee in his bonnet. Music was different now, he said, and we needed to be current. I think maybe he was attracted to the grunge sound because it was dark—it fit with the persona he wanted to project. When I brought in a few songs early in the process, he was very dismissive. "You don't know what's going on," he said. "You don't know what music is like anymore."

I just couldn't picture KISS writing gloom and doom stories. "What are we going to write about?" I asked him. "That our housekeepers didn't show up today? Our limo was late?"

It was ridiculous for me to write gloomy songs—and just as ridiculous for Gene to do it, too. It ain't that dark in Beverly Hills.

I was also skeptical about what all the grunge bands would do on their second albums. There were a lot of great first albums, but what would they do once they were platinum acts instead of kids living in roach-infested garages? I mean, if they were so miserable, once they had money, they could all go see shrinks.

But Gene felt strongly about the project, so I agreed to the plan. He didn't want to do it any other way. I could be proven wrong.

Hey, maybe the album would come out and everybody would say it was a work of genius. I seriously doubted it. After all, it was us impersonating other bands, which made no sense. KISS *celebrated* life—we sang about how great life was and about self-empowerment. Now we had to mope and sing about how miserable everything was? That wasn't us doing what we do well.

I started tuning my guitar down, but I struggled with writing songs I had no real connection to. Meanwhile, Gene reveled in the idea of trying to out-Metallica Metallica. There was already a great Metallica, and we sure as hell weren't going to beat them. We were at our best a great KISS, and that fact seemed lost as we tried to hop on a train that we could never pull. We'd be lucky to be the caboose.

Fortunately, I eventually found a subject I felt connected to: I wrote "I Will Be There" for my new son, Evan. Pam had gotten pregnant again in late 1993, and in June of 1994 we went to the labor and delivery unit at Cedars-Sinai Hospital. Pam was about a week past due, so we went there with an appointment for her to be induced. She wasn't actually in labor, so I had plenty of time to set up my tripod and camera. I'll never forget the last sonogram before Evan was born. The 3D technology was still pretty new, and when the doctor did a close-up of his head, Evan turned and faced the device as if on cue. *Oh, my God, that's my face!*

I'd always thought that having kids someday would be a terrific thing. But until I cut the umbilical cord, I didn't realize the depth of it, the holiness of it, the sacredness of it. Up until that day, life never made much sense to me. You showed up on earth, spent a little time here, and died. It seemed pointless. But as soon as I held Evan in the delivery room and we made eye contact, I suddenly got it: *We don't really die.* We were here on earth to leave the world a better place through our children. And through our children, we lived on. It was stunning to make eye contact with this little person who had just entered the world and to realize that I would continue. This was the cycle that had been going on since the beginning of time. I would live on through *him*.

As we were driving home from the hospital with this new little being in our car, I was absolutely terrified. I probably caused accidents because of how slow I was driving. When babies are born, their necks can't support their heads, and if their heads lean too far one way or the other, they can suffer from lack of blood flow to the brain. I drove five miles an hour, constantly looking in the rearview mirror to make sure his head was upright in the car seat.

I had always considered myself the center of my universe; when Evan came along, I suddenly moved aside without even thinking about it. He became the center of my universe. And maybe he was a second chance for me to experience a childhood the way it was supposed to be.

His birth calmed me and answered a big question: *Why are we here?* We're here to raise children and leave something better behind. The profundity of the moment took me back to Hawaii years before, when I had thought I was drowning. Back then, all I could think about was that it made no sense that the world would go on after I died. Looking into my son's eyes, I went from being the center of the universe to being glad to move aside and cede it to him. It's yours, son.

I am here because of those who came before. And I will go on because of those who come after.

All of a sudden, I slept better.

50.

The KISS conventions came to fruition in 1995, starting in Australia. Ticket presales were strong, so we
weren't anxiously waiting to see whether anyone showed up. The
conventions worked because of the mythology of KISS—that was
the drawing power. The concept was unique and people responded.

And responded in some unique ways. Some people, for instance,
got married at the conventions. That might seem odd to some, but I
saw it as a huge compliment. I never took it lightly that somebody
chose to get married in KISS makeup at one of these events. The
fact that the band meant that much to people was terrific. To have
that kind of impact and be that much a part of the fabric of somebody's life was a special feeling. I loved the looseness and informal-
ity of the format of the conventions, too, with the Q&A sessions we
did and our acoustic performances. We were playing to the most
hardcore fans and not being scrutinized for perfection—the acoustic shows became sonic snapshots.

When we held a convention in Burbank, just outside of L.A.,

Eric Singer suggested that we invite Peter Criss to come. It was a gesture of goodwill—to show Peter that he was part of the family. When he showed up, he was thrilled—grinning ear to ear, punching the air. Peter was older than us, and in the years since he had left the band, the age gap seemed to have increased—perhaps because of his lack of solo success or a dissatisfaction with life in general. I gave him a KISS motorcycle jacket to wear. The only one we had on hand was about four sizes too big, but he was pleased to be flying the colors.

He joined us onstage and sang "Hard Luck Woman." He couldn't remember all the words—we hadn't rehearsed—but it was a warm moment. He looked like a kid who had just gotten the keys to the candy store, and I was glad to see him after all the years.

We had about twenty-five stops across the United States, with the final convention held at Roseland in Manhattan. Alex and Roger Coletti at MTV, both big KISS fans, had gotten wind of our acoustic shows at the conventions and sought us out in New York to ask about doing an *MTV Unplugged* session. In the process of playing all the conventions, we had honed our ability to play the songs acoustically and sing them well. Electric guitars are very forgiving, whereas acoustic instruments have a crispness and clarity that gives you less leeway. The strings are also a heavier gauge, and bending them is challenging at first. We also sang without any effects, though the spaces often created natural ambience and echo. By the end of the long convention tour, the band sounded great. We felt confident about doing *Unplugged*.

MTV wanted the extra hook of a reunion with the original guys. Peter and Ace were both being represented by an old road manager of ours named George Sewitt. He came in with lots of ridiculous terms and stipulations. We had to throw all of that out before we could get Peter and Ace into a studio in New York to try rehearsing together. George's terms and demands kept changing, no matter what Peter and Ace had agreed to, but Gene did a great job of riding shotgun and keeping them under control.

Everybody had their guard up when Ace and Peter sauntered into the studio. Eric Singer and Bruce were both there, but clearly Peter and Ace were feeling the most uncomfortable. Everybody in the current band was approaching the situation from a place of strength. We never thought for a second about not having Eric and Bruce there. Peter and Ace were coming into our house, and Eric and Bruce were residents—they had earned their places.

I had seen Peter and Ace only rarely since the early 1980s. I had heard secondhand stories about how much Peter's playing had deteriorated—how his various bands weren't very good. But there was an exciting and surreal sense of nostalgia in the room when they entered.

Tommy Thayer had once revealed a perception of the original lineup that he probably shared with a lot of outsiders. "I always thought Ace and Peter were the rock and roll guys," he had said, "and you and Gene were the business guys." I had laughed then, and I laughed inside now as they walked into the room. It was true that Ace liked to portray himself as some sort of American Keith Richards, but I knew Tommy was in for a rude awakening. Gene and I had never stopped playing our instruments since the inception of the band. I'd become a much more proficient guitar player after fifteen years of working at it constantly. Ace hadn't played nearly as much, and Peter hardly at all. When they had played, nobody was there to tell them when it wasn't good enough.

Peter seemed to have completely lost it. He had become your slightly nutty uncle. He came in with some silly miniature tribal drums that he held in one hand and boinked with a stick. He wanted to hit them while he sang "Beth." We nixed that idea.

We worked on about four songs with them. The rest of the show would be just me, Gene, Eric, and Bruce.

The studio where we did the *MTV Unplugged* taping was beautifully staged and lit. An audience of die-hard KISS fans packed the place, having heard the rumors of an original-lineup reunion. The floor was covered with a huge drop cloth printed with the *Rock and Roll Over* album cover. We had wax figures of us in makeup—swag from the conventions—set up behind us.

Ace kept gabbing on and on into the microphone, which was distracting and clearly about trying to reclaim more of the spotlight. That got fixed when the show and album were mixed.

When the show was aired in August 1995, it proved to be the second most viewed *MTV Unplugged* in the history of the show. Almost as soon as it aired, speculation about a full-on reunion started to brew. To me, there seemed to be sufficient good feelings to explore the possibility. In fact, I saw it as a logical next step. Also, given the well-documented car accidents and other brushes with death that Ace and Peter seemed to constantly have, the window for a reunion might shut sooner rather than later, as far as I was concerned. One of these guys was sure to kick the bucket, and if there ever would be a time to get back together, it was now.

I also thought a reunion might provide closure. When the band broke apart, we were all young and stupid. Maybe we could get back together having learned from life, and everyone would see the band for the gift it was. Maybe we could see it through to the end and ride off into the sunset together, a band, a team, one for all and all for one, until we called it quits on our own terms.

I started trying to get Gene on board.

He was skeptical, to say the least, and didn't think it would be the financial juggernaut I was sure it would be. We had just done the conventions and sold tickets for a hundred dollars to a pared-down crowd of a few hundred fans in each city. The idea was to get a smaller number of people at a higher ticket price. We weren't trying to sell out arenas. And since we didn't need fifteen buses to move the show from place to place, the overheads were lower than a concert tour. In theory, the conventions could have been quite lucrative. As novel and fun as they were, however, they weren't very profitable.

Given the way concert guarantees and tour merchandising had evolved—this was the era when concert ticket prices suddenly shot up—it was hard to imagine anything like the conventions competing with the windfall of a reunion tour in makeup. It seemed like a no-brainer to me.

Still, Gene was a hard sell. Even as I crunched numbers on the phone for him, his skepticism was unwavering.

I was 100 percent convinced the timing was right. When we went back to L.A., I called Gene and again went over hypothetical numbers based on a possible attendance of ten thousand people, ticket prices, and merchandising statistics for current tours. One example I used was the Eagles. They had reunited in 1994 and continued touring throughout 1995, playing to millions of people and hitting the Billboard charts with a live album. I had personally witnessed the long lines of people waiting to buy T-shirts and merchandise at one of their shows. It was an unprecedented financial success for a band who had also broken up around the time the original KISS lineup started to splinter. Those guys certainly didn't reunite out of a newfound love for one another. And, hey, if *they* could get along . . .

You know how you wet your finger and hold it up to judge the wind? I felt it was now or never—the wind was right. No matter how successful we were in the present, without makeup, I knew there was nothing that could compete with what we had been. The myth. The legend. Once upon a time.

Gene finally agreed to talk with a few talent agencies about the possibility of booking a reunion tour. When we showed up for the meetings, we encountered a perceptible shift in the reception we got. In recent years we had become accustomed to beer nuts and sodas at meetings. Suddenly we were ushered into conference rooms packed with bigwigs. Elaborately catered buffets were laid out in front of us. "Please, gentlemen, help yourselves."

Hot food?

Hmmm, maybe we really *were* onto something big. Gene now smelled the coffee. He was in.

Part V

The highway to heartache

51.

Based on what booking agencies told us, it was clear that a reunion tour was going to be way bigger than we could handle on our own. We needed a new manager. We immediately thought of Doc McGhee. When Bon Jovi went to Europe with us in 1984, Doc was managing them. He took them to superstardom. He had also taken Motley Crue to the top. And we had encountered him even earlier, when he managed Pat Travers, who opened some shows for us during the original makeup era. If anyone would get it, Doc would.

We had our first meeting with Doc at a restaurant on Sunset Boulevard in Hollywood. He immediately started riffing—we would do the "Seven Wonders of the World Tour" and kick it off by playing in front of the sphinx and the pyramids in Egypt. He thought big. Ridiculously big, just like we had. Just like Bill Aucoin had.

Clearly, Doc was the right guy. It was a relief to find somebody who not only got it, but was capable of adding to it, of raising the ante. We didn't take meetings with anyone else.

As the planning started, it became obvious this wasn't going to be one year out of our lives, but rather a chunk of our lives—*years*. Doc was talking about everyone putting all their time and effort into a reunion. Even though Gene was mouthing his enthusiasm, I warned Doc, "I've seen this movie—I know how it ends." Doc assured me that he could keep everyone engaged, but I knew the inevitable truth. I liked shooting for the moon, but it was also imperative for Doc to understand and accept reality.

The adrenaline was flowing, and we were all shooting sparks as we came up with endless ideas. One thing Gene kept bugging Doc about was getting KISS on the covers of *Time* and *Newsweek* magazines. Apparently, Bruce Springsteen had been on both simultaneously at the time of *Born in the U.S.A.*, and Doc now had marching orders to make it happen for us.

"Gene," said Doc, "the only way you're getting on the cover of those magazines is if you shoot the president with your makeup on."

Doc is one of us.

As a reunion became more and more concrete, we had to break the news to Eric Singer and Bruce Kulick. We scheduled a meeting at Gene's house. I don't think those guys thought a reunion was feasible because they had witnessed the state of Peter and Ace's playing during the *MTV Unplugged* rehearsal and taping. I realized later that they expected the meeting to be a game-planning session for the release of *Carnival of Souls*. When we broke the news, they both seemed blindsided.

Eric and Bruce weren't happy, but we told them we would keep them on the payroll while they took some time to figure out their next moves. Eric has always been a little cynical and has always seen himself as a hired gun. Even then, he was already a journeyman drummer who had played with lots of bands—he worked for everybody because he was just that good. And yet, in this instance, he was clearly hurt.

We didn't mean to hurt those guys, but I still felt bad. "They call it the music *business* for a reason," Eric said, as a way of saying he understood the decision. "I appreciate the fact that you guys had the balls to do this face to face." I guess it hadn't always been that way in the course of his career. But that was something important to me. For instance, I would never break up with a girlfriend over the phone, and we had flown out to New York to end things with Bill Aucoin in person. It showed respect for someone. And these guys had made sizable contributions to the band.

Bruce, as always, was a real mensch. "I get it," he said. "A reunion seems obvious—it's the way to go."

Not surprisingly, it took a lot of wrangling with Peter and Ace's representative to get a deal in place. Ace insisted on getting more money than Peter because, as Ace put it, Peter wasn't worth as much as he was. "Peter hasn't done anything," Ace insisted. "He hasn't been playing—and I'm more famous than he is."

Of course, this was all behind Peter's back. For all the times Ace threw Peter under the bus, he should have had muscles like a professional bodybuilder. And yet Peter still saw Ace as his teammate and buddy, no matter how many times Ace offered Peter up as a sacrificial lamb.

In the past, people had told me, "The time to find out that you don't want to be in bed with somebody isn't when your clothes are off." So we spelled everything out in the contracts with those guys—ground rules, consequences for not following them, all the things we would and wouldn't do. And most importantly, we would rehearse and see how everyone responded to working together within carefully spelled-out parameters. We left nothing to chance.

Part of that included hiring personal trainers—not just for Peter and Ace, but for me and Gene, too. We wanted the band to look the way people remembered us looking. The last thing I wanted was people to be disappointed when they saw a bunch of fat guys in tights.

The trainers weren't bodybuilders or anything like that—it was about cardio and basic strength. Even so, the guy working with Peter was aghast—not only at how weak he was and how low his endurance was, but also at how little Peter was willing to work. The trainer said it was like working with an old man. Peter had a tendency to explode at the trainer about nonsense because Peter didn't like working out.

Ace, as usual, was just lazy. But he put in his time.

Alongside the physical training, we also started the rehearsal process. Or tried to. We convened in L.A. in March, planning to rehearse for several months. It was imperative to look and sound great for these shows—we were competing not just with our past, but with people's recollections of our past. That was the challenge as I saw it. We had to re-create the impact our shows had on people at a time when nobody else did what we did. By the nineties, everybody had pyrotechnics, everybody had a show with KISS DNA in it—all it took was money. We had to blow away a new standard.

Then Ace asked, "Why do we need to rehearse? I know these songs like the back of my hand." It quickly became apparent that Ace didn't know the back of his hand very well. And Peter? Peter was another story. There was no point to rehearsing as a band. Peter and Ace didn't know the material, didn't know their parts.

I called Tommy Thayer. Tommy knew our music inside-out and would make a good coach. We wanted to be true to the original *KISS Alive!* versions of our classic songs. "Listen, Tommy," I told him. "We need you to get together with Peter one-on-one in a rehearsal studio. Just you and him. You on guitar, Peter on his drums. You need to go through all the songs with him and make sure he knows what he's doing."

After the first day of working one-on-one with Peter, Tommy called me. "Paul," he said, sounding very serious, "I don't know exactly how to say this."

Uh-oh.

"I want to see this happen more than anything, for the sake of everyone involved," Tommy continued. "But, well, I have to be honest with you: I don't know how you guys are going to be able to do this." He paused. Then I laughed. I assumed he was joking.

"No, I'm serious," Tommy said. "Playing with Peter is like playing with someone who picked up drumsticks for the first time today. It's like he's never played before. He doesn't remember anything, and he can't play."

Somehow this didn't surprise me. Not only had Peter failed to grow musically or to hone his craft over the years, he had neglected it. I still hoped Tommy could bring him around. "Give it a few more days," I said. "You can do it."

Tommy kept at it, recording their sessions on cassette and bringing them over to play for me afterwards or playing them to me over the phone. Listening to the tapes was frustrating. At times, Tommy would gently say things like, "Maybe that last bit wasn't quite right . . . ," and Peter would shout at him aggressively, "Don't you fucking tell me how to play drums!"

It was a thankless job, having to be so diplomatic, having to take Peter's abuse. And for what? So Tommy—a *guitar* player—could teach Peter, supposedly a *professional* drummer, how to play his drums as well as a *beginner* again. In the end, Tommy taught Peter the parts like you would teach a dog a trick. It had nothing to do with music. But, lo and behold, after a few weeks, it started to click. Peter had learned his tricks. He could roll over—and play "Strutter."

We reconvened as a band. Now we realized Ace wasn't there yet, either. I was shocked to see the full extent of the deterioration in these guys—the disrespect they had for their talents and gifts.

I called Tommy again. Same drill. Tommy and Ace sat face to face in a studio for hours a day, two chairs, two Marshall amps, reviewing songs. Ace got up to speed much faster than Peter had.

Again we reconvened as a band. Now things started to sound better. We obviously weren't going to get to the level of the previous lineup, or any previous lineup, honestly, but there was now a bit of chemistry. We had a bit of that ragtag feel like we'd had in the early years.

Finally the day came when we went over to Gene's house and put on makeup and outfits together again for the first time, just to see how we looked. It was like time had stood still. We were those guys again. It was magical. I even let myself daydream about the possibility of not having just this moment, but of having a future— picking up where we had left off.

When we got down to the business of planning the tour, Doc McGhee said, "We'll start at Tiger Stadium."

"Are you nuts?" I said.

I knew it was going to be a big tour, but I didn't see it at that scale. This was well over the number ten thousand that I had pegged when I had called Gene to try to persuade him to consider a reunion tour. Here Doc was having us open at a venue that held four times that number of people. No testing the water on ticket sales. No warming up.

It was chutzpah beyond anything I could muster. Doc clearly knew something we didn't. He was coming off mega-tours with Bon Jovi and Mötley Crüe, and he knew that perception would become reality if people bought into it. Luckily, we deferred to him.

Soon we had offers from venues we had played at the height of things in the 1970s—and this at a time when many of our contemporaries, bands of the seventies and eighties, seemed on the verge of extinction because of grunge and the sea change in the music industry. Meanwhile, we had huge offers on the table. It was unreal. It was like hitting the lottery. Again.

When the tickets for the reunion tour went on sale, usually early in the morning East Coast time, I would get on the phone with Doc in the predawn darkness of L.A. and monitor what was happening at Ticketmaster in real time. Tiger Stadium sold out in less than an hour. As the other shows went on sale, it was the same. "Okay, New York just went on sale . . . okay, sold out, rolling into a second show . . . second show sold out."

The sun wasn't even up where I was, and we had sold out four shows at Madison Square Garden. "Okay, we're into Boston . . ."

It was amazing. Doc had been right.

52

Detroit rock city—back where it all began. Tiger Stadium, sold out, June 28, 1996. Gene, Ace, Peter, and me, together again. Magic. Electricity.

Here we are.

We had arrived ten days earlier—once again leaving nothing to chance—and had done seven rehearsals, including one full dress rehearsal. Ace was late for all of them.

At this point in my life, there were certain perks and prerequisites I felt I had earned and were necessary to make the coming tour manageable. We booked the best hotels; I wasn't going to be staying in hotels with a paper ring around the toilet seat saying SANITIZED FOR YOUR PROTECTION. Ace and Peter hadn't stayed in the upper echelon hotels in the sixteen years since they'd last toured with KISS. Peter in particular seemed completely lacking in world experience. I took him to Starbucks one day, and he was blown away by how good a biscotti was. Quite quickly both Peter and Ace came to resent the fact that they weren't as worldly or savvy when it came to maneuvering in nice surroundings. Peter constantly felt disrespected by hotel staff, for instance, which was simply the result of his feeling intimidated by them—and almost anyone else for that matter.

On the afternoon of the show, we did a sound check. As I stood on the stage, it was still hard to grasp that this baseball stadium would be jammed to capacity in a few hours. We took pictures, enjoying the moment. Peter, who had recently broken up with a girlfriend and was there on his own, seemed uncharacteristically open and grateful. His tendency was always to become dependent on someone and cut himself off from everybody else by using his girlfriend as a buffer—either a good buffer or a bad buffer, depending on the woman's personality. Now, single, Peter let himself bask in the moment.

That night, on our way to the stage, golf carts drove us through the mazelike bowels of the stadium. Suddenly we emerged from one of the access ramps to the area behind the stage, and the air was electric. You could hear the excitement, the anticipation. It was overwhelming. I realized I was suddenly exponentially more important than I had been just a few months before—because I was again a member not just of KISS, but of *this version* of KISS. I could hear the pent-up feelings of the people waiting for the show. People had made the journey from around the world to witness this night. It was deafening.

When the lights went down, it was pandemonium. It seemed like forty thousand flashbulbs went off as people waited for us to emerge.

I knew this show was pivotal. This show would reintroduce the band and the imagery and everything that went with it. This show could allow us to move forward. To continue. It felt like we were in the eye of a hurricane, everything swirling around us as we calmly watched from the quiet of backstage.

As we took the stage—still behind the curtain—I felt an incredible wave of pressure. The sound of the crowd had a tangible force to it. And even as the place went quiet, the noise of forty thousand people breathing created a deafening kind of hush. I had never felt like this before.

Alright, Detroit! You wanted the best, you got the best, the hottest band in the world . . . KISS!

The curtain dropped, and the force of the crowd reaction nearly lifted me off my feet.

I had to fight to be in control of the situation, of myself, of my persona, of the band. I was worried about staying connected to Peter—there was going to be a lot of foot-tapping and hand signals, I knew, in order to keep him with us. Fortunately, he was happy to have the guidance. It wasn't like him, to be honest, to be open to that sort of thing, but for the time being Peter was terrific— working hard, being cheerful and appreciative.

The joy for me was being able to revisit something I'd experienced as a much younger person in a different frame of mind. When I was in the midst of it the first time around, I had the sense it would never end. No matter how thankful I was, I had still suspected it would be endless. Then it had died down. But there on that stage, with KISS reunited, facing that kind of energy again, I felt thankful in an entirely different way. It wasn't about money. It wasn't about fame. I had those things already. This was the chance to read a book that I'd read as a kid, to see a movie that I'd seen when I was younger, to get something out of the experience that I hadn't had the capacity to get or appreciate before.

I was overwhelmed by a sense of gratitude.

As the tour continued, everyone seemed to share that feeling. At least initially. Peter swore up and down that he wouldn't repeat the mistakes he had made the first time around. And for the first few months of the reunion tour, we voted Peter the MVP. He often joined us for dinner. He was upbeat and pleasant to be around. His attitude seemed to mirror mine—we were incredibly fortunate to have this opportunity.

One of the things we had worried about on the reunion was Peter's drum solo. He had wanted to play one from the get-go. In a perfect world, a solo was part of what we did—we had always had a drum solo during the *Alive!* years. Looking back, it wasn't clear why we felt we needed to, but it had become a tradition. In the meantime, Peter's abilities had greatly deteriorated. But since he wanted to do it, and it was part of the tradition, Gene agreed to help him put one together.

Fortunately, by the nineties, you could hit a Coke bottle with a stick and make it sound explosive and powerful if you put enough effects on it. And that's exactly what we did. We put triggers on each individual drum so that when Peter hit one, it activated a pre-recorded drum sound. Although Peter had played with fire in the seventies, he was a shadow of himself now. On the reunion tour he hit the drums like he was worried his arms would snap if he did anything more than barely tap them. His arms hurt, he said. How hard you hit the drums determined the activation of the triggers, but fortunately they could be set to any level of sensitivity. We used to say we had the triggers set so Peter could play a solo by sneezing. I'd hear these huge drum sounds and turn around to look at Peter and see that he was barely moving his sticks.

But we wanted to succeed. And succeed we did.

For a time.

Then came Gigi. She was a born-again Christian who by all accounts had been a dancer before—and I don't mean she was in *Swan Lake*. When Peter got together with her, things started to change quickly. Peter reminded me of a small animal—when it's afraid, it's timid, but when it feels protected, it shows its teeth. Peter latched onto her and started to distance himself from everyone else.

I was amazed that while he and Gigi professed a deep love of God and religion, they inflicted nothing but pain and suffering on all those around them. Suddenly, when I called his room to talk, she would answer and say, "What do you want?"

"Is Peter there?"

"What do you need him for?"

Just get him to the damn phone. You're a guest.

She became a gatekeeper.

The tour might as well have been printing money by this time. Everything was selling out, and we kept adding shows. We were living an amazing life, flying around in a large private jet with a flight attendant, staying at beautiful hotels—we were on top of the world. Peter and Ace made millions of dollars—and they hadn't made squat in the nearly two decades they'd been out of the band. They had nothing before the reunion. And yet, as soon as their bank accounts began to fill up again, they changed.

Peter's hotel requests necessitated Doc printing a multipage handbook that was distributed to hotel staff wherever we went. It contained a set of complicated rules: if Peter put a sign on his door with one symbol, the staff could go in and vacuum, but they couldn't touch the windows; another sign meant they could air the room out, but not touch the towels; he needed to be a certain distance from the elevators; he couldn't be too high up; he made them cover certain windows with tinfoil.

Are you kidding me? This time last year you'd never been to a Starbucks!

One afternoon I heard screams and crashing sounds coming from the hall. I opened my hotel room door and saw Doc running past toward Peter and Gigi's room. Dishes were flying out of the room and smashing against the opposite wall in the hallway. "What's wrong, what's wrong?" Doc shouted.

"They didn't clean my room!" screamed Peter.

"But Peter, you put your sign on the door that means they can't come in!"

The cracks in the band were beginning to show—already.

Some nights Ace nodded out while putting his makeup on—just slumped into his chair with a paintbrush practically stuck in his eye. His use of a variety of illegal drugs was again out of control. He would go through all kinds of contortions—he even managed to get a superficial gun wound in Dallas—and then demand prescriptions for more drugs. Doc would have to blow the whistle and tell doctors not to give him painkillers. As Doc used to say, "Ace has the willpower of a grubworm."

It was sad. And frustrating. This should have been four guys celebrating something miraculous. Instead, it became hard work just to make sure it came off every day—that Peter and Ace got out of their rooms, that we made it to the venue, that we got through a show.

While I traveled with one rolling suitcase, Ace was now traveling with seventeen bags, including one that weighed more than a hundred pounds. In it was a projector and cables so he could run an image of his face and Elvis's face morphing into each other on a loop in his hotel room.

Ace brought along some interesting girlfriends, too. One liked to wander out into the audience with a clipboard and take notes—apparently, she was checking to make sure Ace was mixed loudly enough. Another one must have shot up on the plane, because she left blood all over her seat. She was in such bad shape, we sent a doctor into Ace's dressing room to have a look at her. "If I were you," the doctor told us, "I wouldn't have her traveling with you, because she's going to die." Doc handled that situation, and she was never seen on the tour again.

Needless to say, Doc was increasingly pissed off at Peter and Ace.

"You're going to be changed out," he told them. "This is a business. I'm not an archaeologist, I'm not here to preserve the past. I'm here to make this thing move forward and grow. If you're a hindrance, you're going to go. It would be a shame for you to miss this opportunity. You have a second lease on life—why can't you just ride the pony?"

They hated Doc for saying that, but he was sick of having to drag them through everything and motivate them to do the basic things they needed to do for us to function as a band.

As things went south, though, a lot of the fallout actually landed on Tommy Thayer, who had to take over as tour manager of the operation about six months into the first year of the reunion tour. Tommy spent 90 percent of his time and energy dealing with things a person shouldn't have to deal with—making new arrangements when Peter or Ace missed a flight or didn't show up for a car pickup, making sure the hotel staff didn't take the tinfoil off Peter's windows, whatever it was. Ace was chronically late getting out of his hotel room when we needed to get to a venue or to our jet. For a while, Tommy just lied to him about departure times—pushing them an hour forward so there was a chance of Ace's making the actual time. But when Ace realized that, he got bent out of shape.

At some stage Tommy came to me with the realization I had been waiting for. He admitted that the perception he'd had—of me and Gene as the tight-asses, the business guys, and Ace and Peter as the rock and roll guys—couldn't have been more wrong. Being inept, unreliable, and marginally capable didn't make you rock and roll. It made you inept, unreliable, and marginally capable. Ace was now, in Tommy's words, "a fucking loser."

In early 1997, we flew to Japan, where we were received like heroes once again, huge crowds awaiting us everywhere we appeared. We traveled between shows by bullet train. One afternoon, we went to board a train and an enormous crowd greeted us once again—kids gathered at the station to see us. We walked through the station surrounded by security people, and when we arrived on the platform, it too was mobbed with fans.

It was incredible—again, I felt blown away.

We should wake up every day and thank whatever God we believe in for what we are experiencing.

And at that moment, Peter turned to me and said, "I'm sick and tired of this *Hard Day's Night* shit."

I was speechless.

53·

In April 1997, before a show in Georgia, Peter started grousing that his hands hurt. "I can't do the show," he said, calling Doc from his hotel room.

"Fine," said Doc. He then called Peter's roadie, Eddie Kanon. "Shave your beard," Doc said. "You're on tonight."

Peter heard about it and went ape shit. "The fans will never accept it!" he screamed. "You can't put someone else out there in my makeup!"

"I disagree," said Doc dryly.

Yeah, well, actually, Peter, we have a show to do.

Eddie shaved and put on Peter's makeup.

One, two, three, four, let's go—we launched into the show. I introduced Eddie from the stage and—surprise, surprise—either nobody cared or nobody had time to care. This was the night and this would be the show.

We weren't going to put on a show because Peter's hands hurt? I don't think so, pal. Because the show, as they say, must go on.

Ace started to get paranoid. He had rented an apartment off La Cienega Boulevard in L.A. and spent off-days there. But he was convinced the place was bugged—that he was *being watched*. So he pulled all the electrical wires and phone lines out of the place. The owners went crazy.

Ace also started studying our tour books, which contained the tour itinerary, site specifications—all sorts of pertinent info. He would bring the tour book to the dressing room and say, "How many people paid last night?"

Let's say the answer that night was 18,700. "Bullshit!" he would scream. "It says right here 24,100!"

"Ace," I'd try to explain, "that's the venue *capacity*, not the number of tickets sold, and it's not the capacity for a concert."

"Bullshit!"

Part of Ace's contract included a stipulation that he not get high. But he carried around a shoulder bag that might as well have been made of gold for the way Ace clung to it. He had pills tucked into the sleeves of his onstage outfit. The problem was, how could we enforce the contract? Stop the tour? Fine him?

During the tour Peter and Ace's representative, George, demanded a meeting with the entire band to go over finances. His intention clearly was to show us and his clients that he was a force to be reckoned with. He came in wearing a blazer and tie in an effort to look businesslike, with Ace and Peter trailing behind him. He set up an easel and started pointing at numbers. His grasp of the business was not much better than Ace's. After months of nonsensical requests and suggestions of poor budgeting, we'd finally had enough. We took him apart item by item. He was completely ill-equipped regarding finances or touring, and Ace and Peter were silenced when they saw it.

At the end of the tour, in July 1997, Peter and Ace demanded to be made full members of the band again. "We did things your way,"

Peter said, "and we had a huge successful tour. Now we want to be equals."

Being stunned by one of these guys was an almost daily occurrence, but this dropped my jaw.

Don't you realize the reason it was a big success is because you had no input and no say?

We'd made a lot of money. And we'd made a lot of people happy. Peter and Ace were upset because they were now *rich* again but not *as rich* as me and Gene. There were people richer than I was, and I didn't lose sleep over it. And anyway, I deserved more than Peter and Ace did—I stayed when they left. The door swings one way. I nurtured the band and kept it going. For that alone I deserved to be better compensated. In a million years, I would never have brought them in as equal members. Not a chance.

Peter and Ace were also totally unequipped to be involved in the decision-making process—they had no idea how the concert business and music business were run. And yet they seemed to think they had now earned the right to participate in decision-making in a world they knew nothing about.

It was sad to see. On the one hand, they sometimes acknowledged that they had made bad decisions in life. But on the other hand, they ultimately found solace in believing that they'd been taken advantage of—that they were victims, then and now.

When they'd struck out on their own after leaving KISS, they'd had tremendous advantages—name recognition, notoriety, industry contacts, money—but they could barely get arrested before the reunion tour. And they were broke. They'd been thankful at the start of the tour because they had found a way out of the miserable, marginal lives they were living. Now, just a year later, they were millionaires. But they were bitter. They were defensive. They were unrealistic about their own importance and abilities. They were, in their minds, victims. It was insane.

Ace kept grumbling that if he had retained the name KISS, the band would have been successful without me and Gene. He had another brilliant argument, too. "I'm actually responsible for the whole reunion," Ace said.

Okay . . .

"If I had never quit, there wouldn't be a reunion."

Wow.

"Everybody should be thanking me!" Ace continued. "This tour only happened because I quit."

I didn't know how to respond to that kind of "logic."

Doc suggested we just get rid of Peter and Ace. He always believed we could do it without them. He saw no upside to continuing with them. "If you're a good person, there's very little I can do to make you a bad person," Doc said. "But if you're an asshole, there's very little I can do to make you a good person."

That was his way of saying there was no way around the dysfunctionality if we continued to work with Ace and Peter.

We had another idea: we would make a reunion record. I didn't want to be plagued by thoughts of things I could have done. I didn't want to have regrets about not giving this a real try. When we had put the band back together in its original form, I for one had hoped that could lead us to some spectacular places. I hoped that seeing what we had all learned and bringing all of our experiences to the table would be a winning formula. If nothing else, working together again would alleviate any lingering questions of culpability and show whether there were any mistakes that could be rectified. I was pretty sure I had the answers to those questions after the reunion tour: people don't change, and we separate from them for a core reason. But I didn't want to be wrong, I didn't want to miss out on the chance to take it all the way.

To produce *Psycho Circus*, we brought in Bruce Fairbairn, who had been involved with some very big records from Bon Jovi, Aerosmith, and Loverboy, among others. He turned out to be ill-suited for the job. On his big records of the 1980s, he had worked with a team that included Bob Rock and Mike Fraser, both of whom went on to do tremendous things. Sometimes when a team splits and various members try things on their own, you get a better sense of who did what by who succeeds and who doesn't.

Bruce chose awful songs from the demos to record for the album. The song that eventually made the most noise turned out to be the title track, "Psycho Circus." Bruce wanted to leave it off the album. He was so far up Gene's ass he not only couldn't see, he couldn't hear.

One day I finally had to say to Bruce, "This is your first KISS album. This is my eighteenth. You will leave here and go on to something else. I won't. I have to stand by this record, so I'm going to do what I want."

I went into the studio that weekend and recorded "Psycho Circus."

Making the album was a disaster all around. Peter and Ace didn't show up. I don't think Bruce would have used Peter anyway, since he couldn't play much beyond the dog tricks Tommy had taught him to get through the reunion set list.

Instead of working with Ace and Peter, we spent all our time talking to their attorneys. I wish their attorneys could have played on the album.

It would have been cheaper.

54.

I realized one day near the end of the tour that I had to use one hand to support the other arm when I reached up to grab something from a shelf. By the end of the tour, I couldn't raise my arm. When I got home I went to see a doctor, who said I needed an operation to repair a badly torn rotator cuff. I told Pam I had to have surgery. When the day of the surgery arrived, she told me she had an audition the next day. She had already shipped Evan off to her parents' place in Texas for a few weeks.

"I don't want to compromise the audition," she said, "so I'm going to stay in a hotel tonight and work on my scene." Pam drove me home from the hospital and then left.

The doctor who performed the surgery sent me home with a prescription for Vicodin and a cooling system that pumped ice water over my shoulder from a bucket. I took my painkillers and refilled my bucket of ice water by myself throughout the night in a dark and empty house.

I can't believe I'm alone. I can't believe she did this.

Pam wanted to believe she had given up her career for me or for Evan, when the truth was that her career had given her up. She just wasn't getting work. I guess it was easier to blame me. Of course, I was to blame—but for different reasons. I had been intent on settling down, and even though Pam was a good person, she wasn't the right person for me to do that with. I was bullheaded about making it happen and making it work in spite of things I saw from the very beginning that were contrary to what I wanted.

"Before I was married I could go to Europe whenever I wanted," she said one day.

"Yeah," I said, "ten years ago I was banging women whose names I didn't know. Great. But that's not now."

Clearly, neither of us was happy.

Pam had become friends with an actress whose career suddenly surged when she was in her forties. She came to be seen as a symbol—her success represented a victory for middle-aged women against the stereotyping that many of them faced. I didn't think she was particularly warm or particularly bright. Her husband, who struck me as a spoiled rich kid, didn't make me feel any warmer about the couple. The actress had been invited onto Oprah Winfrey's TV show as part of an ongoing segment on how various women managed to balance their independence with success and home life. In the run-up to her appearance, she said to me, "I don't know what to say!" and asked me to help. So I wrote some pap for her that read like a bad episode of *Kung Fu.*

If you think of yourself as a tree, your family are your roots, and the deeper your roots go, the more fruit the branches can bear.

She actually used what I had written on TV. Oprah and the audience lapped it up. Wouldn't it be hysterical if all the people watching realized that this liberated, intellectual woman had been spoon-fed her lines by that male chauvinist bozo from KISS?

At one point Vanna White, another friend of Pam's, recommended that we go see the marriage counselor she and her husband were seeing. He looked like Curly from the Three Stooges and wore *Star Wars* ties and had *Star Trek* memorabilia around his office. Here we were sitting with Captain Curly on the Starship *Enterprise* and I was thinking it was all nuts. Vanna and her husband, incidentally, split up.

Pam and I went to another therapist during our first trial separation. She had us do exercises together—like pretending we had just started to date each other, or making gifts or drawing pictures for each other.

Great, when are we making pot holders?

Counseling with her went on for quite some time. But it struck me as a waste of time. The counselor may have meant well, but she should have been more direct. We didn't deal with the core issue— the fact that we were on fundamentally different pages. If we had acknowledged that, perhaps we could have split up neatly. Maybe part of marriage counseling should be helping people to divorce well rather than having them make doodles for each other.

During the separation, Gene generously offered me his guesthouse. I appreciated the offer and gladly accepted. When I first showed up, his kids, Nick and Sophie, greeted and welcomed me. It was a lovely gesture. My room felt like a college dorm, and it was the perfect place to reflect on my life.

A few months later, when the therapist suggested that Pam and I move back in together, I couldn't see why and resisted. Nothing had changed. Nothing had been resolved. What was the point? Reluctantly, I agreed to move from the frying pan into the fire.

When *Psycho Circus* was ready for release, Doc booked us a Halloween show at Dodger Stadium on October 31, 1998, to kick off a tour to support the album. We put on a real spectacle, with circus sideshow acts on the huge stage. The Smashing Pumpkins opened the show and, in the spirit of Halloween, dressed like the

Beatles circa 1964. As I got ready to walk to the stage, Pam let me know she was pissed off that I was distracted and not paying enough attention to her. I said my best bewildered apologies and headed out. It was another night of glorious pandemonium as the curtain dropped and the bombs went off.

We had booked rooms at the Sunset Marquis in Hollywood so we could all get ready together as a band and have a place to clean up afterwards. At the end of the show, we all hopped straight in a van in full makeup and costumes to return to the hotel. As we got near the Sunset Marquis, the streets became clogged. Soon, the van couldn't move at all; thousands of people were out in the streets. Somehow, we'd forgotten the Hollywood Halloween parade. We were about seven blocks from the hotel when it dawned on me that we could get out and walk. "Come on, let's go," I said.

What? We're in full gear!

"It's Halloween. Everyone's dressed up. It'll be okay."

We had no choice anyway. We climbed out of the van and started walking down the crowded street along with the costumed

Me, Gene, Sophie, and Evan at the beach. Good times.

crowds. Soon, though, a few people stopped and stared at us. "Wow, man, great costumes! You really look like them!"

"Thanks a lot!" I said.

We kept walking. Other people gave us thumbs up.

"Cool costumes, guys!"

Nobody had a clue we were the real KISS, walking back from playing to forty thousand people.

As the *Psycho Circus* tour went on, it was clear to Doc, Gene, and me that we couldn't continue. Ace wanted out to work on his fabled solo album—the one he had been working on since the 1980s. Peter had Gigi running interference for him and whispering in his ear.

The only way to keep the tour going was to talk about ending things. At some point I pulled Peter aside and told him, "You're doing it again. You're doing what you said you would never do again. You're not the same happy guy who came to the reunion saying he had blown it the last time around. You're doing the same thing all over again."

Musically, we were regressing. At times Ace played songs in the wrong key without even realizing it.

Throughout the various reunion tours I had insisted on building in off-days to allow me to get home for visits with little Evan. He remained my priority—I thought the initial bonding time was critical. Once in a while Pam also traveled to meet me on the road. She was going to join me in Florida in January 1999, and I wanted to surprise her with a gift for her upcoming birthday. I had gotten her a Jaguar sedan a few years before, and the lease was coming to an end. She had always loved the two-seater Mercedes SL coupe, so I decided to buy her one for her birthday. I made some calls and arranged the whole thing. When she arrived on tour I told her, "I wanted to do something special for your birthday, but I didn't want you to have to wait until then. You won't get it until you're back home, but I wanted you to know—I got you a white Mercedes 320SL." Then I handed her the color brochure I'd been carrying around in anticipation of this moment.

"A 320?" she said. "I don't want some *small* Mercedes."

Oh, no.

I wanted validation. Instead, I had to explain to her all the details about the car, how the 320SL was the same body and interior as a 500SL but that it had a six-cylinder engine instead of a V-8, which made no difference for the way she used her car around town. But as I began to explain all this, I suddenly changed my mind.

I could explain. I could apologize. I could change the order. But it didn't matter. It was ruined.

"Forget it," I said.

Happy birthday.

On the way home from another tour leg where Pam joined me, she told me she had lost her engagement ring. I couldn't believe she could lose a five-carat diamond, but she started sobbing. "Don't worry," I told her.

I'll just get a new one.

The day I picked up the new ring from the jewelers, I spotted Pam and her parents driving down Beverly Boulevard. I flagged them down. I couldn't wait. I got out of my car and went over to hers to show her the ring.

She looked at it and said, "Oh, the setting isn't what I expected." I felt deflated.

Don't I ever get the cookie? Don't I ever get the pat on the head?

There was a lot of sexual temptation on tour, amplified by the way things were going with Pam. When it came to sex, I was an alcoholic, and touring was an open bar. But if my marriage wasn't going to work out, I wanted to be clear on *why* it didn't work. What was true of the band—and the reason I wanted to try to make an album with the original four guys—was true of my marriage: if I was going to walk away from something, the most important thing was to know I did everything I could to try to make it work. I didn't want any lingering what-ifs. I didn't want my marriage to end and wonder whether part of the reason was because I had cheated. So I didn't. I would have hated myself. It would have confirmed my worst feelings about myself.

It was depressingly familiar territory. Dysfunction in the band, dysfunction at home, feeling lonely, and hating each day for the mess I had created.

55.

At the end of 1998, I got a call from my agent at CAA, the talent agency that represented us. "Are you interested in theater?" he asked me.

"Maybe," I said.

"Well, you would have to audition."

"What for?"

"*Phantom of the Opera.*"

Wow! Phantom!

"Absolutely! Where and when?"

I realized immediately this was a case of "stunt casting," that is, bringing in somebody from a realm other than Broadway or the legitimate theater world in order to spur ticket sales. My fame got me the audition. But I wasn't insulted. This was *Phantom*! The masked musician whose hideous deformed face was revealed. The show that had taken my breath away in London ten years before. *Phantom*!

Even so, I wouldn't have agreed to audition if there had been conflicting plans for the band. But we would have a big block of free time once the *Psycho Circus* tour ended, and it would be a long time before I would think about making another album. A very long time indeed.

The audition was for the Toronto production, which was then in its tenth year. If I made the cut, I would take over the role in May 1999. The *Psycho Circus* tour ran through the end of April, and then we were pretty much off until 2000, when we would go back out for a Farewell Tour that was already in the works. Who knew what would happen after the Farewell Tour? Musical theater was an avenue I now wanted to explore—I might need a second act soon enough.

KISS had the month of January 1999 off before playing the Super Bowl pregame show on January 31. The audition was scheduled to take place in New York, since all principals in the show had to audition and be signed off on by Hal Prince and his staff, who did the casting worldwide. Rock star or not, they weren't going to jeopardize a billion-dollar franchise.

I spent weeks practicing the three songs that were required for the audition. Playing the Phantom meant so much to me that I also wanted to try to control the audition situation as much as possible to give myself the best shot. I realized the singing would be only one of the determining factors in getting the part.

When I finally went to the audition, I walked in and made small talk with the staff. I flirted a little with the woman who was there to sing the role of Christine with me. People were sitting at desks like judges at the Olympics, as if they were waiting to hold up numbers after I sang. I spoke to them, made some jokes, and, knowing I would get only one chance, waited until I felt comfortable and ready.

Don't blow this.

When I finished a full audition of songs and scene blocking, I knew I had nailed it. Sure enough, my agent called me soon after to tell me I'd been offered the role.

To make it official, I did a press conference after the *Psycho Circus* tour resumed. As I talked with reporters on the conference call, the same thoughts kept going through my head:

I'm fucked. I can't get out of this now.

It would be a trial by fire, because there was very little time between the end of the KISS tour and my *Phantom* debut. I had muscled my voice through the audition, but could I really do it night after night?

I had to learn the entire show while on tour. I memorized the melodies and lyrics during downtime and off-days, and I tested myself during KISS shows. I sang songs on the side of the stage whenever I had a break—like when the other band members had their solos. I figured that if I could still focus in the midst of complete bedlam and chaos, I really knew the material.

KISS wrapped up the *Psycho Circus* tour in Mexico City; right after the show I cut my hair and headed up to Toronto. Rehearsals started immediately at a studio used by theaters and the local ballet company. When I walked in the first day, the only person there was the show's musical director. He seemed like a bit of a tight-ass, and it was clear we were from different musical backgrounds. I was pretty sure he saw me as somebody without any pedigree coming in to desecrate the theater. The first thing he said was, "Where's your script?"

"I memorized it," I said.

He looked at me like I was nuts. I told him, "I may be a mutt in a kennel of purebreds here, but if you tell me what you want, I'll give it to you."

He sat down at a piano and we started working, just the two of us.

It was the hardest work I've ever done. Six hours a day. I went home every night slumped in the back of a taxi, exhausted emotionally and—because of the demands of singing a different way and the physicality of the role and the staging—physically. I'd be damned if I was going to go in there and turn the show into the *Rocky Horror Picture Show*. This was a big, legit show with tremendous history, and I wasn't going to do a rock version of it.

Almost immediately I saw some problems navigating certain vocal passages. I had to figure out the breath control to make it through lines I hadn't written. I guess without thinking about it, when you write songs, you write what you can sing. Now I was singing lines that involved things beyond my experience, things that weren't intuitive.

With just a few weeks to go before I had to take the stage, I decided I should reach out and get help. I had never had much luck with vocal coaches before, because they generally tried to completely change the way I sang—they used a cookie-cutter approach and gave rock singers stilted, pseudo-operatic voices, disregarding what anyone had built naturally. You often hear those voices in bands that sing about slaying dragons and other mythological pap. After meeting another one of those typical coaches, I asked the musical director of the show for a recommendation. He suggested Jeffrey Huard, the previous musical director of *Phantom*.

Jeffrey was very encouraging and supportive. "They hired you *because* of the way you sing," he said. "Your voice is terrific, and we don't want to throw away the engine. We'll just fine-tune it."

From that point on, during the morning hours before rehearsals, I worked with Jeffrey on my technique and comfort. He took me through exercises and scales and helped me with the phonetics and word pronunciation of musical theater.

As I worked on scenes at rehearsals every day, I wore a T-shirt and jeans and a cape, and they handed me things to use as props. Here's a broomstick—it's an oar. Here's a cardboard box—play it like it's an organ. If I could turn those things into the objects they were supposed to be, that reality would only be reinforced once I was onstage with the actual props in hand.

The Pantages Theatre, where the show was staged, was a beautifully renovated space with an orchestra pit and a marquee out front—with my name on it. It was all about to happen! But days before opening, when we started to rehearse key scenes in the theater with the orchestra, I suddenly had problems because I couldn't hear on my right side. I hadn't realized my deafness would be so difficult to deal with. The orchestra was far enough away and I was singing loud enough that it was very hard to hear the monitors and stay with the orchestra. But I found I caught on pretty fast after I looked like an idiot a few times.

Toward the end of the theater rehearsals, a couple of women from the theater company came to watch. When I finished the final act, they were in tears.

That's a good sign . . .

Well, either that or I'm horrible.

I'd been told that the role of the Phantom was the loneliest role in the show, because most of the time when the Phantom was onstage, the rest of the cast was off; when the Phantom was offstage, the rest of the cast was on. You rarely met anyone else. And then it was opening night, and I was waiting in the wings ready to do my first scene, standing behind a mirror.

The only way out of this now is to do the show. When I leave, it's going to be after the curtain comes down.

There was no editing, no second takes, no cutting to a different camera. This was it. I used the techniques and visualizations that Jeffrey had helped me with, and even though I wasn't as good as I would get as the show went on, I didn't fall on my face. As I settled in, I loved it. I loved giving something this level of concentration and trying to immerse myself in the character—despite a few devil horn salutes I saw in the audience that first night.

Then came the moment in the production that had caused me to gasp the first time I saw it—when Christine rips off the Phantom's mask. I cringed as she took my mask off to reveal the horrid makeup beneath. I *knew* this scene. It was the scene I had feared my entire life: scrutinizing eyes staring at Stanley the one-eared monster. Betrayed and exposed.

But then . . .

Christine tells the Phantom his face "holds no horror" for her. It's in his *soul* that the true distortion lies.

When she finally makes herself available to him, it is the Phantom who recoils and is unable to hold her.

When I performed in KISS, I was constantly interacting with the audience, bringing them to a certain level of excitement, leading them, cajoling them. Now I ignored the audience. People in the theater had to buy into what I was doing, and I couldn't get them to do so by winking at them. For me it came down to abandoning the audience and abandoning any sense of performance and just being that character and finding the truth in that moment. That was why the show that night—and almost every night thereafter—ended with me completely sweat-soaked. And in tears.

After that first night, the cast was great to me. I know they appreciated my dedication. Suddenly I was captain of the team, and everybody wound up hanging out in my dressing room. This may have been stunt casting, but as the shows sold out—eight of them per week—I was helping to keep hundreds of people in work.

My parents came to see the show early on, and I felt as if doing theater validated me in their eyes. No matter how ambivalent I felt about my parents, I realized in that moment that ultimately their approval was something I wanted. And when they saw me getting a standing ovation from a sold-out house, it felt terrific.

Gene came to see me as well. It wasn't his cup of tea, but he seemed astonished. When he came to my dressing room after the show he said, "Where did you learn to sing like that?"

Peter came, too. He showed a side of himself I rarely saw anymore. We went out for sushi after the show, and Peter was joyous and beaming, saying how proud he was of me. Every once in a while he would show flashes of warmth—whether it was at the beginning of the band or at the beginning of the reunion tour—but his insecurity usually kept him too defensive and isolated to be warm and open. On that night, in a context away from the band, a context that didn't threaten him, I guess, it was truly enjoyable to be around Peter. He felt like an old friend for a change.

Revisiting the stage of the Pantages Theater in Toronto, where I starred in Phantom of the Opera *from 1998–99.*

My son Evan came, too. I was worried that he might be scared—he wasn't yet five years old, and the face I revealed when the mask was torn off was grisly. So I had him come to my dressing room at the Pantages Theatre and watch them put my makeup on when the show was in previews. I wanted him to know it was still me underneath. I think it unnerved him a little.

At one point he looked at me and said, "I love you, Daddy."

"It's still me," I said. "It's just makeup. And I love you, too."

I had done something similar before the *Psycho Circus* tour. I figured at age four Evan was finally old enough to see a show, but I worried about him seeing me in makeup without warning. I took my makeup box home before the tour, and we played with it together. I showed him how I put on the star and showed him photos of me in full regalia. I wanted him to connect the dots before he saw me like that at the show.

After Evan saw me in *Phantom*, he started to sing the songs. I got him his own mini-me outfit, with mask and cape, and he strutted around and sang.

Every night when I occupied that character, I tapped into things buried deep inside me.

The mask. The hidden facial disfigurement.

It haunted me.

The Phantom had it wrong. Christine recoiled in horror not at his face, but at his soul.

Was it possible that the Phantom was . . . in a way . . . *me*?

The mask. The hidden facial disfigurement. Why had I never confronted the birth defect I had covered for my entire life? Why had I cowered in fear of it? Why had I let it keep me from sharing myself with people, from embracing people—from embracing the fullness of life?

The mask. The hidden facial disfigurement.

Was the problem really in my soul, too? And if so, could I exorcise it?

56

I was supposed to have been the second-to-last Phantom before the show closed after its ten-year run in Toronto. But things went so well that the theater bought out the contract of the actor poised to replace me and had me take the show to the finish line in October 1999.

I enjoyed the pressure of knowing some people wanted me to fail, and of changing the minds of others who thought I was some bozo ruining their favorite show. Of course, it wasn't always smooth sailing. One night during a scene where I was hooded and singing "Point of No Return"—a hushed moment, with just the Phantom and Christine onstage—I went absolutely blank. I was walking toward her, singing solo, and I forgot the words. I knew from rock concerts that people notice your reaction to mistakes more than they notice the actual mistakes, so I just kept singing—in gibberish. Eventually my mind cleared.

After the show I went to see Melissa Dye, the great-looking woman with an incredible voice who played Christine. Melissa was a joy to work with, and her support and friendship made the whole experience that much more fun. Plus there was something between us that under different circumstances, I definitely would have pursued. "Wasn't that unbelievable?" I said to her.

"What?" she said.

"I was just singing nonsense during 'Point of No Return.'"

Melissa looked confused. She hadn't noticed.

Other people in the cast told me that they'd had similar experiences and sung about chickens or ducks—whatever came into their heads.

Before shows, the staff often dropped off letters that had been mailed to me at the theater company's office address. I liked to read them. One woman wrote that she had seen the show many times—it was her favorite musical—and that her sister had recently bought her tickets for her birthday. When she found out I was playing the lead, she had been disappointed. She was expecting the worst but was completely won over when she saw the show. And she wanted me to know that.

Another letter—the one from the woman who worked with AboutFace—changed my life. The woman, Anna Pileggi, wrote that when she watched me play the Phantom she had the impression that I identified with the character in a way she hadn't seen in other actors.

Wow.

It was true, of course, that I identified with the character—the mask, the hidden facial disfigurement—but how did she figure it out? I rarely mentioned my birth defect to anyone, and these days I had the surgically created ear where earlier there had been the stump. It felt as if Anna had pulled aside a veil and seen the real me. She knew my secret.

The woman's letter went on to describe AboutFace, the organization that helped children with facial differences. Would I have any interest in learning more about the organization or perhaps even working with them?

I called her.

Her connection to young people struggling with facial abnormalities struck me immediately.

She didn't know my secret, of course, though I quickly told her about my microtia and the surgeries I'd had. She had just seen something based on her work—perhaps she had recognized the pain of reality in the way I played the role.

She described some of the programs her organization undertook. Eventually she asked if I might be willing to talk to kids and their parents about my experiences.

Here, perhaps, was a way to help heal my soul.

I took a deep breath.

"Yes," I said.

Speaking about my birth defect would have been impossible when I had been in the midst of pain and turmoil. My life had evolved, however, and I was now in a better position to be open. I suppose I could have gone to speak to the kids and just offered a cheering up from a so-called celebrity. But I knew I wasn't going to do that. I wasn't going to just speak to the kids; I was going to reveal something about myself. This was an opportunity for me to gain something by sharing with them what I had been through.

I agreed to go to the AboutFace office and meet with a group of children and their parents. I had some anxiety leading up to that first meeting and talk, but my overwhelming and yet unanalyzed compulsion to do it eclipsed any fear I had. I didn't know what I would get out of the initial talks, but I knew I was compelled to do it.

As monumental as my own condition seemed to me, I knew from speaking to Anna that many of these children dealt with far more severe facial differences. I didn't want them to think that I placed myself on the same plane as them, but I wanted to let them know what I had been through emotionally and where I had ended up. One thing I had noticed as a child was how much more difficult it was when nobody acknowledged the reality of the situation. There was nothing more isolating than having everyone act as if my missing ear and my deafness were no big deal. It didn't help me tackle the reality that I faced every day. So I wanted to explain that my life had been tough, lonely, and painful; I also wanted to acknowledge that it wouldn't be easy for them. Maybe nobody had ever told them that. Perhaps it would be a breath of fresh air for them to hear, "Yes, success is more difficult to achieve for someone with a facial difference. Happiness is more difficult to find. The odds are worse."

I also hoped to encourage the parents of the children to acknowledge these things, too. I wanted to impress upon them that it wasn't about tough love. It wasn't about sticking their heads in the ground.

As soon as I started publicly talking about my ear, I felt a huge weight lift off of me. I realized that you couldn't appreciate others when you were immersed in your own misery. Perhaps that was what Christine meant about the distortion of the Phantom's soul.

Suddenly the world looked different to me. Helping others helped me heal myself. I felt freed from something that had been so painful and all-encompassing my whole life. Simply putting the truth out there in front of these kids and their parents had set me free.

The more work I did with AboutFace, the better I felt.

Eventually we came up with an education program to try to help kids who didn't have facial differences change their attitudes toward those who did. In a video presentation, I told kids to imagine wearing what they thought was a special shirt and then realizing everyone was snickering and laughing at their shirt. "You can go home and change your shirt," I explained. "But kids with facial differences can't change their faces."

I had never been so calm and centered as I was during those months in Toronto. A big part of it was finally coming to grips with my birth defect. Another part of it was doing something that demanded a lot of thought, effort, and discipline. Whatever the cause, the effect was to take me completely out of myself and allow me to think about my life and my relationships with some critical distance—with the kind of objectivity that's impossible when you are caught up in things.

It felt like a time for self-evaluation and, perhaps, renewal.

I had always thought my marriage was about breaking through a wall. Pam and I were going to resolve everything and finally push through to a great place on the other side. Then, sitting in my hotel after a *Phantom* show one night, it suddenly occurred to me: the nature of our marriage was banging our heads against the wall, not pushing through it.

There is no other side.

It was a heartbreaking realization.

Another thing that occurred to me was that I had failed to break the pattern I had seen at home growing up. In some ways, Pam was very much like my mom—distant, cold, unsupportive, and not one to give a compliment. It was a shock to realize that the dynamics in my own marriage mirrored something I had sought to avoid.

When I got back to L.A. from Toronto, I had some questions for my dad, as well. There were pieces of the puzzle that seemed missing, and feelings I was unable to identify. As my dad got older, it became clear that a day would come when I wouldn't have the option to ask him to fill in the blanks.

One day when he was visiting me, I told him that I had been thinking a lot about the past as I stumbled into the future, and that I wanted to ask him some uncomfortable questions. Thankfully, he said he was willing to try to help.

So I asked him about the time he had come home late smelling of booze, when my mom was out of town, and told me that we all did things we regretted. "What was that all about?" I asked him.

He paused. Then he said, "I was in love with another woman."

I was floored. I couldn't recall any instance when I had heard him say he loved my mother. He went on to tell me that he'd had a girlfriend for decades. He wanted to leave his family for her, but he couldn't do it.

It suddenly flashed in front of my eyes: the time when my dad had spit his words at me for seeking psychiatric help—"You think you're the only one with problems?"—it was because he didn't want to be there and he was living a double life. A lie.

My stomach started to knot up, but I was determined not to let my face give away my shock and bewilderment. I wanted to hear as much as I could.

"She taught me the meaning of love," he continued.

This was so far beyond the realm of what I considered possible. Skepticism flooded into my mind. Love was something you built over time through shared experiences with someone. My dad had never spent a night away from home, so it struck me as odd to place that kind of value—love!—on something that was never tested beyond years of trysts. Was my dad describing it this way to justify his actions or sanitize his desire for sex?

I felt that for my dad, his affair had to be sugar-coated, given redeeming value, as opposed to just accepted for what it was—sex, which under most circumstances doesn't need any justification. Of course, in the context of a marriage, there are very few circumstances to justify an affair, though my dad seemed to be trying his best.

One thing was clear: this was tangible evidence of what I'd picked up at home as a child. The more he revealed, the more I understood that those unspoken undercurrents, conflicts, and tensions that I'd grown up with hadn't been my imagination.

I did not tell Pam about that conversation. Yes, my dad had made huge and stunning revelations, but Pam no longer felt like my partner. It would have felt like a breach of confidentiality to tell her. I wanted to talk about it, but I couldn't with her. If anything, that conversation with my dad spurred me on to avoid repeating the mistakes I'd witnessed as a child.

I didn't want to get stuck in a loveless marriage.

I'd been on such a high when I came back from Toronto, but I'd arrived at a house while hoping to return to a home. Whenever I tried to talk to Pam, she blamed our lack of closeness either on some outside issue she was dealing with or on me, telling me all the ways in which I was falling short of her expectations. Most of the issues she brought up were everyday aspects of life, basic things that went along with living with someone—not things I felt were at the core of our problems.

Finally, I said something to her in a way I thought would be very clear, expressing as basic a truth as possible. "You can choose to be happy," I said, "or you can choose to be gone."

It's funny. Even though we had separated before, I thought that if I made the choice as basic and clear as possible, the answer would be

Celebrating the Fourth of July—"Uncle Gene" holding Evan in 1999,
one of the times I was separated from Pam.

obvious: she would choose to be happy. I was surprised when ultimately she figured out that she'd rather be gone. In hindsight, with the exception of Evan, that was the greatest gift she ever gave me.

I didn't want Evan to have to deal with a divorce while I was away, however, so while Pam and I agreed to end things, we also agreed to wait a year until I was home fulltime, after the conclusion of the imminent tour.

The clock was now ticking. Soon, both my marriage and my band would be finished. Everything in my life was suddenly in flux as KISS set out on the Farewell Tour in March 2000.

57.

Peter posted a sign every day counting down the number of days left on the Farewell Tour. He started painting a teardrop below his eye. I thought it made him look like Emmett Kelly's famous Weary Willie character, the tragic clown who toured with the Ringling Bros. and Barnum & Bailey circus. And as for the rest of his makeup, it was as if he had forgotten how to do it. He started to look like a panda bear, with big rectangles around his eyes.

The tour was horrible. Constant drudgery and misery. We spent all of our energy trying to coax Peter and Ace out of their hotel rooms. Ace sucker-punched Tommy at one of the shows. Peter had his usual handbook detailing how hotel staff had to treat him and which windows had to be covered with tinfoil and all that. There was no reasoning with either of them. We never knew if we'd make it to a show on time, and once we got onstage we never knew whether we'd get through the show. I mean, if a guy has trouble putting on his makeup, how is he going to play? Not surprisingly, the shows could be pretty awful.

I was angry at Peter and Ace for being disrespectful toward everything we had accomplished and everything the fans were giving us.

I bought into the idea that this really was it. The end of KISS. There was no place to go. It was unbearable.

We were stuck in a rut musically as well—basically playing the same seventeen songs we'd taught them for the initial reunion. This was the third tour with the same set list. Peter and Ace just couldn't master any more. The needle was already into the red. I had to come up with nonsensical interview responses to questions about why we were playing the same songs. I couldn't just say, "Because Peter and Ace can't learn any others."

One night during a show Doc McGhee tried to get my attention from the side of the stage, gesturing up at me and holding his nose.

Huh?

"You stink!" he yelled. I walked over to him during a break between songs. "What did you say?"

"You stink!" he repeated.

"Fucking Peter is playing too slow," I told him.

Doc ran around behind the drum riser and started making the same gesture at Peter. "Peter, you're playing too slow!"

"Well, so are they!" Peter shouted back.

"What are you talking about?" Doc screamed. "You're the fucking drummer!"

Another night Peter had a new problem. He stopped playing in the middle of a song and just held his sticks up and looked at me like a deer in the headlights. I yelled, "Play!" and started tapping my foot so at least he would start hitting the drums again. That happened on more than one occasion.

A well-known musician—who had seen the band many times—approached me one night and said, "I can't come to any more shows. It's just too painful to listen to."

The worst feeling was reading reviews trashing the shows and thinking, *That's spot on.* It was such a shame because the band could have been great and wasn't. The drama offstage and the hostility and resentment and backstabbing were taking a heavy musical toll. And then there were the drugs. When Ace had an off night and made a lot of mistakes, we would joke that his mixture was off.

It would have been great to go out in a blaze of musical glory; instead, we were dragging our asses. At one point we put aside a few days to brush up on songs and tighten things up. Ace didn't show for one of the rehearsals. He said he wasn't feeling well because he had Lyme disease—an illness brought on by the bite of a deer tick. Peter, brainiac that he is, said, "That's bullshit! He was never bitten by a deer!"

Am I living in an insane asylum?

On August 11, 2000, we had a show in Irvine, California, after a week off. Ace had spent the week in New York. We had a rule that if anyone was going to fly cross-country on a commercial flight to get to a gig, he had to get there a day in advance—just to be safe, in case there was a storm or a mechanical issue or whatever. We didn't want to have to cancel shows.

The day before the Irvine show, Tommy had arranged for a limo to pick Ace up and take him to his flight. He always had the limo show up hours early because it was the same chore to get Ace out of his house as it was to get him out of a hotel. Then all of us sat around waiting for updates on Ace's progress. Ace's pickup was scheduled for noon East Coast time. At 1:30 P.M. Tommy called the limo. "Mr. Frehley needs to get going."

"Um, sir, he hasn't come out of the house yet."

Another half an hour passed. Tommy and Doc tried to get Ace on the phone, calling his house. No answer. After calling his house five more times, they finally got him on the line. "Ace, you have to get in the car—you're going to miss your flight."

"There's a problem . . . uh . . . and I'm sick . . ."

Millions of excuses.

They kept rescheduling Ace on later and later flights. The limo went back each time. It got to be 7 and then 8 P.M. "Passenger has not left his house, sir," reported the limo driver each time.

Tommy managed to get Ace on the phone again. "There's one more flight out tonight, last one."

"Okay," said Ace. "I promise."

But again at the appointed time, nothing happened. "Passenger still not out of his house, sir."

Flight missed.

The next day was the show. Ace started the day on the other side of the country. By some minor miracle, however, he made it to the airport in the morning, was met by the on-site rep, and was escorted onto his plane.

Traffic from LAX airport to the venue was going to present a serious problem. So we arranged for a helicopter to sit at Terminal 4, where Ace was arriving, and shuttle him to the venue by air. That way he could probably make it in time for the concert.

Then we got a call. "Well, there's good news and bad news."

Okay.

"The good news is that Ace really is on the plane. The bad news is that the plane has a mechanical problem and is delayed." At that point Doc told Tommy to drop what he was doing and get to the venue. He was going to have to play the show.

We traveled with a Spaceman outfit custom-fitted to Tommy—as an insurance policy. A brand-new outfit, boots and all, tailored to Tommy always came along in one of the wardrobe crates. We knew Tommy could do it, but he had never actually done it.

"You guys are like superheroes," said Doc. "So Tommy Thayer is playing Batman today? It's still Batman."

Tommy got made up and dressed. And meanwhile we were getting updates on Ace's location as the start time of the show approached. *He's landed . . . passenger is in helicopter . . . fifty miles away . . .*

Ace walked into the dressing room about twenty minutes before the show was scheduled to start. He looked at Tommy—fully dressed and made up, with his guitar on, ready to go—and just said, "Oh, hey Tommy, how you doin'?"

We delayed the show an hour, Ace got into his makeup, and we played the concert.

The fact that we traveled with a costume for Tommy didn't seem to faze Ace. He thought it was a ploy—something between a joke and an empty threat. But we were 100 percent ready to go on with Tommy. We didn't have him suit up to teach Ace a lesson; we did it because we had a concert to play. The same reckless behavior that had led to a decades-long downward spiral was threatening to sink the ship. Here was a life preserver.

Still, Ace continued to think and act like he was irreplaceable. He continued to show total disregard for everyone else, continued to act as if we were blessed to have him. He congratulated himself on making it to the show.

"This will not do," Doc said to me and Gene. "These guys are just terrible. I run a management company, not the Red Cross. They don't send me into destroyed countries to rebuild things. I don't save people. You have to make changes."

But still Gene and I clung to the idea of the four of us being together.

"You've already given it three more years than I would have," said Doc.

We decided to take the Farewell Tour to Asia in early 2001. Ace was on board. I personally offered Peter a million dollars to play eight shows in Japan in March 2001. He made the brilliant business decision to say no.

"Peter," I told him, "I want you to understand: you get one million dollars or you get nothing and the train leaves without you." Still no. Once again, what I was making was more important to him than the seven figures he would sock away. I told him I would call Eric Singer.

"The fans will never accept it," said Gigi, who was now married to Peter. "Peter's the most talented one in the band."

I just said, "Okay."

Initially, Doc's talk about getting rid of Peter—and Ace, for that matter—had been wishful thinking. No longer. This time we'd all had it. It's one thing to put up with somebody who's a virtuoso and a prick. It's quite another to put up with somebody who can barely play his instrument and is a prick.

I called Eric Singer, just as I had told Peter I would. To Peter's shock, the tour would go on. And Eric would wear the Catman makeup. At that point it was clear that compromising the four iconic characters had been a mistake the first time around, and we wouldn't repeat it. The Catman, the Demon, the Spaceman, and the Starchild were far more important than Peter, Gene, Ace, and Paul. Nobody in KISS is irreplaceable—and I definitely include myself in that calculation. All around the world people can identify a picture of the band KISS without necessarily knowing any of the members' names. So be it.

Gene, Ace, and I got together with Eric to rehearse in L.A. before we left for Japan. What a breath of fresh air. The reality of playing without Peter was freeing. Peter was marginal when the reunion started, and his playing had gone downhill since. His drum solos were an embarrassment. Eric hated drum solos. That kind of tells you everything you need to know about Eric.

Without Peter, the musical standard quickly improved. Even Ace picked up his game with Eric behind him. Even so, I wasn't sure what the reaction of the fans would be. Just as I hadn't been sure what the reaction would be when we took off our makeup years before. But overall, fans didn't seem to care. We didn't use any sleight of hand about the change. We introduced Eric by name at every show, and he got the applause he deserved for his playing. Nobody put a gun to people's heads and forced them to buy tickets, and yet the shows were just as full.

We had labored unnecessarily under a self-imposed concept. It turned out there had been no need. Few missed Peter—and Ace wasn't one of them. "I don't want this to get back to Peter, but I'm glad he's not here," Ace said one night. "He got me all worked up—I'm having a whole lot more fun now."

With Eric back in the band, Ace actually started socializing with all of us again. He liked Eric on all levels and loved playing with him. We had band dinners again and hung out together in Japan and Australia, where we added additional concerts into April 2001. Everyone got along better than ever. And in concert, Ace played the best he had since 1996. The vibe was great—until the last show in Australia on April 13. Ace had a rough show that night, and in some ways he was never the same again.

The plan was to say farewell in Europe after that, but we had trouble pinning Ace down. He would say yes and then change his mind. Eventually, he dropped completely out of sight. Nobody could get ahold of him, not even his lawyer. Finally he showed up for a meeting to discuss another proposed European farewell, and he was shockingly thin. Over the years he'd had a tendency to blow up and then get skinny again, careening back and forth depending on what he was ingesting at the time. But now he looked like he was going to die. And it was obvious that he was out of it. "My God, Ace, how'd you get so thin?"

"Yoga," he slurred.

The shows never got booked.

58.

With the European farewell canceled, I had the time I felt was essential for me to help support Evan through the traumatic upheaval that lay ahead for him. After having it looming in front of me for a year, the time had finally come for me and Pam to divorce.

The way I see it, we shared equally in all that happened. We chose each other, and from the very start we rarely met the other's needs or expectations. We chose poorly. Pam was a beautiful woman who was emotionally unavailable to me, which was a familiar dynamic. I was once again drawn to a challenge, seeking validation where it wasn't going to be given no matter what I did or didn't do. As for Pam, I know she felt minimized by my fame and success, although I'm sure she had hoped it would have the opposite effect on her. It was all futile and pointless; that was the lesson learned. We had been brought together to create and bring an extraordinary child into the world and then to parent him without compromising him in our divorce or separate lives. We accomplished that admirably, and I will always be grateful to Pam for her commitment in making that our priority.

Still, I had no idea how painful it would be.

Pam and I sat at the dining-room table with Evan, who was six, and explained that Mommy and Daddy weren't going to be together anymore. "We're still going to be your mommy and daddy, and we still love you and will always be there, but we won't be living together."

He burst into tears.

I told him that yes, it was horrible, and that yes, Daddy cried, too. I never tried to minimize what he was going through. I tried to acknowledge the pain and share it.

Strangely, during our separations, Pam and I had been building a house. I'd found a spectacular piece of property in Beverly Hills with unobstructed views of the ocean. By the time all the red tape had been taken care of, plans had been drawn up and approved by the city, bids for the construction decided on, and actual ground broken, our marriage was descending into crisis. But the work was in full swing by that point and was best left to continue. At the time of our divorce, the house looked complete on the outside, but it was just a shell—as incomplete as our relationship.

As Pam and I began the divorce process, it knocked me off my feet to find that the person I'd seen as my partner now saw me as her enemy. I had faith in Pam because of what she had told me years ago—about not wanting anything if things didn't work out between us—and since in my mind this wasn't going to turn into a typical Hollywood scenario, I hired a very civil and reasonable lawyer. But then I found myself sitting in a conference room in a mediation office, facing her and her attorneys and her forensic accountant advisor, feeling like I was having surgery performed on me without anesthesia.

Finally I said, "There must be a misunderstanding here, because

Pam would never go along with what you're proposing."

. Pam looked at me and said, "I know exactly what they're saying. This is business."

My jaw dropped.

My mind raced back to the unsigned prenuptial agreement and Pam's declaration that where she was from, your word was your bond. Apparently, *now* she was from Beverly Hills, a place where words and bonds were quickly forgotten. Evan was never an issue. He was my son 100 percent, and I would pay all his costs and expenses through adulthood without hesitation. Additionally, I had offered Pam a $2 million house and told her I would pay her expenses for five years and fund any classes she might want to take to prepare for the future. I didn't expect her not to want anything, of course. But I was shocked when the mediator asked her what she wanted and she said, "I want the same as he has."

What!?

I had gambled my future because of this dream that I believed in, and she wanted the same as I had? How could she rationalize something like that? An astute attorney later told me, "I've never met a woman who thought she got too much."

But the law was on her side. To be in a room and have no control over my destiny was a situation I had never been in. I just had to sit there as people sliced pieces off of me.

At some stage, my lawyer said, "You might have to sell the house."

"Absolutely no way," I said. About that one point I was adamant. The house meant more to me than its monetary value—it was the culmination of all my decades of hard work and my surgically repaired body—in addition to the shoulder work, my knees and hip were wrecked. It represented the freedom I had worked my entire life for.

"I'll do whatever I have to," I said. "That house is mine."

I ended up buying Pam a sixty-eight-hundred-square-foot house, sight-unseen, that she chose in a gated community. It was important to me to have Evan nearby to make it easier for him to go back and forth between us. I almost felt guilty about the house that she said was "just okay" until I actually saw it. The place had a tennis court and a pool and was beautiful.

When it was all settled and I was home one night—alone, without Evan—I collapsed to the floor in my empty house. I was devastated. There was a voice to the pain that came from deep inside—a guttural sound from someplace that you never reach at other times. It happened several times; I would just buckle over and sob, and this sound would come out.

I felt a sense of failure even though I knew—at least in retrospect—that the marriage had been doomed from the start. We had failed to see that marriage should be the confirmation of a great relationship as opposed to a way to fix the problems of a relationship that wasn't great to begin with. It should never have happened—though I wouldn't trade a minute of it because Evan became a part of my life through the relationship.

I thought back to my own childhood and something my mom used to say: "Nothing bad ever happens." I hated hearing that back then. But now I understood what she really meant: *Everything leads to something else*. Evan was a gift from God, and having him come into my life was worth whatever it now cost me in pain—or dollars.

In fact, the thing that hurt the most was the fear that I had betrayed my son. I had vowed never to hurt him. Yet I couldn't protect him from this. The most horrific realization was that I wasn't going to be able to see him every day. That I couldn't be with him whenever I wanted. Or whenever *he* wanted.

In the wake of my divorce, people in the same situation told me that I needed to go out and start dating. You know, "You need to have a life, too."

No, I don't.

I saw other people go that route, based on one rationale or another, but at the end of the day, I saw it as selfish—it didn't take into account what was best for their children. My child was going through incredible trauma, and my only concern was to make him feel safe. Bringing other people into the equation because I wanted to have company or get laid would be insane. How selfish could you get? The only thing that mattered at that point was Evan. My decisions would have a huge impact on him. I wanted to spend all my time with him, talk with him about whatever was on his mind. I bought a book called *When Children Grieve* that helped explain how children process and deal with grief and loss. I studied it.

One afternoon I was sitting outside my house thinking about all of this when one of the guys who had worked on the house came by unexpectedly to fix something. I didn't know him beyond a nod of "hello" here or there. But he must have known what had happened and seen how distraught I looked, because he came up to me.

"I hope you don't think I'm overstepping my bounds," he said, "but I can see what you're going through. I know you're going to think that I'm crazy, and that this won't be true for you, but I got divorced, and it felt like the world had ended. I didn't know what I was going to do. I just want you to know that I'm happily married now to the most amazing woman and have the most fantastic life now. And you will, too."

Just as he predicted, the first thought that went through my head was, *You're crazy.* I had no band. I was divorced. I had betrayed my kid.

What the fuck am I going to do now?

Through this period of intense pain, I still had few people to talk to or confide in. Divorce for me was something very solitary. Gene was on his own journey with his own way of protecting himself, his own armor. Therapy continued to be a haven for me, a place where I could talk honestly and express the stupidest, craziest thoughts. One of the things that therapy always did for me was to allow me to see that I wasn't as nuts as I feared I was—that my reactions were normal, or rather, that there was no such thing as "normal" despite appearances to the contrary.

Perhaps the person who helped me most of all was Michael James Jackson, the producer we had used for *Creatures*, *Lick It Up*, and *Animalize*. He's very intellectual and well-read and seems to see life in a more multilevel, complex way than most people. He knew I had been an art student and had noticed me sketching all the time during downtime in the studio. One day he said to me, "You need to paint." I was taken aback. "You need to get some of this out and explore some of it by painting," he continued.

The idea resonated with me. Soon Michael gave me some art books to try to inspire me, including a coffee-table book on Mark Rothko.

Finally I went out and bought some supplies—canvases, brushes, a pallet knife. I had no idea what I was going to do, but I was determined to give it a try. The first time I set things up and started to paint, it was like an out-of-body experience. I watched my hand move without thinking, and when it was done, I had a self-portrait.

I felt a sense of relief and satisfaction. So I started another one, and another. I suddenly had a need to paint.

Painting was like stream of consciousness with color. A purging. It allowed me to explore emotions without words. And then, in a sense, I could step back and look in the mirror—to see what was going on in my life or how I was feeling. It was almost like an exorcism. I would exhale and sigh when I finished a canvas; I had a sense of having gotten something out of me.

Eventually I realized I hadn't heard that guttural sound in a few days, and then I hadn't heard it in a few weeks. I licked my wounds and moved forward.

I started cooking a lot, too. It was important to me that Evan see that he and I could be self-sufficient. Not to mention that I wanted to feed him healthy meals and give him the calm and stability of eating together. I learned to make chicken parmesan and pancakes, I learned to prepare different types of fish and vegetables, I mastered the waffle iron and the muffin tin. My meatballs became things of beauty.

One of my favorite things to prepare was a Brussels sprouts dish I invented myself. Even people who didn't like Brussels sprouts—like Evan when he was a child—loved that dish. I cut the sprouts in half and pan-fried them with balsamic vinegar, dried cherries, and prosciutto, then finished them with parmesan cheese and lemon zest.

I found great pleasure in cooking and serving food—in giving.

Evan liked to help with the cooking. It was just the two of us in the house most of the time, but cooking together helped make the place feel like a home. A family home. Once when my dad was at the house and Evan and I were cooking and playing, he said, "Don't you give him too much love?"

"You can never give a child too much love," I said. "You can only give them too little love. Love doesn't make a child weaker, it makes a child stronger."

That was an odd one for my dad to hear.

If I ever heard someone telling Evan not to cry, not to be a baby, anything like that, I made a point of telling Evan the truth that I had discovered: people who hide their emotions are weak.

You find strength and peace by being open.

59

After my divorce, I might as well have worn a hat that said NO DRAMA on it. That became a mantra. I didn't want actresses and models; I didn't want anyone whose sense of self or mood was subject to whether or not she got a part or did well at an audition. I now knew that the drama I had earlier mistaken for fun, exciting, and normal—a basic component of a relationship—was actually tumultuous, counterproductive, and unnecessary. Emotions, yes; drama, no.

I wasn't going to waste time, I wasn't going to compromise myself or portray myself as something I wasn't. I wasn't going to second-guess people and try to be what I thought they wanted.

No drama.

I knew now that I should expect someone to love me for who I was.

One night in late 2001, I met Michael James Jackson for dinner at Ago restaurant, on Melrose. A group of women sitting at the next table included Tracy Tweed, whom I had dated, the sister of Gene's longtime girlfriend, Shannon. We said hello, and I went back to my conversation with Michael. Then another friend of theirs came bounding into the restaurant and over to Tracy's table. I was absolutely captivated by her. I decided I had to talk to that woman. I was compelled as if by an unseen force.

If there was ever going to be a moment that proved to me the existence of God—and I do believe there is a God—then this was it. Sure, some people might choose to call it luck. To me, luck is taking advantage of a situation God puts in front of us. The woman's name was Erin. She was as tall as me and had a great laugh. And she was a practicing attorney.

I called her the next day and asked her whether we could have dinner—either we could go out or I would cook for her on a night when Evan was with his mother. "If you like seafood, I could make swordfish with Dijon mustard and capers, maybe serve it with some pasta and, oh, I don't know, maybe broccoli with garlic and lemon and olive oil?"

She agreed. Apparently, her friends had already given her the green light. They told her it was safe to hang out with me. She went for the swordfish and came over to my house, where we drank wine and ate—and talked for six hours straight. My newfound love of cooking was paying off.

From the moment Erin and I met, we were totally honest with each other. She knew what I was going through, and I was very clear about my parameters for a relationship. I let her see everything about me. But she was understanding and nurturing, and she wasn't threatened by who I was or what I'd done. She was extremely bright and was confident in who she was. If anything bothered her, she told me about it; there was zero drama. We didn't rush into a monogamous relationship, but on all levels, there was definitely a great attraction there.

Meanwhile, there was a little burst of activity on the KISS front. In February 2002 we were scheduled to play "Rock and Roll All

Nite" for the closing ceremony of the Winter Olympics in Salt Lake City. The Sunday broadcast was supposed to attract something like a billion viewers, so even though it was a lip-sync job, we wanted to rehearse it beforehand on Friday and Saturday. Gene, Eric, and I all arrived as planned on Friday, rehearsed that day, and rehearsed twice again on Saturday. Ace was still a no-show on Saturday, so we had to call Tommy, who was on vacation with his family in Hawaii. Poor Tommy had to fly in and stand by to fill in, since there was no way to know whether Ace would turn up in time. In the end, Ace did appear at the last minute on Sunday and perform the song with us.

He was severely testing my low tolerance for drama.

We'd also been asked to do a private gig in Jamaica about two weeks after the Olympics debacle. A Russian oligarch offered us $1 million to play for about three hundred people at his thirtieth birthday party. Ace wouldn't do it. He was so paranoid by that stage that he thought the whole thing was a dastardly plot to get him out of the country so Gene, Doc, and I could have him assassinated. That way, we could replace him and not have a problem.

Replacing him was easier than all that. If Ace didn't want to go, Tommy could do it. End of story. Again, this was no mystery. Tommy had his own costume already, which was no secret to Ace; Tommy knew every song the band had ever recorded. I had no doubts about Tommy. We wouldn't have had him suit up all those times if we weren't confident in him.

Without demeaning the role of actually being in the band, Tommy just shifted from one position to another. He was already part of the family. And now he took a step to the right—from being next to the band to being in the band. He was more equipped for the task than Ace ever was.

The gig itself was strange. Everyone who wasn't a guest had a gun.

Eric and Tommy opened the door to spontaneity. With them, we could play a song we hadn't played in ten years. They both had the knowledge and ability to spit out a song from any era of the band.

After those gigs, on the heels of the Farewell Tour, I truly bought into the idea that this was the end of the band. It was a shame. Because even though it was a spur-of-the-moment thing, with Eric and Tommy the band was firing on all cylinders. In a lot of ways it was the band I had envisioned when we started the reunion—an idealized version of the band, with the iconic characters and the chops to match.

Damn.

I had no idea what I was going to do next. I thought about making music on my own. I thought about doing more theater. Losing KISS was like losing a family member. It had been such a big part of my life. I felt a huge void.

One afternoon later in 2002 I took my car to the carwash and one of the workers said to me, "Paul, the Farewell Tour was great. When are you doing the thirtieth anniversary tour?"

What? That would be okay? You mean you still want us?

The guy at the carwash really opened my eyes. He still loved the band. He wanted to know what was next.

I'm the one closing the door. I'm the one throwing the baby out with the bathwater.

But why?

All of a sudden, I wondered what we were really saying farewell to. Maybe the Farewell Tour was better envisioned as a farewell to those two guys? A farewell to compromising ourselves musically? A farewell to *drama*?

The idea of throwing it all away because of a pair of jerks who never valued the band suddenly seemed crazy. We had existed without them before. Now, because those two had come back into the fold, I was going to let them have their way by causing the demise of KISS?

Why stop now?

We had built the band back and people had embraced it. Hell, put on a good show and KISS could go on for another two hundred years. And without the weak links, this band could put on a *great* show.

I didn't want to give up something I'd spent thirty years busting my ass for.

I'm not done.

Part VI

Forever

60.

How much could we alter the equation in KISS? That was the question the Aerosmith camp raised when the idea of a co-headlining tour was floated. Doc was sure he knew. Gene and I were sure, too.

Under other circumstances, both Ace and Peter would have been out for the 2003 tour. But for whatever reason, the Aerosmith camp wanted at least three original members involved. By this point, Ace had already made it clear he was done. Which left Peter as the third member. *Ugh.*

There were contracts to be signed by Peter, Gene, Tommy, and me. Of course the four of us discussed it, and the members of the band were spelled out. After the Jamaica gig, it was a given that Tommy would wind up in the band. It was a logical progression, so much so that we never even spoke about it. After Jamaica we knew we didn't need to audition for a new guitar player. Tommy was the answer.

Tommy had been a great tour manager—not because he was destined to be a great tour manager, but because he gave himself totally to anything he did. And when he officially joined the band as the new lead guitarist, it wasn't that we took our tour manager and dressed him up in a Spaceman outfit. Tommy wasn't a doppelganger or a substitute; he was the next step and had proved that he deserved to be in the band and that he enhanced it musically.

As we started out on our co-headlining tour with Aerosmith, however, I have to say that Tommy and Peter didn't feel like the secret formula to me. It still felt transitional. It felt like the wound was only partly healed. Certainly we had somebody who wanted to be there, who knew the songs, who could play them consistently night after night. And I didn't wake up every morning wondering how the day would go and how the show would go. Fifty percent of the uncertainty and chaos had been eliminated.

Peter, on the other hand, was up to his same old tricks. He had Gigi pouring a little more poison down the well each day; he complained incessantly about being disrespected by hotel staff; he bitched about the smoke from the pyrotechnics. The hotel guidebook was back, too, along with complaints that his room was too dark or it was too far down the hall, the shows were too long, his hands hurt. On and on.

But the response from audiences was encouraging. There were cheers for Tommy, everybody on their feet, just as it had always been. If it sounded like KISS, looked like KISS, and commanded like KISS, it *was* KISS.

Meanwhile, Peter had his attorney trying to negotiate a contract extension during the tour. His demands, as usual, were absurd. I think they figured we would cave because Ace wasn't around anymore. Who knows what they were thinking? I knew by then that KISS was bigger than any of the individuals. And I do not mean "except me." I have a high regard for what I do, but I don't fool myself by thinking I'm the only one who can do it. Strangely, the longer the negotiating went on, the more Peter and his attorney seemed to think they had us over a barrel. We went along with it.

When the tour was over and Peter's contract expired, I told him we had decided not to renew his contract.

"You're not happy. You say the shows are too long. Your hands hurt. You want to play other kinds of music. We want to continue. I think it's best for everyone if we just call it quits, Peter. It's time for us all to move on."

I didn't have much to say beyond that. It wasn't that we were just going to become a different KISS or a new KISS; we were going to become a better KISS.

I couldn't change Peter any more than I could have changed Ace or Bill Aucoin or Donna or Pam. What I could do, however, was stop battling someone whose agenda was resolutely negative, someone who seemed intent on sabotaging everyone and everything around him—and then blaming anyone but himself. Fuck that.

The idea that we would stop using any of the four iconic images was as ridiculous as the idea that we would stop playing any of the songs. Interestingly, years before, when we decided to try to buy the rights to the Catman and Spaceman images, Peter and Ace dealt their characters away as if they had no value. To them, they were mere bargaining chips. The fact that they so readily relinquished them showed me how little they cared about them. I was glad that those guys couldn't start turning up at Halloween conventions signing autographs in tattered KISS outfits and makeup. I valued the images and wanted to protect them.

Eric Singer had been phenomenal when he filled in on the Farewell Tour, and again it was a case of not needing to look any further. We had our man for the future.

It was such a relief.

Touring was a part of my life that Erin knew nothing about. Back on the road I missed her and wanted her to be with me and experience it firsthand. It seemed strange to see her walk into this until-then-unknown realm of my life. She was a joy. When Erin came to her first KISS show, I remember seeing her in the audience dancing. She wasn't showing off; she was reflecting the elation I felt onstage.

During a break from that tour I took Erin to a charity dinner as my guest. When the host of the dinner mentioned me by name, Erin was the first person standing and clapping. I had never experienced anything like that. She was so secure in herself that she could happily give like that without feeling she was compromising who she was.

The first trip we took together was to Las Vegas. We went to my favorite restaurant at the Bellagio, called Picasso, and I was thrilled that she loved the whole fine dining experience and meeting the executive chef there, Julian Serrano, who had become a friend of mine. As we were lying in bed later that night watching TV, I said I was thirsty. Erin said, "Oh, I'll get you a drink."

I thought it was just an empty gesture and said, "No, don't be silly." But she got up and looked for the mini-bar. There wasn't one.

"I'll go down to the lobby and get you something," she said, pulling on some sweats.

"You're going to go down to the lobby and get me a drink?"

I don't mean to sound like a kicked dog, but nobody had ever done something like that for me before.

Erin would never do something that took away her pride, but she wasn't tangled up in bullshit—being kind and giving wasn't a negative to her and didn't chip away at her sense of self. From time to time we talked about the state of our relationship—where she was, where I was, how my home situation was unfolding. We always remained on the same page.

A healthy relationship makes you healthier. I guess I realized only in retrospect that a dysfunctional relationship is a pretty good indicator of where you yourself are. Only someone in turmoil stays in a tumultuous relationship. Erin wasn't like that at all. I had really never met anyone like her.

For the first year she and I dated, I never took her home when Evan was there. He had gone through a calamitous event in his life, and he needed to know he was safe rather than seeing me bring women around. Evan was in a situation he hadn't asked for, and the idea of "getting on with my life" without paying attention to his needs seemed transparently self-serving.

I wanted Evan to know that our home was for the two of us—it was our world. One way I tried to declare this was to have a massive floor-to-ceiling fresco of the two of us put into my bedroom. The house was not a home when Pam and I divorced, so I decided to make this fresco the centerpiece—both as a way to lay claim to the space and to illustrate the world I wanted to create for Evan. It was based on a nineteenth-century oil painting—a hunting party, Greek gods, nude maidens, cherubs, the works. Only I had the artist place me and Evan front and center, wearing togas with laurel wreaths around our heads. In the landscape around us were horses and dogs and dozens of bare-chested nubile maidens.

An extreme example of poor bachelor-pad taste? No way. No, no, no. For some reason, I thought this massive fresco was absolutely spectacular and something to display with pride. Erin, it would turn out, did not share this opinion.

After Erin and I had been seeing each other for more than a year, I thought it was time to introduce her to Evan. But again, I didn't want him to feel threatened. So I decided to have them meet in a neutral location. I told Evan I had a friend who, like him, loved candy. I said we were going to visit a candy store at a shopping center and she was going to meet us there. She came and met Evan, but I never held her hand or kissed her. Only slowly over the course of many months, as Evan learned to get used to her and like her, did we start to reveal our affection a little more. As he became closer to

Erin, I allowed him to see me and her becoming closer as well. It was a parallel course—I hoped that in his eyes our relationship was evolving in front of him.

Pam and I never badmouthed each other to Evan, and for that I'm so grateful to her. Neither of us wanted him to become a pawn in any disputes between us. I see things very simply. If you want to take it to logical extremes, it all boils down to one basic question: do you hate your ex more than you love your child? As long as you love your child more, there's no basis for bad words or denying access or anything like that. Which also meant Erin never represented a replacement or a threat.

Further on down the road, Erin, Evan, and I took a trip together. I wanted him to see that Erin slept over sometimes, but again, I wanted it to happen in a neutral setting. We checked into a resort in Santa Barbara, and when we went into the room, Evan asked, "Where's Erin going to sleep?"

"With me," I said.

"Oh," he said, without any surprise or discomfort. And we moved on.

By that time in my life I firmly believed we heal ourselves by helping others. My making Evan the center of things for me benefited everyone. It was such a joy to see a happy child.

When Erin and I finally moved in together, she told me she wasn't crazy about the fresco in the bedroom. "We don't have to lose it," I said. "I mean, we can add you into it. You can be one of the maidens. You live here now—you can be on there, too."

"I hate it," she finally admitted. "I've always hated it."

I was shocked. Then suddenly I found myself chuckling. When I stepped back, it *did* look like something from *This Is Spinal Tap*.

"Why didn't you tell me sooner?" I asked.

Then I went to the storage room and grabbed some paint and a couple of paint rollers and we painted over the thing together.

61.

Sometime after Erin moved in, Evan, who was about ten at the time, accidentally locked himself out on the balcony off his bedroom. Erin and I were downstairs and didn't realize it. At one point I heard a noise but couldn't place it.

Wait, was that somebody shouting?

Suddenly it dawned on me that Evan might be locked out. Erin and I ran upstairs. Evan was beside himself out on the balcony. We opened the door. And he came running in—right past me and into Erin's arms.

Some parents might have felt insulted by that, but I thought it was the greatest thing that he felt that way about her. It assured me that their relationship was strong and loving, too.

While on vacation with Erin in Hawaii in 2003, a gallery owner approached me and asked about doing something for his gallery—something like signed guitars. "I paint," I told him. He asked to see some of my paintings. After I showed him photos, he wanted to mount a show.

Me? An art show?

It sounded odd. Now granted, this wasn't some swank New York gallery. But still.

We organized the show and I went back to Hawaii for the opening. We sold $35,000 worth of paintings, which certainly exceeded all my expectations, since I had never expected to sell anything. It was quickly clear to me that if credibility came from being a starving artist, I would have to cross that off my list.

After that, I had the bug. I wanted to do the same thing on the mainland. Soon enough, I had a deal in place with a chain of galleries around the country. We did a series of shows, and I felt as if I was exposing some people to a potentially enriching aspect of culture—the visual arts—who might not otherwise get exposed to it. The same thing had been true when I did *Phantom of the Opera*, where I'm sure some KISS fans made their first foray into musical theater. I felt I was breaking down some of the snobbery that I think ultimately does a disservice to the arts. People sometimes would come up to me at a show and tell me, "I don't know anything about art, but I like this piece."

"What do you need to know?" I would say. "Something either moves you or it doesn't."

I found it gratifying when people said a piece made them think of something from their own lives or sparked them to tell me a story about their own families. Seeing people affected by my paintings validated my work in a way I probably never would have experienced otherwise.

Bill Aucoin came to one of my art shows. He had leveled out, and it was great to see him. Bill was warm and supportive. As the friendship was rekindled and KISS began to tour again—with Eric and Tommy—Bill came to a few concerts as well as more art shows. Over time we did a good deal of talking about the past. He told me how he had seen me as defensive and unhappy in the early days—

unfulfilled, guarded. He loved the transformation he saw in me, what he called growth. He loved Erin, and he made a big point of how happy it made him to see that I had evolved to a better place. I was touched.

Eventually I would take a break from showing my art, even though my sales had by then passed the $2 million mark. I had started painting as a way to let off pressure. It was something I did without a schedule, without anyone asking questions. Painting was a big commitment since I had no training—it took a lot of time and effort and thought. There was no need for me to turn it into a business. I didn't want it to become a chore, especially as the band began to tour regularly again.

One day back in L.A., Erin and I were chatting about the state of our relationship. We started talking about her mother, who had spent decades working as an elementary school teacher. "So what does your mom think is going to happen between us?" I asked. "What does she think of this whole thing?"

"Oh," Erin said, "my mom thinks either it will move forward at some point or it will fall apart."

I love this photo. It says it all to me.

ZEN TODD

It hit me at that moment: *This isn't going to fall apart.*

I couldn't imagine not being with Erin. I knew then and there that I wanted to be with her forever.

We'd been together several years at that point. It wasn't a passing infatuation. Our relationship wasn't about love at first sight. The depth of my feelings for her grew out of our experiences together. It built over time.

I called a jeweler in New York City and asked them to send me one of their booklets. A ring jumped out at me immediately. Next, I picked out a stone.

When the ring was finished, I carried it around waiting for the right moment to ask Erin to marry me. But I couldn't find that moment.

We took another trip to Vegas in 2005 and returned to Picasso for a great meal. We both loved the place and were enjoying ourselves and drinking the wine pairings. I got pretty buzzed, in fact. I had figured this would be the place to pop the question, but I wanted to propose to her with a clear head.

The next day, I kicked myself.

Fuck, when am I going to do this?

A friend of mine had lent me his private jet to fly home on—which is something I never imagined I'd say in my life. I thought perhaps that would be the perfect place—the sunlight at forty thousand feet would make the ring really shine. But when we got on the plane, all my neurotic tendencies came into play: *Damn it, these windows are polarized, I won't get a sparkle on the ring.*

We landed back in L.A. and drove home.

I have to do this!

We got home. Off our bedroom is a balcony overlooking the pool and guesthouse—more things I never envisioned in my life. It was a beautiful sunny day. "Come on out here," I called to Erin from the balcony. "We should go for a swim."

She walked out onto the balcony. We had literally just walked into the house, but I couldn't wait any longer. She was leaning over the railing looking down over the pool, and I stood behind her, wrapped my arms around her, and held the ring before her eyes.

Her reaction was a cross between panic and crying as she blurted, "Oh, my God!" She didn't seem to know what to do.

"Will you marry me?" I asked.

"Yes!" she said.

Then we called her mom to tell her the news—that we were moving forward, not falling apart.

We planned the wedding in a single afternoon. Everyone said they'd never seen anything go so quickly. But I thought, hey, if we want peach-colored flowers, what does it matter what kind they are? People tend to get hung up on minutia when it's really about celebration. *Oh, we need to have these certain flowers from Africa . . .* Screw that. I did spend time picking every song the band would play, however, and since I wanted to go deep into the Motown catalogue, we got a horn section, multiple singers, and percussionists. It was an incredible sound, gloriously loud and unrelenting.

The outdoor wedding took place at the Ritz-Carlton in Pasadena in November 2005, with a relatively small group of friends and family.

As thin and beautiful as Erin is, she loves candy. So we arranged to have a candy bar there—every kind of candy, stuff I'd never seen, stuff that looked to me like a science project. She was in heaven.

And so was I.

We danced and danced and danced.

62.

Tommy and Eric came to the wedding, but Gene wasn't invited. I told him well in advance. I didn't want to go through the motions of inviting him just because he was my musical partner. He didn't belong there. He was well known for his views on marriage—calling it an "institution" that he didn't want to live in.

"Your views on marriage are your own," I told him. "But when you insult and demean people who get married and ridicule or dismiss the idea of marriage, you have no place at a wedding."

How somebody votes in a presidential election is one thing. But why ridicule people or the validity of their beliefs? It would have been insulting to have such a vocal opponent of marriage—somebody who went out of his way to say things I found offensive about the rationality and importance of marriage—at my wedding.

He got it.

But his opinions on marriage also began to shift. By the next year, when Tommy got married in 2006, Gene was very supportive. And Gene eventually married Shannon Tweed, his girlfriend of more than twenty-five years, in 2011.

Two months after Erin and I were married, we found out she was pregnant. We were ecstatic. Having children was always our plan, and we weren't waiting to get started—I was fifty-three and Erin was thirty-three. During the pregnancy, reading books, going for sonograms, and searching for possible names only bonded us more. Erin looked incredible pregnant and loved every minute of it, which made the time all that much more joyous. Evan, too, was thrilled with the news, which put to rest any fears of mine that he might be angry or resentful. His only demand was that he be the first one to join us in the delivery room to greet his new sibling.

Once we found out we were having a boy, we went through hundreds of names and combinations before deciding on Colin Michael. Funny how after he was born, all of the other possibilities we had considered seemed so wrong.

Colin's birth was a completely different experience from Evan's. Erin started having contractions in the middle of the night, and I was there with a notepad timing the contractions and writing everything down. Eventually we drove to the hospital; again, I set up my tripod and video camera. I told the doctor who was going to deliver the baby that I wasn't squeamish and wanted to be involved in the delivery as much as possible. When Erin was in the final minutes of labor, the doctor turned to me and said, "get your gloves on." After a brief moment of panic, I pulled on some gloves, and as this little miracle began to emerge, I was told to pull him out. It was surreal as I lifted this little life out of the only world he had ever known and brought him into ours. Colin's birth was another moment of deep connection with God and all the generations before me. He, too, would be my legacy and my connection to both past generations and future ones.

I had sometimes worried during Erin's pregnancy how I could love another child with the same depth and effortless commitment to giving my all with which I loved Evan. That fear evaporated as I held Colin and realized that we have an unlimited capacity to create and give love. I would dedicate myself yet again to another amazing little boy, and together we would find out all that we could learn from each other.

Outside my growing family, Gene and I still fought on occasion. His use of the KISS logo and makeup and his self-promotion in the press escalated throughout the late nineties and beyond. I saw the term "marketing genius" used in reference to Gene quite frequently in the wake of subsequent tours. It turned my stomach. Contrary to the notion that Gene spearheaded or maximized our merchandise empire, the truth is that over the years the vast majority of licensees have sought us out and all solicitations go through our product development team. Neither Gene nor I has had an active hand in any significant deals. He was no marketing genius. He just took credit for things. It was unwarranted, selfish, and hurtful, and there was no way to excuse it. Calculated strategist? Sure. Genius? No.

After the Farewell Tour I saw sketches of a concept for a cartoon series Gene had sold. The cartoon character was basically Gene in KISS makeup. It was about a guy in a band. "Hey, man, that's a KISS entity," I said.

"Oh, no, this is not a KISS image," he said. "It's totally different."

That kind of stuff still riled me up. There he was sitting across the table from me lying about something that clearly fell under our partnership agreement, and he knew it. "Do you think you're talking to one of the other idiots you're in business with?" I asked him. "Are you kidding me?"

That got settled real quickly. Fairness prevailed, but not by Gene's volition.

Beyond the anger I felt each time he showed such blatant disregard for our partnership, my feelings were also hurt that the guy with whom I had built all of this would treat me—when it served his purposes—with the same indifference I often saw him exhibit in his dealings with people I knew he didn't care about.

Still, despite the hiccups, Gene and I have never gotten along better than during the past decade. We have very few points of contention these days. We've been friends for more than forty years and have built great lives for ourselves. I think that over time I came to recognize the fundamental difference in our personalities. I wanted to improve myself and remedy the issues that plagued me. But he chose to ignore his underlying issues and instead committed himself to creating an external façade and persona that, unfortunately, he felt required him to knock down anyone who threatened his singularity in the spotlight. Earlier, I could never understand why he didn't want to resolve issues he had. I could never understand why someone so intelligent wouldn't do something to make life easier for himself—and probably for me and other people around him. After all, I know the never-ending effort it takes to keep up a persona and maintain a front to shield yourself.

Somewhere along the line I came to understand that his attitude was, "Why bother?" Once I reconciled myself to how different we were in that regard, our relationship became easier. Gene and I are very different, and that chemistry and contrast continue to be keys to our success.

These days, we laugh at each other's quirks.

Another thing that has changed is what I expect from Gene. I expect less; I'm more realistic. I'm very clear about what's acceptable to me and what isn't. I found the secret to a great partnership was knowing its limitations. If you don't ask of a relationship what it can't give you, you won't be disappointed. Forty years on in an immensely fruitful and successful partnership, I express my thoughts regarding Gene with acceptance as opposed to animosity. He continues to have his meetings sitting behind a big desk in an office surrounded by wall-to-wall cases filled with KISS merchandise, never clarifying the fact that rather than being the creative force behind it all, he is in reality just one of the four faces on each box. This stuff still goes on, but I'm okay with it.

I still want credit for what I do and achieve. But in the wake of all the positive changes in my personal life, I have stopped caring as much. I now consider my life to be so rich that many of the other concerns that once were so important seem like a waste of precious time. What I have gained—inwardly and outwardly—from a happy marriage and family far outweigh whatever I might have been looking for as far as perceptions about the inner workings of KISS. Those perceptions were—and are—far more important, and perhaps fulfilling, to Gene. Life has to be about what you get in exchange for what you give up, and the things I now hold dear aren't worth giving up for fleeting publicity hits. If you define yourself by deals and media coverage, you're always searching for the next fix. That's life on a hamster wheel. If you can't stop running, you aren't really free. You remain a slave if you don't figure out something internal to make you happy.

The same is true as far as touring is concerned. We don't have to tour all the time. We are our own bosses.

KISS is my work, and it's spectacular and rewarding work in so many ways, but there is room for a life outside the band. Every week I spend on the road is a week I don't spend with the people who matter most in the world to me. Those seven days are more precious to me now than ever before. After I married Erin, I began to put parameters on what I was willing to do and who I was willing to spend time with. There would be no compromises; life was too short for that.

KISS isn't life. It's a facet of life.

At times, when Doc came to us with proposals for things, I began to say, "I'd rather be home." Gene was always puzzled by this.

"You're going to say no to money?" he would ask in utter disbelief.

"Yeah," I said. "The question is, What's more money going to get me? And what will I have to give up to get it?"

For him, it was simple. As Doc jokes, when Gene is ninety-five years old, he'll be standing at the end of his driveway with his walker, flicking his tongue at passing cars. We all deserve to find happiness, and I hope Gene does, now and in the future.

But to me, there's more to life. The money I lose by not doing a show won't change my world, but being away from my family will. I weigh one against the other. How much do I need? Sure, I'd always like to have more—who wouldn't? But I don't *need* more if the sacrifice is too great—not just to my wife and kids, but to me. Sometimes what I would miss out on isn't worth the money.

My children turned out to be the ultimate resolution to issues that plagued me my entire life. You can't change your past, but you *can* change your life and the lives of those around you. I've come to terms with things about myself that I've had to wrestle with, and as a result I have more to give—because I know myself more. Having children allowed me a second chance at the childhood I never had. It's cathartic to raise my kids in a loving and nurturing way that I myself never knew. I've been able to give my kids the life I didn't have, by treating them the way I wished I had been treated, by helping them feel the way I wished I had felt.

Maybe not everyone is affected in the same way by what a family and a deep relationship can offer. As the things I missed most in life until very late, they mean the world to me. Truly sharing with somebody, baring your soul to someone, having someone know your vulnerabilities and weaknesses and fears—and doing the same for that person—offers a calm and a sense of refuge that no hotel, no matter how luxurious, can rival.

63.

All my feelings of love and pride for KISS were amplified by starting to tour with Tommy and Eric as permanent members. I quickly realized that I would rather not perform anymore than have to deal with people I didn't want to be around. I could never go back to the drama, the lowered standards, the disrespect for the craft. It would be whoring myself.

It was amazing to have people in the band whose mentality was, *What can I do to make the band bigger?* instead of, *What can I do to make myself bigger?* You accomplish the latter by the former anyway, but if you make the latter your priority, it doesn't work. With Ace and Peter, that's the way it was. With Tommy and Eric, there was a work ethic—and it started with taking pride in what they did individually and what we did as a team.

Of course, a certain segment of the audience didn't want the reunion era to be finished. People occasionally dismissed Eric and Tommy as imposters. But when I stood onstage with them, I had the opposite impression: if anyone had been imposters, it was Peter and Ace during the reunion tours. Whatever ability those guys may once have had was long gone—or rather, long discarded. They were a distortion of anything they had ever been. With apologies to anyone who doesn't want to hear it, Ace and Peter simply couldn't play their instruments by the end. And they didn't care, which in my mind was perhaps an even bigger sin. If people want to talk about seeing the band as a meal ticket, they can't point at me or Gene. We were already eating well. Only Peter and Ace treated KISS as a meal ticket, and even then, they couldn't recognize their good fortune sufficiently enough to punch it.

The new lineup of the band was much more the band as I envisioned it—and the way people heard it in their minds. I always wanted the audience to feel that we surpassed their expectations, and it had been a long time since we had been able to do that. With Tommy and Eric, we did it. The band could sing so well, in fact, that people constantly asked us whether we used prerecorded background vocals. Nope. We just finally had four strong band members.

Through all of this, KISS wasn't just surviving, it was thriving.

Once I rekindled my friendship with Bill Aucoin, he continued to come to occasional concerts. I loved the fact that we had both come to terms with personal demons; I loved where we both had ended up—both in stable relationships and peaceful mental states. In a way, I found with Bill what I wasn't able to find in the band reunion. We were able to bring things full circle, put things to rest, and look back and enjoy what we had created together.

Then over lunch in Florida one afternoon, he told me he had advanced-stage prostate cancer. I asked what I could do to be helpful, and Bill told me he worried about his partner, Roman, and what would happen to him if Bill lost his battle. I talked to Gene, and we decided to buy the condo they were living in and give it to Roman.

At the end of a European tour in 2008, I rented a beautiful villa in Tuscany. The place looked like a three-story museum in the middle of the countryside. I made arrangements for Erin, Evan, and Colin to join me there, along with my parents, Erin's mom, her mom's husband, and my good friend and security man, Danny Francis. Erin and I had been holding off telling everyone some big news until we were all around the kitchen table eating a home-cooked dinner. We started our meal with a couple of bottles of lambrusco, a bubbly red wine with no pretenses of chic or airs of high society. Then we told them: Erin and I were expecting a baby girl!

Funny thing about choosing names. We just weren't cool enough to name our children Pineapple or Astro Girl. We loved old-school names and chose Sarah Brianna for our first girl. Colin's delivery had been an easy twenty-five minutes of pushing for Erin, and we assumed Sarah's would be similar. No such luck. Sarah wasn't in the proper position in the birth canal, and ultimately a C-section was needed. Watching it performed was shocking and certainly bore no resemblance to natural delivery, but at the end of it, there was Sarah—who was absolutely gorgeous. Everyone commented on her angelic face and perfect upturned nose.

There were some post-surgery complications that led to days of unspeakable pain and very real danger for Erin—including the risk of losing a kidney—and so I called some "big guns" I thankfully knew. A group of specialists descended on Erin's room like a SWAT team, and a series of quick tests found the root of the problem.

Erin endured weeks of risky surgery to reattach things and reroute the problems. But thanks to a stellar team that included Dr. Stephen Sachs and Dr. Ed Phillips at Cedars-Sinai Hospital, Erin made a slow but full recovery. Once she and Sarah were finally home, I got to experience a bond I had always heard was so unique—the bond between a father and daughter. Sarah melted my heart and awakened a spot in it that she alone owned.

In 2009 KISS went back to South America and found ourselves treated like visiting dignitaries. When we arrived in São Paulo, one of the world's most populous cities, it was rush hour and the freeways were gridlocked. Suddenly about three dozen motorcycle cops shot ahead of our vans and cleared the entire highway between the airport and our hotel. The overpasses, on-ramps, exits— everything was blocked by the police so we four idiots could get to our hotel. It was unbelievable. Certainly the motorcade of the President of the United States of America wouldn't have gotten better traffic control. At the end of the ride, we took photos with the cops. They were fans.

Despite the fact that the new KISS lineup proved an immediate success and also had long-term durability, it wasn't clear we needed to go back into the studio. We certainly didn't need to do it for the money. And besides, the experience of *Psycho Circus* had left a sour taste in my mouth and totally turned me off to the idea of recording. I couldn't have articulated what exactly it would take to change my mind, but over time I began to figure out a set of prerequisites that might make it possible for me to make another KISS album.

For one thing, I needed to have final say. I wasn't going to work on something I couldn't be proud of. I was through second-guessing things or being second-guessed. At least if we did something I loved, there would be one big fan regardless of what else happened.

For another, I wasn't going to work on an album unless everyone put in the same amount of effort. There wasn't going to be any sense of entitlement or special treatment. Everyone would have to earn their place, and I wouldn't put up with any mediocre songs just because of a sense of job tenure.

And finally, I wanted to produce any new record. The idea of needing an intermediary between me and Gene or anyone else was ridiculous. I was too old for that nonsense. If there was going to be another KISS album, it was going to be done properly without politics or ulterior motives. It was going to be great material and great playing, all brought together with a vision.

I did believe that this team—Gene, Tommy, Eric, and me—could put together a really great KISS record. With the changes in the industry, we also had the chance to have total control—from the songs and recording process to the marketing and distribution. And I thought it would be a shame to let *Psycho Circus* be our final statement. I knew that times had changed, so I had no expectations of sales at past levels. Success in my eyes would be measured in quality and realizing my own standards and expectations.

The current band is so impressive and cohesive.

We owe it to ourselves to step up to the plate.

So in 2009 it was time to make a new KISS album. Everyone got together to start writing songs—another stipulation was that we do it all together as a team with no outside writers. When we finished *Sonic Boom,* we did a deal directly with Walmart to have not just our new album on sale there, but a store-within-a-store, with all sorts of merchandise and back catalogue items alongside *Sonic Boom.* And when it was released, we debuted at No. 2 on the charts.

Bill Aucoin flew in for our show at Madison Square Garden in October 2009, just after the release of *Sonic Boom.* He said he was going to beat the cancer, but he was clearly very sick. He planned to come to our show at Wembley Arena in London in May 2010, but he had to cancel. A few weeks later, Roman told me that Bill's condition had taken a turn for the worse and he was in the hospital. I called Bill while we finished our European tour, and Gene and I made plans to fly to Miami to see him as soon as the tour was over.

When I checked back with Roman soon after, he said Bill was unconscious. He had developed sepsis. Roman put the phone to Bill's ear for me, and I thanked him for everything he had done for KISS. Regardless of what had happened later, none of the good things that happened in the formative years would have happened without him, I told him.

"I love you, Bill" I said.

The last concert of the *Sonic Boom* tour was in Belgium in June, and Gene and I stayed up all night after the show to catch the first flight to the States in the morning. We phoned Roman to let him know we'd be at Bill's bedside by that afternoon.

When our flight landed and I turned on my phone, I saw there was a missed call from Roman. I checked my voicemail. Bill had passed away while Gene and I were on the way to say good-bye to him.

Good-bye.

64.

My life was as full as I could ever have hoped for with Erin and my children. Evan and I shared a growing musical bond in addition to our bond as father and son. Colin, my little dynamo, was a perfect blend of rambunctiousness and cuddling who wrestled me with laughter and a determination to win. Sarah had grown disarmingly beautiful, a little drama queen who danced, sang, and had her mother's daring and spunk. What more could I have wanted or needed?

Erin was very vocal about wanting to have one more child. I couldn't imagine having yet another, but judging by how quickly she was again pregnant, God had other ideas. And once our daughter Emily Grace arrived, I couldn't imagine life without her. She's clearly part of a plan I didn't understand. Although she strongly resembles me, she's blessed to be another stunner like her sister. Stubborn, secure, and always laughing, Emmie is my angel. My four children have made me wealthy beyond anything I ever could have imagined. And it's a gift to *know* that.

As I got older, my mother said on many occasions that I should call any time and at any hour if I needed to talk. I always found comfort in that, and when I felt the need, I did call her without hesitation. My parents' desire to be there for me as an adult was unfortunately often sabotaged for all of us by a disconnect in their own lives decades past, but I never doubted their love for me. How much could I really have hoped for when their own experiences from a young age left them unable to help themselves or each other? My mom and dad were good people who over the course of their lives

Mom and Dad. Despite everything, together to the end. My mom passed away at eighty-nine on September 29, 2012. I will always miss her.

tried to make their way as best they could with the cards they had been dealt. Frustrating and unsuccessful as many attempts were, they—like me—never stopped trying, and that is what I keep with me.

When KISS decided to start making another album, *Monster,* in 2011, the ground rules were the same as for *Sonic Boom*. Gene said in a few interviews that he didn't have the time to do the production work because of all the other things he had going on, which I of course found undermining and designed to imply that I was producing by default. The truth is, neither of those albums would have been made if I hadn't produced them. I wasn't aiming to be a dictator, just demanding to be a director.

We went into the studio with a sense of pride, not with a sense of obligation. We wanted to challenge ourselves as well as build on what had come before. The long journey through different players, different lineups, different tours and albums had gotten us to the real KISS.

This is *the* band.

The four of us had a ball making the record. We collaborated as a band. A song like "Wall of Sound" began as an idea Gene brought to the table. Then Tommy found the riff, and I added the lyrics. Eric said, "Let's make a song with a bit of the feel of the MC5" and came up with the drum part that became the foundation of "Back to the Stone Age." The album came together from all of us working together, plain and simple.

Monster isn't just classic KISS, it's classic rock. It reminds me of why I love rock and roll and of what made the bands that inspired me so great. Between Eric's authority, Tommy's fire, and Gene's undeniable ferocity—both in his bass playing and his vocals— *Monster* has a rare vitality. It sounds like the work of a new band. In fact, the album probably would have had a bigger commercial impact if it had been released by an unknown band.

I get it.

There's no getting around the fact that nothing KISS does in the future will have the impact of the things we did in the past. Those things took place in a different era: the world was different, the music business was different, the monolithic nature of pop culture was different. In addition, of course, the magnitude of something gets enhanced by the simple passage of time. As good as it is, "Hell or Hallelujah" can never be "Love Gun." The classic songs have already been the soundtrack to people's lives for forty years in some cases. There's no way to compete with that. None of the newer material has time on its side. But then again, when we play "Lick It Up," it goes over gangbusters—what was once considered one of our "new" songs has long since acquired classic status to people who came to the party a little later. The song "Psycho Circus" is now a show opener and goes over better now than when it came out. Time is the ultimate judge.

As we hit the road to celebrate *Monster,* one of my favorite parts of the tour quickly became the "meet-and-greet" before each show when we played an unplugged show, without makeup, in the afternoon for a small group of fans who had bought special VIP packages. We couldn't possibly have done the meet-and-greets with Ace and Peter. For one thing, they wouldn't have shown up. For another, they didn't know enough songs to do what's most fun about these gatherings—letting the fans make requests and then hashing out the songs on the spot, sometimes after not having played them for decades. It's a thrill to see the reaction of the fans, and we have a blast jamming there with them as if we're all in a living room. The band is so comfortable now. And capable. Admittedly, the VIP packages aren't cheap, but people actually thank us after the meet-and-greets. That, to me, is the ultimate testament to what we're doing—if someone pays you and then thanks you, you've done a good job.

The current lineup of KISS has built a broad sense of community that wouldn't have been possible when we were burdened by all the inner turmoil of the old lineup. Doctors come up to me at shows and say, "You got me through med school." Former convicts say, "You got me through prison." People tell me KISS helped them deal with the deaths of loved ones or battles with cancer.

At a concert in St. Louis in 2012, I had arranged complimentary meet-and-greet tickets for a young man incapacitated by ALS, or Lou Gehrig's disease. He couldn't move or speak, but I thought I detected the hint of a smile in his eyes when we took photos with him. Also in the VIP tent that afternoon was a married couple who were buying an electric guitar I would play later that night onstage. Following our unplugged set, I talked to the man and woman for a while and determined how they wanted their guitar inscribed. After the wheelchair-bound man with ALS left the tent, the husband of the couple turned to me and said, "We bought a second guitar for that young man."

That stopped me in my tracks. The guitars I sell are intended for collectors and cost thousands of dollars. This couple didn't know the man in the wheelchair. They didn't know what his ailment was or anything else about him. They had simply seen him across the room.

I told them I was moved by their gesture.

"We're very lucky people," explained the husband. "We like to pay it forward."

Their reward was the act of giving. Mine was to reimburse them the cost of the guitar.

That same year I met a woman in San Antonio who came to the show to celebrate her cancer being in remission for a year. Another night, coming offstage in Las Vegas, a police officer came up to me with a huge smile on his face. "*Destroyer* was my first album," he said. "The show was amazing . . . oh, my, God . . . I can die now."

"Please don't," I said. And then we hugged.

I know I'm not Florence Nightingale. And obviously, KISS never was and still isn't a philanthropic movement or a humanitarian effort. We're four guys who play instruments. We're a rock band. And yet, to realize our band can be an inspiration and raise awareness and contribute significant sums to worthy causes like the Wounded Warrior Project and various cancer charities is both humbling and deeply rewarding.

Early in KISS's career I thought it was cool to see people at the shows having fun. Now I see the part I play in making them happy and find that very fulfilling. The time and consideration I can give to people—people who, for instance, are returning from military service or have gone through tough times of one kind or another—mean so much to me now. It was nice when I was young, but it didn't go to the core of my being the way it does now. The more opportunity I have to treat people the way I wished I myself had been treated, the better I feel. It's also amazing how little it takes to have a huge effect on someone's life. It's tempting to say it would be sinful not to take advantage of such opportunities, but then again, there's a selfish element to it—I feel that I gain as much as the other person.

I've taken some big leaps in my life, and the biggest ones have been in the past fifteen years. Learning the value of kindness was a gift that came to me late, but it changed the game. Doing for others is now the most satisfying thing in my life, the gift I never knew. It's fulfilling in a way I could never have imagined when I was young.

Back then, I thought I knew everything. It's amazing some of the things I thought I knew. That was sheer audacity. Being judgmental was a defense mechanism and a way to avoid looking at myself. It was rooted in fear and self-doubt. I didn't like myself.

I'm Jewish and I believe in God, but I don't picture God as an old man with a beard and a robe sitting in heaven judging us. The thing I love about Judaism is that it's not about being good because of the consequences of being bad; it's about being good because it's the way we are *supposed* to be. Being good is its own reward. I'll buy that. When Evan was born, I read a book on interfaith marriages that said the problem in such families can be that children often don't feel fully part of one religion or the other because of tensions between the parents. When children fear they might be angering or betraying a parent, they're paralyzed. In our family, our kids aren't 50 percent Catholic and 50 percent Jewish; they're 100 percent both. I grew up around people who had numbers tattooed on their arms from being in concentration camps, and I feel a responsibility to them, and to the 6 million others who were killed, to keep their stories alive and make sure my kids know the history of Jews and Judaism. But ultimately, I'll let my children come to their own conclusions as far as what they want to participate in and believe, and I'll know they are deep, wonderful people regardless of their choices.

I gave a speech at a high school graduation ceremony in June 2012 that emphasized the need to show compassion. I talked about my ear deformity and deafness and the way I shut myself off from others as a result. And then I came to the most important part—the part about realizing how I can help myself by helping others; how I can free myself from harsh judgment by not judging others. When someone asks for a handout, I said, it's easy to look down on that person or to say, "Get a job." America is a land of opportunity, yes, but not everyone gets the same chances. You have no idea what got that person into his or her situation. You don't necessarily solve anything by helping the person, but if you provide even a moment's respite from difficulties and pain, it's worthwhile. Plus, you'll feel good about it. That lost soul is one of God's children, and by being compassionate and kind, you open yourself to a feeling of peace and contentment.

Who am I to look down my nose at somebody?

Judging others and being quick to criticize just pollutes your life. Learning how to open your hand is the best thing you can possibly learn.

That lesson has been brought into our home, as well. From a very early age, Evan's birthday parties were no-gift parties. What kid needs thirty gifts? How about learning what it means to give to others instead? Each year for his birthday he picked a charity, and we collected money at his party to donate to his chosen cause. I would kill to be able to play guitar the way Evan can now, but I'm far more proud of the hardworking and compassionate human being he has grown up to be. As Erin and I have nurtured our three younger children, we've tried to make them aware of their part in the world, too, and the responsibilities that come with it.

To paraphrase Bob Dylan: You may know what you want but not what you need. We all run around wanting certain things, but when you reach a point where you can distinguish between the things you thought you wanted and the things you actually need, that is an epiphany.

In my case, it may have been necessary to get what I wanted in order to learn what I needed. Achieving all those things that I thought would make me happy—fame, wealth, desirability— confronted me at each milestone with the fact that what I had chased wasn't the solution. In each case, I may still not have known what I needed, but I could scratch another potential solution off the list. *Not* fame. *Not* wealth. *Not* desirability. I had to go through it all to find the truth. Fortunately, just because something turns out ultimately not to be the right road doesn't mean it ain't fun driving on it.

I'm a firm believer that everything in my life has led me to where I am today. I have few, if any, regrets; after all, if I'd done things differently, perhaps I wouldn't have made it here at all. There were times when it was tough to get through the day, but even on those days I knew that if I fought my way through, there was something better ahead. When faced with misfortune, you can either sit in the shit or you can clean yourself off and move forward. In my case, I always chose to move forward. I didn't know how hard it would be to find my way, but I knew I wouldn't stop until I had.

It was just a question of work.

My quest to perfect myself—or whatever you want to call it— ended up teaching me the impossibility of that goal. It's not about being perfect, being normal, or seeking approval; it's about being forgiving of imperfection, being generous to all sorts of people, and giving approval. That, too, takes work.

I'm not what I call a passive optimist. I don't believe everything will work out if I wish for it hard enough. I'm a realistic optimist: I know that as long as I'm realistic about my capabilities, I can make things work out, or at the very least, I can try to steer things in the right direction. On the one hand, no matter how hard anyone pictures himself or herself, say, flying, it's not going to happen. You can do something ten thousand times and still be bad at it if you have no aptitude for it. As far as I'm concerned, if you pursue something that's out of your reach, then you're a fool; time is irreplaceable, and you are the only person who will bear the brunt of your misjudgments. On the other hand, realistic goals can be achieved through hard work. There's nothing wrong with limitations. If anything, you get farther when you realize what your limitations truly are. It's just that many limitations are either self-imposed or based on what other people believe them to be. You need to determine your own limitations and then work toward their outer limits.

Evan called me from his dorm room during his first semester at college in the fall of 2012. He'd just had breakfast with Jimmy Page.

ROSS HALFIN

Out to dinner in London with Jimmy Page.

Yes, *that* Jimmy Page. I thought back to being Evan's age: I'd been a lost teen with a dream and a commitment to making it come true, and Led Zeppelin was my biggest influence. Now Jimmy had one of my paintings hanging in his country home, and my son—the same age I was when, as a total outsider, I stared in awe at Zeppelin—hangs out with him. Funny how things can come full circle. Your life and destiny are determined to a large extent by your participation in the outcome. Think big, work hard . . .

"Dad?"

I snapped back from my reverie. Telling me about his breakfast with a legend wasn't why Evan had called me. The real reason he called was because he wanted to cook brussels sprouts in his dorm room. *Dad's* brussels sprouts—the way I made them at home. He needed the recipe.

How cool.

I explained how to panfry them and told him how much balsamic vinegar, dried cherries, and prosciutto I used. "And don't forget to top them with some grated parmesan cheese and a little lemon zest."

My younger children already like to help me cook. Lately, they've become interested in gardening. We decided to plant a family vegetable garden. Erin and I went to a nursery and bought heirloom seeds and together with the kids planted tomatoes, sugar snap peas, strawberries, carrots, and broccoli. I watched in astonishment as these things that looked like lint balls eventually started to send up green shoots as the kids watered them day after day. As the plants started to grow, I found I too had a desire to nurture them so they would grow up big and strong. It was something I could never have imagined myself feeling.

One afternoon Colin, who is in elementary school, told me, "I have some important work to do." Then he scurried out the back door. After a few minutes, I went out and checked on him. What could he be doing that was so important to him? He was kneeling in our vegetable patch pulling weeds.

Soon enough we had a bumper crop of tomatoes, and the kids and I made huge vats of tomato sauce. We froze some, but we used a lot in lasagna and on pizzas we learned to bake together. I found a recipe for a thin-crust dough; we all sat around mixing and rolling, and then we topped our pizzas with our homegrown tomato sauce and grilled them in a wood-burning stone pizza oven we had built in the backyard.

There's something wonderful and almost therapeutic about making your own food, from seed to table. If you told me fifteen years ago that I would have photos on my phone of the lasagna I made with my kids, I would have called you crazy. But the photos are there.

We have a family-friendly, food-friendly, wine-friendly household. We sit and eat together as a family, and I look forward to it every day. Sometimes I'm reminded of a sunny afternoon in the 1980s when I watched from the pool at the Sunset Marquis as the band Mike + the Mechanics checked in with their kids and strollers and nannies. I remember shaking my head, thinking it was the most uncool thing I had ever seen. These days there's nothing I consider cooler than being on our jet with the kids running up and down the aisle. Or standing onstage in front of one hundred thousand people at the Download Festival while my kids watch and wave from the side of the stage. Or walking backstage and seeing Emily, Sarah, and Colin in their pajamas. It's amazing.

And to have it at my age is even more amazing. Perhaps it's unusual to be sixty-two years old and have a two-year-old. Certainly, I feel blessed. People equate getting old with shutting down, with the joy seeping out of your life. But me? I'm in love with my wife. I love my kids. There's a part of my life that's over, but what's taken its place is so much more fulfilling. Sure, every once in a while I look at a hot young woman and think for a fleeting moment about what I will never again have. But when I think of what I have instead, it's no contest.

That's also why I finally decided to write this book. Because despite the odds, I managed to go from a very unhappy place to a peaceful, harmonious place. If *I* found a path—no matter how long and arduous—to happiness and satisfaction, I firmly believe others can, too. It may not be an easy road, but sticking to that road and pushing forward is the most worthwhile thing you'll ever do.

We tend to compromise through life and lower the bar; we settle for relationships or jobs because we're not sure that we can do better—or that we even deserve better. But we *can* do better, and we *do* deserve it.

Life is not about surrendering.

65.

Because of the makeup, KISS today looks pretty much the same as we did forty years ago. But the longer I keep at this, the more I realize that I'm not invincible. It's an ever more daunting task to get up there and sing and play guitar and dance and do it in a way that appears effortless. Nobody wants to see somebody killing himself onstage. I enjoy every minute of performing, but it has always been physically grueling, and it certainly is more so now.

When I was younger, people asked me, "Doesn't it hurt when you jump up in the air and land on your knees like that?"

"No," I said.

Well, I wish I had their phone numbers. Because all those years of doing jumps without pain have left me with a reminder: my knees hurt now.

I don't know whether people in the audience can fathom just how difficult it is—or the extent to which they themselves make it possible. I could never jump around like that at a rehearsal. I depend on those people. I depend on the rush of adrenaline I get from them. Every night I find myself up there with a huge smile on my face, laughing, having a great time.

It's a gift, and it's terrific that I love it and have fun doing it, and it's doubly terrific to look out into the audience and see other people loving it, too.

I never understand bands who say they're sick of playing their hit songs. I'm thrilled to play our big songs. I'm proud of those songs. And the people at our shows deserve to hear the music the way they love it. God knows how many times I've played "Firehouse" over the course of the past forty years, but I still love it. When Gene, Tommy, and I rock back and forth to "Deuce," it's the ultimate middle finger to the people who don't like us and the ultimate salute to those who do. Each night is the only night that counts to the people at that show. They weren't at the show the night before, and they won't be at the one tomorrow. I won't let them down.

Most rock and roll is so age-specific or demographic-specific—your favorite band can't be your older brother's favorite band, and god forbid it be your parents' favorite band. A KISS show is different: it's a gathering of a large, long-lasting society that transcends any demographics.

There's nothing better than seeing people holding up their children during a show. People want to share this cult of millions with their kids—it means that much to them. Those people are happy. They're getting a break from whatever else is going on in their lives. Even as citizens of the world with a sense of morality and purpose, everyone is entitled to a day off. All the problems of the world will still be there tomorrow.

What KISS does is timeless. We sing about self-empowerment, celebrating life, believing in yourself—and sex.

It ain't a crime to be good to yourself.

Is there anything more truthful than that?

We're all here one time, and why should anyone but you get to decide who you love and how you spend your time?

We sing about the joys of being alive.

On the *Sonic Boom* tour, Gene, Tommy, and I would get into a caged-in platform behind Eric's drums before the first song started. As we played the first song, the platform would go up and over the drums and eventually put us down at the front of the stage. It was a spectacular effect. I can't tell you how many times, as we came over the top and I first saw the audience, I got choked up and teary eyed.

I looked out over the crowd and was amazed.

What a blessing.

My God.

Had somebody told me KISS was going to last forty years with no end in sight—that I would be wearing the same outfit and not getting laughed off the stage, that on the contrary, we'd be selling out arenas and stadiums—I would never have believed it. I think the longer we've survived, the more potent we've become. There's something inspiring about longevity. There's something inspiring about going against the odds and thriving.

Perhaps the best way to win is not to play the game.

Twenty or thirty years ago, I couldn't imagine the *world* without me, much less the *band*. But at some point, you can't ignore the reality of your own mortality. I won't be physically capable of performing in KISS forever. Something I've come to understand, though, is that I'm not immortal—the band is.

Nowadays I don't confuse my role in the world or the band. I realize that KISS could—and should—go on without me. KISS isn't like other bands. We've never subscribed to the limitations other bands impose on themselves. People come to see the characters we created and what those characters represent. It's not me they're coming to see, but what I embody.

There was a time when people said nobody in this band could be replaced. It had to be the four of us. Well, they're already 50 percent wrong. And they're going to find out at some point that they're 75 percent wrong, and then 100 percent wrong.

I'm objective enough about myself to realize that no matter how good I am—and I think I'm damn good—there's somebody else out there who can do something equally valid. I think that being replaced would be a huge compliment, not a detriment. It's part of what I hope we've built—an ideal that goes far beyond me.

Causes go on. Political parties go on without their founders. I think someone could come along who would be capable of carrying the flag just as well if not better—someone who can build on the foundation. I look forward to the day that I'm replaced in KISS. Not because I want to leave, but because it will prove I'm right: *KISS is bigger than any of its members.*

I've always said that I'm not just a member of KISS; I'm a member of the KISS Army. I look forward to watching the band I love continue to rock and roll all night long after my body is too shot to make it to the party every day.

About the Author

Paul Stanley is the frontman and rhythm guitarist for KISS, which he cofounded in New York City in 1973. He is the designer of numerous KISS album covers, costumes, and concert stages, in addition to writing many of KISS's most successful songs. With sales of more than one hundred million records worldwide, KISS sits atop the list of American bands, with the most gold-certified albums earned in history. Along with his bandmates, Stanley was inducted into the Rock and Roll Hall of Fame in 2014. A painter, with art sales reaching two million dollars; a solo musician; a musical stage performer; founding partner in Rock & Brews restaurants; and co-owner of the Arena Football League's L.A. KISS, Stanley is a committed and active supporter of various Wounded Warrior Project organizations. He lives in Los Angeles with his wife, Erin, and four children.

About the Collaborator

Tim Mohr is an award-winning translator of novels by such authors as Alina Bronsky, Charlotte Roche, and Wolfgang Herrndorf. He has also collaborated on best-selling memoirs by Gil Scott-Heron and original Guns N' Roses bassist Duff McKagan. He spent several years as a staff editor at *Playboy* magazine, where he worked with writers including Hunter S. Thompson, Matt Taibbi, John Dean, and George McGovern. Mohr's own writing has appeared in the *New York Times*, the *Daily Beast*, and *New York* magazine, among other publications. Before starting his writing career, he made his living as a club DJ in Berlin, Germany.

Acknowledgments

Telling my story has been another milestone in my life. Incredibly rewarding in its connecting me through reflection to my life, its challenges, and its ultimate arrival at a pinnacle I never thought possible.

Over the years I've had no interest in adding my name to an ever-growing list of celebrities whose autobiographies seemed little more than a self-serving platform to brag and boast of supposed accomplishments.

With time, I came to envision telling my own story in a book that might possibly empower and inspire others to meet and overcome their own obstacles head-on and with hard work, as I believe I have.

Life, I have found, is a team sport, and I would need a small but dedicated and talented team to see this through.

I want to thank each of them:

On an intuitive gut hunch I contacted Tim Mohr as a possible collaborator. Within an hour of meeting we had rolled up our sleeves. He was totally dedicated to my story being in my words and my voice and helped put it into the best and most effective form possible. Tim's opinions and point of view were indispensable. As if that alone wasn't enough, he constantly left me both repulsed and in awe as he bravely sampled all kinds of questionable street foods during our travels abroad. Thank you, Tim.

Once I signed on with a publishing company, building a new relationship initially had to be based on what was said seeming simpatico between us, and ultimately on faith. Roger Freet, HarperOne's executive editor, became a close ally who cheered me on, supporting me and implementing my ideas in all phases and aspects of *Face the Music*. When things got bogged down he was there. Thank you, Roger.

Thank you, Bill Randolph, for your guidance and work on my behalf to bring this project to both a start and a finish.

Thank you, Michael Levine, for your early belief that I had a story worth telling and helping me find a platform for it.

Thank you to all members of KISS over the years, but especially and with full appreciation to my brother to this day, Gene.

Thank you to my parents, William and Eva Eisen. Everything they did in my life was done always with the best of intentions. They gave me many gifts and I am here and who I am directly and indirectly because of them.

It seems almost redundant to thank my incredible wife, Erin, and wondrous children, Evan, Colin, Sarah, and Emily, who are at the very core of this book, but I can never thank them enough. Thank you again for your endless support, inspiration, and love.

And last but never forgotten, my fans. You made this road trip possible, and every mile I have traveled these past forty years is a direct result of what our relationship has enabled me to do. You remain in my thoughts and in my heart. I have always been humbled when told how I may have helped some of you on your road. Maybe you knowing me better now means we can still go further together. I hope so.